German

An Essential Grammar

German: An Essential Grammar is a practical reference guide to the core structures and features of modern German. Presenting a fresh and accessible description of the language, this engaging grammar uses clear, jargon-free explanations and sets out the complexities of German in short, readable sections.

Suitable for either independent study or students in schools, colleges, universities and adult education classes, key features include:

- focus on the morphology and syntax of the language
- clear explanations of grammatical terms
- full use of authentic examples
- detailed contents list and index for easy access to information.

With an emphasis on the German native speakers use today, *German: An Essential Grammar* will help students to read, speak and write the language with greater confidence.

Bruce Donaldson is Principal Fellow in the Department of German, Russian and Swedish Studies in the School of Languages and Linguistics at the University of Melbourne. He has been a prolific author of language learning and teaching materials, including the following publications: *Mastering German Vocabulary* (2004), *Colloquial Afrikaans* (2000), *Dutch: A Comprehensive Grammar* (1997), *Colloquial Dutch* (1996) and *Colloquial Dutch 2* (2005).

Routledge Essential Grammars

Essential Grammars are available for the following languages:

Chinese
Danish
Dutch
English
Finnish
Modern Greek
Modern Hebrew
Hungarian
Norwegian
Polish
Portuguese
Spanish
Swedish
Thai
Urdu

Other titles of related interest published by Routledge:

Basic German: A Grammar and Workbook
By Heiner Schenke and Karen Seago

Modern German Grammar: A Practical Guide, Second Edition
By William Dodd

German

An Essential Grammar

Bruce Donaldson

LONDON AND NEW YORK

First published 2007
by Routledge
2 Park Square, Milton Park, Abingdon, Oxon, OX14 4RN

Simultaneously published in the USA and Canada
by Routledge
270 Madison Ave, New York NY 10016

Routledge is an imprint of the Taylor & Francis Group, an informa business

Transferred to Digital Printing 2010

Typeset in Sabon by
Fakenham Photosetting Limited, Fakenham, Norfolk

British Library Cataloguing in Publication Data
A catalogue record for this book is available from the British Library

Library of Congress Cataloging-in-Publication Data

Donaldson, B. C. (Bruce C.), 1948–
German : an essential grammar / by Bruce Donaldson.
p. cm. -- (Routledge essential grammars)
Includes bibliographical references and index.
1. German language – Grammar. 2. German language – Textbooks for foreign speakers – English. I. Title. II. Series: Essential grammar.

PF3112. D66 2006
438.2'421--dc22

2006012912

ISBN10: 0–415–36603–8 (hbk)
ISBN10: 0–415–36602–X (pbk)
ISBN10: 0–203–01858–3 (ebk)

ISBN13: 978–0–415–36603–8 (hbk)
ISBN13: 978–0–415–36602–1 (pbk)
ISBN13: 978–0–203–01858–3 (ebk)

Contents

Introduction

There are numerous German grammars on the market, so why this one? This book has been written specifically with the needs of the intermediate learner at secondary or particularly tertiary level in mind. It is intended to be used as a reference grammar, which does not mean that it is utterly comprehensive, but it does cover everything that might be called 'essential' knowledge for someone who has reached the intermediate level.

So what constitutes the intermediate level? That depends of course, but it would certainly apply to anyone who has completed an elementary course in German at a university, i.e. people who are in their second or third year of tertiary German, having started it at university without having done it at school. Students at advanced secondary level, however, would also qualify as intermediate and will thus find this book pitched at their needs, as will those teaching themselves who are progressing beyond what one might call beginners' level. Once you have mastered the contents of this book, you will have reached a point in your learning of German where you are able to express yourself at quite a sophisticated level. Needless to say, you will also need to be concentrating on building up your vocabulary – grammar is useless on its own.

Other than being a book pitched squarely at the needs of the intermediate learner, what does this book offer its readers that other similar books may not? It has been written by someone with nearly forty years of experience in teaching German and Dutch at tertiary level, specializing in teaching students in their second year of German at university. The author is all too well aware of the shortcomings of the many textbooks available for the learning of German – take for example the way in which nearly all such books tackle German plurals. They nearly all fail to help the learner see through to the underlying system and thus fail to illustrate that plural formation is not nearly as arbitrary as it often appears to be to the newcomer to the language. How many books, for example, in their first introduction to plural formation, mention that **Mann** has a plural in **Männer**, but fail to mention that there are only about ten masculine nouns in the entire language that have a plural in **¨er**, which is otherwise an ending limited to neuter nouns? How many grammars tell you, to take another example, that possibly no more than 10 per cent of German nouns are neuter? So, if forced to guess a gender, it would be safer to assume the noun is masculine or feminine before assuming it is neuter. These two examples are typical of many of the underlying truths about German grammar that one discovers only through learning and teaching the language. These are also things which seldom strike the native speaker and why, at certain levels of learning a language, one may be better off with non-native teachers – they have been through the mill, as it were, which natives by definition have not. This book contains numerous such insights into German, acquired over many years of involvement with the language, both as a student and as a teacher. The author has applied his insights and long experience in explaining the intricacies of German to English-speaking people in as simple a fashion as the often complex material permits. German is certainly not simple – but then no language is – but it can be explained in a simpler, more palatable fashion than many books do.

Learning German is a challenge, but the rewards are great. No language other than English is of more use to you when travelling around Europe. Not only are there many more Germans (82 million) than there are French, Italians or Spaniards, for example, but the countries of Austria, Switzerland and Luxembourg further swell those numbers by several million native-speakers, not to mention the German-speaking minorities living in Russia, Romania, Hungary, Italy, Belgium and Denmark. All in all, the number of native-speakers of German living in Europe is nigh on 100 million. But go travelling through eastern Europe and you will be amazed at how well Poles, Hungarians and even Latvians, for example, can speak German too; their German is often much better than their English. Germany is an economic power of enormous importance and lies both physically and philosophically at the heart of the European Union. If you are interested in Europe and seek to broaden your linguistic and cultural horizons, you need look no further than German.

Other books you might refer to may use different names for several of the grammatical concepts dealt with in this book. Particularly in the American and British English-speaking worlds different terminology is often used for various concepts. For this reason, where alternative terminology exists for a given concept, it is briefly discussed before proceeding with the issue under consideration and all grammatical concepts can be accessed under all alternative names via the index.

There is an old German maxim: **ohne Vergleich kein Verständnis** (without comparison, there is no understanding). The approach to German grammar adopted in this book is strongly contrastive with English. English and German are after all, as languages go, very closely related and have a great deal in common. Look, for example, at the past tenses of irregular verbs (**trinken/trank/getrunken**) and the forms and functions of modal verbs (**kann/muss/will**). These are grammatical complexities that clearly stem from a common source, namely the Anglo-Saxon invasion of Britain in the fifth century AD. And then there is all that common vocabulary dating from the same time, e.g. **Mutter, Vater, Sohn, Tochter, Hund, Katze, Schwein** etc. All that the two languages have in common is a godsend to the learner, but then there is so much that the two do not (or no longer, as is often the case) have in common and this is where taking a contrastive approach can be invaluable. However, in order to do so, you need to be aware of exactly what the grammatical situation is in English with regard to a given issue. There are issues of which a native-speaker is often unaware. This is all the more so these days, when English at school level throughout the English-speaking world seldom includes analysis of formal grammar the way it used to. Generally speaking, this now means that the only people who leave school or university with any formal knowledge of English grammar are those who have learnt a foreign language and have therefore had to comprehend the intricacies of English grammar in order to access those of the foreign language being learnt. This is an added bonus in the learning of a language like German. English and German are oh so similar and oh so different. Unlocking the door to those similarities and differences is something this grammar sets out to do.

This book is intended as a reference grammar of 'essential' German and, as such, does not set out to be comprehensive, as previously mentioned. All the important concepts of German grammar are dealt with in considerable detail, with only minor exceptions and subtleties of grammar being left uncovered. The advanced learner who has mastered the contents of this book and who wishes to progress to a fully comprehensive reference grammar of German is advised to consider M. Durrell's *Hammer's German Grammar and Usage* (Arnold, London, 4th edition 2002).

German: An Essential Grammar only addresses grammatical issues, but many of the intricacies of mastering German are more lexical than grammatical in nature. The reader is referred to another work by the author of the current book in which such lexical problems are addressed, namely B. Donaldson's *Mastering German Vocabulary – A Practical Guide to Troublesome Words* (Routledge, London/New York, 2004).

If you've been looking for a challenge, you need look no further. You've found it. Learning German is intellectually very rewarding and terrific fun. It is like unravelling a complicated puzzle, one with an underlying code that needs to be cracked. Penetrating the thoroughly logical system that underlies the intricate weave of grammatical inflection that is the result of gender and case, combined with a myriad of word order rules that are at odds with what prevails in English, constitutes the challenge. Mastering this system is a form of mental gymnastics beyond compare and constitutes a feat that will give tremendous intellectual satisfaction as well as enabling you to converse with 100 million Europeans in their own idiom rather than lazily expecting them, as the overwhelming number of English speakers do, to converse with you in your mother tongue. And it is an effort that you will find is greatly appreciated and admired by German speakers.

About the author

Bruce Donaldson was born in Perth, Western Australia, in 1948. He did honours in German at the University of Western Australia, his MA in Old Germanic Languages at the State University of Utrecht and his PhD on Afrikaans at the University of the Orange Free State in Bloemfontein, South Africa. In 1973 he was appointed as lecturer in charge of Dutch and Germanic historical linguistics in the then Department of Germanic Studies at the University of Melbourne, from where he retired as associate professor and reader in 2004. For the last twelve years of his career, after the abolition of Dutch in 1992, he lectured in German, specializing in the intermediate level. He is currently a principal research fellow in his former department. He has written numerous monographs on Dutch, Afrikaans and German language issues, most of which have been published by Routledge. The author is interested in receiving constructive criticism for the improvement of any future editions of this work and can be emailed at bcr@unimelb.edu.au.

Abbreviations

>	produces, gives rise to
<	is derived from
acc.	accusative
dat.	dative
f.	feminine
gen.	genitive
lit.	literally; literary
m.	masculine
n.	neuter
nom.	nominative
pl.	plural
pron.	pronounced
sing.	singular
s.o.	someone
s.t.	something

Chapter 1

Pronunciation

German does not contain many sounds that are difficult for English speakers to pronounce; **ch**, **r** and **ü** will probably prove the hardest to conquer, but even these are soon mastered with practice.

The only reliable way of committing sounds to paper is via the International Phonetic Alphabet (IPA), but only those studying linguistics as an academic discipline are likely to have the IPA at their disposal and for this reason it is not referred to here. This means, however, that phrasing such as 'compare the vowel in tray' and 'compare the vowel in lot' has its limitations. Those English words may well vary in the way they are pronounced depending on where in the English-speaking world you live. Every care has been taken to make comparisons which are valid regardless of whether you speak British or American English, although the author is a speaker of the former, but then the Australian variant thereof. For this and numerous other reasons there is, of course, no substitute for getting assistance from a native speaker, keeping in mind, however, that German is spoken over a very large area by European standards and thus shows considerable regional variation in the way it is pronounced. Some attempt to cover the prime regional differences in pronunciation is made in 1.5. What should help in describing the sounds of German without being able to resort to the IPA is the fact that this book has, after all, been written for the intermediate level and so this chapter is seldom going to have to serve the needs of the raw beginner. It is assumed the vast majority of readers will already have some idea of how German is pronounced.

1.1 Vowels

Most vowels in German have both a short and a long variant. Clearly distinguishing between the two is very important. In German spelling two consonants after a vowel will normally indicate it is short (e.g. **Kamm** 'comb'), whereas only one consonant indicates it is long (e.g. **kam** 'came') (see 2.1).

a **a** is pronounced short in words like **Hand**, **Mann** and **statt** – compare the vowel in 'but'.
a is pronounced long in words like **kam**, **Vater** and **zahlen** – compare the vowel in 'father'.

ä **ä** is pronounced short in words like **lässt**, **kälter** and **Männer** – compare the vowel in 'bed'. It is identical to German short **e**.
ä is pronounced long in words like **gäbe**, **Hähne** and **Väter** – compare the vowel in 'hair'.

e **e** is pronounced short in words like **Bett**, **Henne** and **Sekt** – compare the vowel in 'bed'. It is identical to German short **ä**.
e is pronounced even shorter in words like **Beruf**, **Tante** and **zahlen** where it is unstressed – compare the vowel in the first syllable of 'believe' or the last syllable of 'wooden'. In all words ending in **e** like **Schule** and **Kassette** the **e** must be pronounced and not merely dropped as in 'cassette'. It is similar to the second syllable in 'rubber' as it is pronounced in British English.
e is pronounced long in words like **lesen**, **Planet** and **Tee** – compare the vowel in 'tray', but keep it pure, i.e. do not diphthongize it at all.

i **i** is pronounced short in words like **bitter**, **ich** and **Pilz** – compare the vowel in 'pit'. In very few words such as **Liga** and **wider i** is pronounced long – compare the vowel in 'read'.

ie **ie** is always pronounced long, e.g. **liegen**, **lieh** and **sie** – compare the vowel in 'fee'.

o **o** is pronounced short in words like **Loch**, **Schloss** and **Stollen** – compare the vowel in 'lot'.
o is pronounced long in words like **Floh**, **rot** and **Ton** – compare the vowel in 'post', but keep it pure, i.e. do not diphthongize it at all.

ö **ö** is pronounced short in words like **Löcher**, **Töchter** and **zwölf** – compare the vowel in 'bird', but keep it short.
ö is pronounced long in words like **Flöte**, **Löhne** and **schön** – compare the vowel in 'bird' but with the lips as rounded as you can make them.

u **u** is pronounced short in words like **Butt**, **Truppe** and **Zunge** – compare the vowel in 'put'.
u is pronounced long in words like **Buch**, **Fuß** and **gut** – compare the vowel in 'food' but with less lip rounding. Make sure you clearly distinguish between this sound and long **ü**. This sound is commonly pronounced too short by English speakers.

ü **ü** is pronounced short in words like **fünf**, **Flüsse** and **Pfütze** – compare the vowel in 'too' but make it shorter and with the lips as rounded and tightened as you can make them, as if trying to whistle.
ü is pronounced long in words like **fühlen**, **Füße** and **trübe** – compare the vowel in 'food' but make it longer and with more lip rounding and tightening, as if trying to whistle.

1.2 Diphthongs

German has only three diphthong sounds, i.e. **ei**, **au** and **eu**. English has quite a few more.

ei **ei** in words like **Blei**, **Stein** and **Verleih** is identical to the vowel in 'fight'.

ai **ai** in words like **Hain**, **Laib** and **Mai** is identical in pronunciation to **ei** and occurs in very few words.

au **au** in words like **aus**, **Auto** and **Traum** is very similar to the vowel in 'house'.

eu **eu** in words like **euch**, **Feuer** and **heute** is identical to the vowel in 'boy'.

äu **äu** in words like **enttäuschen**, **Kräuter** and **Schläuche** is identical to **eu**.

1.3 Consonants

There are few problems lurking here for English speakers.

b **b** in words like **Bein**, **Krabbe** and **loben** is identical to that in 'bed'. At the end of a word as in **ab**, **Lob** and **ob** a **b** is always devoiced, i.e. it is pronounced as a 'p'.

c **c** in words like **Cicero** and **Mercedes** (both foreign words) is pronounced like a German **z**, i.e. as 'ts'.

ch **ch** in words like **Bach**, **Loch**, **Buch** and **rauchen** (i.e. after **a**, **o**, **u** and **au**) is pronounced as in Scottish 'loch'. The Germans call this the **ach-Laut**, a hard sound.
ch in words like **Blech**, **ich**, **lächeln**, **Schläuche**, **Löcher**, **Bücher**, **welche**, **manche** and **durch** (i.e. after **e**, **i**, **ä**, **äu**, **ö**, **ü** as well as the consonants **l**, **n** and **r**) is a softer sound than when it follows **a**, **o**, **u** and **au**, i.e. it is pronounced with the tongue curved, hugging both the soft and hard palates. The Germans call this the **ich-Laut**, a soft sound. It must be clearly distinguished from the more guttural **ach-Laut**. The two **ch** sounds can alternate within variations of the same word when it is inflected, e.g. **Buch** (with the **ach** sound) and **Bücher** (with the **ich** sound).
The combination **chs** is pronounced like English 'x', e.g. **sechs**, **Dachs**, **Fuchs**. Compare **sechs** (6) with **sechzehn** (16) and **sechzig** (60) where **ch** is pronunced as in **Blech** above.
The diminutive ending **-chen** is also pronounced with this soft variant of **ch**.
ch at the beginning of loanwords is pronounced like 1) English 'k', 2) English 'sh' or 3) soft German **ch**, depending on the source language, e.g. 1) **Chaos**, **Chlor**, **Charakter**; 2) **Chance**, **chauvinistisch**, **Chef**; 3) **Chemie**, **China**.

ck **ck**, found in the middle and at the end of words, is pronounced 'k', e.g. **lecker**, **Fleck**.

d **d** in words like **denken** and **Feder** is pronounced as in English.
At the end of a word as in **Glied**, **Gold** and **Hand** a **d** is always devoiced, i.e. it is pronounced as a 't'.

f **f** in words like **Frosch**, **Pfeffer** and **Schiff** is pronounced as in English.

g **g** at the beginning or in the middle of words, as in **Gang**, **gießen** and **fliegen**, is pronounced as in English.
At the end of a word as in **Tag**, **Teig** and **Zug** a **g** is always devoiced, i.e. it is pronounced as a 'k'. However, the ending **-ig** is pronounced like German **ich**, e.g. **König** and **lustig** (see 1.5).

h **h** at the beginning of a words, as in **Haus**, **Horn** and **Hut**, is pronounced as in English. After a vowel it is not pronounced but simply serves to show that the vowel is long, e.g. **Floh**,

sehen, **Schuhe** (see 2.1). Sometimes this **h** is superfluous to pronunciation but spelling requires it, e.g. **sieh** and **sie** are pronounced the same, as are **liehst** (< **leihen** 'to lend') and **liest** (< **lesen** 'to read').

j — **j** is pronounced 'y', e.g. **Jahr**, **jeder**, **Joch**.
j in French loanwords is pronounced like the 's' in 'leisure', e.g. **Journalist**.

k — **k** is pronounced as in English, e.g. **Katze**, **Klasse**, **kommen**.

l — **l** in all positions is pronounced as in 'light' never as in 'well', i.e. it is never a 'thick l', e.g. **Lohn**, **Licht**, **wählen**, **wohl**.

m — **m** is pronounced as in English, e.g. **Mann**, **Lämmer**, **Lehm**.

n — **n** is pronounced as in English, e.g. **nein**, **Tonne**, **zehn**.

ng — **ng** is always pronounced as in 'singer', never as in 'finger', e.g. **Finger**, **lang**, **Sänger**, **Zeitung**.

p — **p** is pronounced as in English, e.g. **Penner**, **Lippe**, **kaputt**. At the beginning of a word, where it is rare, it is lightly aspirated, as in English.

pf — **pf** is pronounced as the spelling suggests, i.e. both the **p** and the **f** are articulated, but this can be hard for English speakers at the beginning of a word, e.g. **Pfeffer**, **Tropfen**, **Kopf** (see **pf** under 1.5).

ph — **ph** is still used in some loanwords and is pronounced as an 'f', e.g. **Photograph**, **Philosophie**.

q — **q** always occurs in combination with **u**, as in English, and together they are pronounced 'kv', e.g. **Qualität**, **Quelle**, **Quadratmeter**.

r — In most of the German-speaking region **r** before a vowel is pronounced by slightly trilling the uvula in the back of your throat, but there are areas where, and individuals who, pronounce it by trilling their tongue against their alveolar ridge, i.e. the ridge of gum behind the top teeth, as in Italian. Either way **r** must be trilled, which usually means most English speakers have trouble with this sound, e.g. **Reh**, **reißen**, **Brot**, **schreiben**.
After a vowel an **r** is vocalized, i.e. it is pronounced as a vowel, e.g. in **er**, **mir** and **Uhr** you pronounce the vowel as you

would expect it to be pronounced and follow it by 'uh', as in the colloquial question form 'huh?,' i.e. air-uh, mee-uh, oo-uh. The common ending **-er** is simply pronounced 'uh'; alternatively you could say it resembles the second syllable in 'teacher', but imagine this being spelt 'teacha', e.g. **Schuster** (shoos-tuh). The ending **-ern** is pronounced 'airn', not trilling the **r**, e.g. **wandern** (vundairn).
Note how **-er** and **-e** differ in pronunciation at the end of words: **Mütter/Feuer** (with 'uh'), but **Hütte/Treue** (with the vowel in the second syllable in British English 'rubber'; in American English this final 'r' is pronounced, but not in British English).

s **s** at the beginning and in the middle of a word is pronounced 'z', e.g. **sollen**, **lesen**, **Gänse**. **S** at the end of a word is pronounced 's', e.g. **es**, **Gans**, **Glas**. The spelling **ss** is always pronounced 's' too, e.g. **Flüsse**, **Guss**, **schoss**.

ß **ß**, which only occurs in the middle and at the end of words, is always pronounced 's', e.g. **bloß**, **reißen**, **schießen**. **ß** indicates that any vowel preceding it is long (see 2.5).

sch **sch** is pronounced 'sh', e.g. **Schule**, **fischen**, **Tisch**.

sp **sp** at the beginning of a word is pronounced 'shp', e.g. **spät**, **Spaten**, **Spatz**. This is also the case in compounds and derived words where the **sp** is still seen as being at the 'beginning' of the word, e.g. **Aussprache**, **verspätet** (< **spät**).
In the middle of a word, however, **sp** is pronounced 'sp', e.g. **lispeln**, **Wespe**.

st There are parallels here with the way **sp** is pronounced. At the beginning of a word it is pronounced 'sht', e.g. **Stadt**, **stehen**, **stoßen**. This is also the case in compounds and derived words where the **st** is still seen as being at the 'beginning' of the word, e.g. **Ausstoß**, **Großstadt**, **verstehen** (< **stehen**).
In the middle and at the end of a word, however, **st** is pronounced 'st', e.g. **Gast**, **gestern**, **bist**.

t **t** is pronounced as in English, e.g. **Tag**, **rot**, **bitte**. At the beginning of a word it is aspirated, as in English.
In French loanwords ending in **-tion**, **t** is pronounced 'ts', e.g. **Nation**, **national**.

tsch **tsch** is pronounced like 'tch' in 'butcher', e.g. **Deutsch**,

Dolmetscher, **Quatsch**. It only occurs at the beginning in foreign words, e.g. **Tschechien**, **tschüs**.

v — **v** is pronounced 'f' in true German words, e.g. **Vater**, **von**, **Volk**. At the beginning of loanwords **v** is pronounced as in English, e.g. **Vase**, **Veteran**, **Video**, **Violine**.
v occurs at the end of some loanwords, in which case it is pronounced 'f' (i.e. it is devoiced), but when **v** is no longer in final position, it is pronounced 'v', e.g. **aktiv**, **passiv**, but **aktive**.

w — **w** is pronounced 'v', e.g. **Wasser**, **wir**, **Wurm**.

x — **x**, which is rare in German, is always pronounced 'ks', e.g. **nix**, **Xylophon**.

y — **y** is pronounced the same as long **ü**, e.g. **typisch**, **Zylinder**, **zynisch**.

z — **z** is pronounced 'ts', e.g. **Polizei**, **zählen**, **zittern**. Sometimes it occurs together with **t** but the pronunciation is still 'ts', e.g. **Glotze**, **Platz**, **Spritze**.

1.4 Stress

As a general rule the first syllable of a German word bears the stress, e.g. **ankommen**, **Bruder**, **Rathaus**, **Wörterbuch**.

The verbal prefixes **be-**, **emp-**, **ent-**, **er-**, **ge-**, **ver-** and **zer-**, which are also found in nouns derived from verbs, are never stressed (compare the stress in 'believe', 'release', 'forgive' in English), e.g. **Bezug**, **empfehlen**, **entkommen**, **erreichen**, **gestehen**, **Verkauf**, **zerbrechen**. Some additional verbal prefixes are not stressed, e.g. **durchsuchen**, **vollenden**, **widersprechen**, while others are, e.g. **anrufen**, **ausgehen**, **wiedersehen** (see separable and inseparable verbs 10.9.1 to 10.9.3).

Many foreign loanwords, usually of French origin, stress the final syllable as in the source language, e.g. **Agent**, **Akzent**, **Bäckerei**, **kaputt**, **Partei**, **Pelikan**, **Philosoph**, **Planet**, **Satellit**, **Student**. Loanwords ending in **e** stress the second last syllable, e.g. **Forelle**, **Garage**, **Kassette**, **Kusine**.

Verbs ending in **-ieren**, mostly derived from French, are also stressed on the second last syllable, e.g. **buchstabieren**, **renovieren**, **studieren**.

1.5 Regional variants

As German is spoken over a very wide area and in several countries, there is great variety in regional pronunciation. Some of these variations are considered standard, not dialect; only these variants are dealt with here.

In the north of Germany long **ä** is pronounced 'eh', i.e. the same as German long **e**, and thus the distinction between **gäbe/gebe** and **nähme/nehme**, for example, is not made.

In the north of Germany many long vowels in closed syllables (i.e. those ending in a consonant) are pronounced short, e.g. **Glas, Tag, Zug.**

In the north of Germany final **g** is pronounced like German **ch** (both **ich-** and **ach-Laut**, depending on the preceding sound), e.g. **Tag, Teig, Weg, zog, Zug.**

In verbs before the endings **-t** and **-te/-ten** etc. **g** is also pronounced in this way, e.g. **liegt, gesagt, legte, sagte**; in standard German the **g** in these words is automatically pronounced 'k' due to the influence of the following **t.**

In the north the ending **-ung** is often pronounced 'oonk', e.g. **Zeitung, Rechnung.**

Over large areas of northern and central Germany **pf** at the beginning of a word is likely to be pronounced 'f', e.g. **Pfeffer, Pfund.** If you are having trouble pronouncing **pf** in such words, simply say **Feffer** and **Fund** and no one will even notice you are not saying **pf.**

In southern Germany and Austria, **sp** and **st** are pronounced 'shp' and 'sht' in all positions, not just initially, e.g. **bist, Australien, Wespe.**

The reverse can occur in the far north of Germany where **sp** and **st** might be pronounced 'sp' and 'st' in all positions, e.g. **Stadt, spät.**

In the south of Germany and in Austria **k, p** and **t** are commonly pronounced in a way that makes them barely distinguishable from **g, b** and **d** respectively, e.g. **kaufen** > **gaufen, Parade** > **Barade, trinken** > **drinken.**

Chapter 2

Spelling

Generally speaking, German is written as it is pronounced, each spelling having only one possible pronunciation and each pronunciation being written in only one way. There are very few exceptions to this, and they are dealt with here.

2.1 Indicating vowel length

Vowel length is inconsistently represented in German spelling – compare the following where all words contain the same long **a**, **e**, **o** or **u** sound respectively: **Saal, Stahl, Tal; Tee, Mehl, beten; Boot, Lohn, bot; Fuß, Schuh.**

h is commonly used after a vowel to indicate that the vowel is long, although this indication is usually superfluous, e.g. **mahlen** (to grind) and **malen** (to paint), **sieh** (look) and **sie** (she/they). This is called in German a **Dehnungs-h** (< **dehnen** 'to lengthen, stretch').

In a minority of words **a**, **e** and **o** are doubled to show they are long, e.g. **Saal, Beet, Boot.** Otherwise a single consonant following **a**, **e** and **o** usually indicates that those vowels are long, e.g. **Tag, Gen, Kot, Vater, beten, boten.** Conversely, a short vowel is usually followed by two or more consonants, which may be the same or different, e.g. **Männer, Pommern, sprechen, fanden, Stadt, Wespe.**

2.2 Use of the Umlaut

German only uses one diacritic, the Umlaut. It appears in printed matter as two dots over the vowel, but in handwriting is best written as two short strokes, not dots. Umlauts are only possible on the vowels **a**, **o**, **u** and the diphthong **au**, which are all vowel sounds pronounced in the back of the mouth. For historical reasons, in derived forms of words containing **a**, **o**, **u** or **au**, the vowel is brought further forward and/or higher in the mouth and this is reflected in the spelling by umlauting these vowels. This is best illustrated by comparing the singular with the plural of certain nouns, e.g. **Bach** > **Bäche**, **Loch** > **Löcher**, **Buch** > **Bücher**, **Bauch** > **Bäuche** (compare 'goose > geese'). In the examples given, the change in vowel also causes a change in pronunciation of the **ch** from the hard to the soft variant.

2.3 Use of capital letters

All nouns are capitalized, e.g. **Bruder**, **Mutter**, **Sofa**.

Adjectives of nationality are not capitalized, but nouns are, e.g. **eine deutsche Frau** (a German woman), **Sie ist Deutsche** (She is a German).

'To write with a capital/small letter' is expressed by the verbs **groß-** and **kleinschreiben**, e.g.

> **Er kann Deutsch; hier wird 'Deutsch' großgeschrieben.**
> He speaks German; here 'Deutsch' is written with a capital letter.
>
> **Beethoven ist ein bekannter deutscher Komponist; hier wird 'deutsch' kleingeschrieben.**
> Beethoven is a well-known German composer; here 'deutsch' is written with a small letter.

Because, for historical reasons, modern German uses the word for 'they' as the polite form of address, to distinguish between 'they/them/to them/their' and 'you/to you/your' the latter are all written with a capital letter, i.e. **Sie/Ihnen/Ihr**.

2.4 Use of the hyphen

Compounds are seldom hyphenated as in English, where we often vacillate between using a hyphen in a given compound, writing it as two words or writing it as one word, e.g. **Wohnzimmer** (lounge-room, lounge room, loungeroom), **Küchentür** (kitchen door), **spottbillig** (dirt cheap). There is no limit to how long such compounds can be in German, e.g. **Gerichtsberichterstatter** (legal correspondent, lit. court report compiler).

When a hyphen is used, as in **an Sonn- und Feiertagen** (on Sundays and holidays) and **auf- und zumachen** (to open and shut), it is understood that this stands for **an Sonntagen und Feiertagen** and **aufmachen und zumachen** and saves repeating the second part of the compound.

2.5 The new spelling

German reformed its spelling (**Rechtschreibung**) in 1998 for the first time in almost a hundred years. The reform, called **die Rechtschreibreform**, has aroused a great deal of controversy. Although all government agencies, schools and publishers adhere to the new recommendations, many individuals refuse to do so, and of course anything published prior to 1998 is in the old spelling. The differences are, however, minimal.

By far the most important change to the spelling in 1998 was in the use of **ß**, called either **scharfes s** or **ess tset** (i.e. German for 'sz', as the symbol is derived from a long s and a z in old German printing and handwriting).

Under the new rules **ß** is only used after long vowels and diphthongs, e.g. **schießen, Spaß, stoßen, draußen, fleißig, scheußlich**. Thus the spellings **Schoß** and **schoss, Fuß** and **Fluss** indicate to the reader that there is a difference in vowel length. Sometimes **ß** and **ss** alternate within a word family, indicating the length of the vowel, e.g. **schießen** (to shoot), **schoss** (shot).

Under the old spelling **ß** was used after long vowels, as now, but also at the end of words, regardless of the length of the preceding vowel, and before the verbal endings **-t** and **-te/-ten**, e.g. **schoß, Fluß, paßt, mußte** are now all **schoss, Fluss, passt, musste**.

The only other important spelling change relates to the use of capital letters where a certain inconsistency had evolved. It was decided that any word that can possibly be perceived as a noun should be capitalized, something which had previously been somewhat inconsistent, e.g. **auf deutsch** > **auf Deutsch, heute abend** > **heute Abend**.

The other changes are so trivial as not to warrant mention here, but if at times you see inconsistencies in spelling (e.g. **wieviel/wie viel** 'how much', **radfahren/Rad fahren** 'to cycle'), the chances are you are witnessing the differences between the old and the new spelling. Just take note whether your dictionary, any other textbook you are consulting or book you are reading was printed pre or post-1998. This book does of course observe the new spelling.

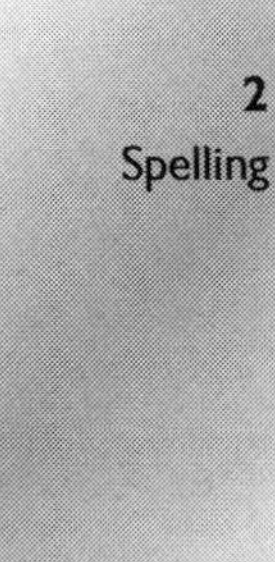

2 Spelling

2.6 The alphabet

The combination 'eh' in the pronunciations given below approximates the vowel in English 'bay' but without any tendency to diphthongize – it is a pure long vowel.

a	ah	n	en
b	beh	o	oh
c	tseh	p	peh
d	deh	q	koo
e	eh	r	air
f	ef	s	es
g	geh	t	teh
h	hah	u	oo
i	ee	v	fow
j	yot	w	veh
k	kah	x	iks
l	el	y	üpsilon
m	em	z	tset

If spelling out a word with an Umlaut in it, read the letters as follows: **kämpft – kah, air, em, peh, ef, teh**. This is more usual than **kah, ah-Umlaut, em, peh, ef, teh**, which is however also possible.

Letters of the alphabet are neuter, e.g.

> **Das I im Wort Voigtländer wird nicht ausgesprochen.**
> The i in the word Voigtländer is not pronounced.

Chapter 3

Punctuation

Generally speaking, German punctuation does not differ greatly from that of English. It is only the comma which is used somewhat differently but a couple of other punctuation marks can differ slightly from English usage too. Only those punctuation conventions that differ from English are described here.

3.1 Commas

Commas are determined by grammar in German, not by the writer feeling a pause is appropriate, as is so often the case in English, e.g.

Er wird aber innerhalb von vierzehn Tagen zurückkommen. (aber = however**)**
He will, however, return within a fortnight.

In German you must always insert a comma between an independent and a dependent clause, however short they are, e.g.

Ich will das Buch nicht übers Internet kaufen, obwohl es dort billiger wäre.
I don't want to buy the book over the internet although it would be cheaper there.

Er wusste, dass ich es war.
He knew that it was me.

When joining two independent (main) clauses by means of a coordinating conjunction, a comma must be inserted between the two if the second clause has its own subject, e.g.

Er fliegt heute nach London, aber er kommt morgen schon zurück.
He's flying to London today but (he) is returning tomorrow.

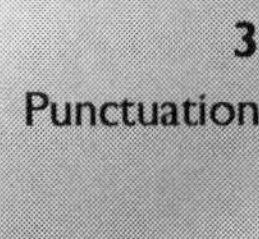

But if the subject of the first clause also serves as the subject of the second clause, which is a possible stylistic variant in both German and English, you cannot separate that second finite verb from its subject by means of a comma, e.g.

Er fliegt heute nach London aber kommt morgen schon zurück.
He's flying to London today but (he) is returning tomorrow.

The post-1998 spelling rules have introduced two small changes here. Just with the coordinating conjunctions **oder** (or) and **und** (and) a comma has been made optional even if the subject is mentioned (see 11.1), e.g.

Meine Festplatte funktioniert nicht mehr richtig(,) und ich muss sie reparieren lassen.
My hard disk is no longer working properly and I have to get it repaired.

The other small change since 1998 is that a comma is now also optional before an infinitive clause (see 11.3) consisting of more than **zu** plus an infinitive, e.g.

Er hat probiert(,) ihr zu helfen.
He tried to help her.

No comma was ever required when the infinitive clause was not expanded beyond **zu** plus an infinitive, e.g.

Er hat probiert zu helfen.
He tried to help.

When a subordinate clause precedes a main clause in a complex sentence, the comma is an indispensable reading tool to indicate which verb belongs to which clause, e.g.

Wenn er mir damals geholfen hätte, hätte ich ihm gestern mit dem Umzug geholfen.
If he had helped me back then, I would have helped him with moving house yesterday.

But even when the order of the clauses is reversed, a comma must of course be used, e.g.

Ich hätte ihm gestern mit dem Umzug geholfen, wenn er mir damals geholfen hätte.
I would have helped him with moving house yesterday, if he had helped me back then.

In English in such cases it is up to the writer to decide if the sentence is long enough to require a comma for the sake of clarity or not and no two people's comma style is the same. This is definitely not the case in German.

3.1.2 *Commas with relative clauses*

A comma must be placed at both the beginning and the end of a relative clause (see 7.6), clearly delineating it from the main clause in which it is embedded, e.g.

Der Kuli, mit dem ich den Scheck unterschreiben wollte, war leer.
The biro/ballpoint I wanted to sign the cheque with was empty.

3.2 Colons with direct speech

When speech is reported by means of clauses such as 'he said', 'she wrote' etc., a colon is used in German where in English we use a comma, e.g.

Sie schrie: „Wach auf!"
She shouted, 'Wake up.'

But if the direct speech precedes the verb of reporting, a comma is used, not a colon, e.g.

„Mach schnell", sagte er.
'Hurry up,' he said.

„Der Vertrag ist unterzeichnet worden", berichtete der Journalist.
'The contract has been signed,' the journalist reported.

3.3 Inverted commas/quotation marks

German places the first inverted commas or quotation marks of a set on the line and the second where it is in English, e.g.

„Mach schnell", sagte er.
'Hurry up,' he said.

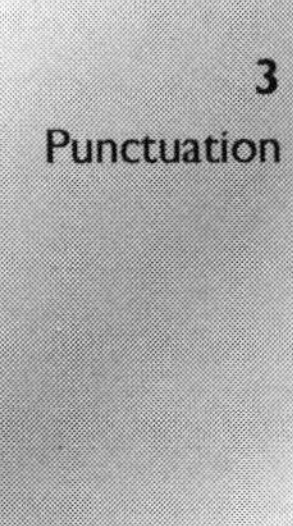

3.4 Exclamation marks

An exclamation mark is used after exclamations, as in English, e.g.

Um Gottes Willen!
For god's sake.

It is also used after imperatives in German, although you may find some inconsistency in use here, e.g.

Setz dich!
Sit down.

Komm nach dem Abendbrot zu uns rüber, wenn du Lust hast(!)
Come over to us after dinner if you feel like it.

Traditionally an exclamation mark was used at the beginning of a letter after the name of the addressee, and the first word in the next line was capitalized, as were all familiar pronominal forms (i.e. **Du, Dich, Dir, Dein**), e.g.

Lieber Franz!

Ich habe Deinen Brief vom 11. März dankbar erhalten.
Dear Franz,
Thank you very much for your letter of the 11th of March.

These days a comma has replaced the exclamation mark but the first word of the next line is not capitalized as in English, because the first word in the letter is regarded as the beginning of the sentence, and all forms related to **du** are written with small letters when not at the beginning of a sentence, e.g.

Lieber Franz,

ich habe deinen Brief vom 11. März dankbar erhalten.

Chapter 4

Case

German is a so-called inflectional language. Inflections are grammatical endings. The plural endings of nouns (books, children, oxen) and the endings of the various persons of the verb (I go, he goes) are examples of inflectional endings that both English and German share. Case is another form of inflection. At its simplest level case is the distinction between the subject (the nominative case), the direct object (the accusative case) and the indirect object (the dative case, i.e. 'to') in a sentence, e.g.

Der Vater hat seiner Tochter eine Email geschickt.
The father (nom.) sent an email (acc.) to his daughter (dat.).

This sentence shows case being applied to nouns, **der**, **seiner** and **eine** being the indicators not only of the gender of their respective nouns, but also of their case, something which English can only indicate with word order. But look at this variant:

Seiner Tochter hat der Vater eine Email geschickt.

This sentence means the same as the former although the connotation is different, i.e. it was his daughter he sent an email to and not anyone else. The forms **seiner** and **der** clearly indicate who is doing the sending (the subject or nominative) and who the email is being sent to (the indirect object or dative). One advantage of case, as this simple example illustrates, is that it can give the speaker a greater choice of word order.

English has only preserved separate case forms in its pronouns, i.e. 'I/me', 'he/him', 'she/her', 'we/us', 'they/them'; only in the second person, i.e. 'you/you', is no distinction made any more, although previously it was 'thou/thee' and 'ye/you'. English uses 'me', 'him', 'her' etc. in both the accusative and the dative, e.g.

Ich habe ihn zu Hause besucht und ihm einen Scheck für €55 gegeben.
I visited him (acc.) at home and gave him (dat.) a cheque (acc.) for 55 euros.

The difference between 'who' and 'whom', which is now waning in English, is also an example of case, i.e. nominative versus accusative/dative, e.g.

Who lives here?
Wer wohnt hier?

Who(m) did you visit in Berlin?
Wen hast du in Berlin besucht?

Who did you give the cheque to?/To whom did you give the cheque?
Wem hast du den Scheck gegeben?

The fact that 'whom' is fast dying out in English provides a living (just) example of the fate of case distinctions in English. But the point is that these distinctions are still very much alive and kicking in German and contribute to what English speakers find difficult about learning German. But once you have got your mind around the concept of case, it is extremely logical and getting it right is one of the great satisfactions of learning German.

In German, case endings don't just apply in the above instances. Adjectives take case endings, and verbs and prepositions can require that the pronouns and nouns that follow them take either the accusative, dative or genitive case, e.g.

Unser alter (nom. m.) **Nachbar hat einen sehr netten** (acc. m.) **Sohn.**
Our elderly neighbour has a very nice son.

Er hat mir geholfen. (The verb **helfen** takes a dative object.)
He helped me.

Meine Frau ist böse auf mich. (böse auf + acc. = angry with)
My wife is angry with me.

4.1 Case endings on nouns

In a few specific cases the nouns themselves take case endings, not just the determiners (i.e. indefinite and definite articles, possessives etc.) standing in front of them as illustrated above. These few cases need to be noted.

All masculine and neuter nouns take an **-(e)s** ending in the genitive case in the singular; monosyllabic nouns may take **-es** rather than simply **-s** in more formal sounding language, but you will never be wrong if you simply add **-s**, except if the noun itself ends in **s**, **ß** or **z**, when **-es** must be used, e.g.

der Name seines Sohn(e)s
his son's name

der Anfang des Gebets
the beginning of the prayer

die Größe des Kreuzes
the size of the cross

In very formal written style and in older texts monosyllabic masculine and neuter nouns in the dative singular optionally take an **-e** ending, e.g.

hinter dem Baume
behind the tree

auf dem Meeresgrunde
at the bottom of the sea

Dem Deutschen Volke
To the German people (written on the façade of the Reichstag)

Generally speaking, these days this ending is limited to standard expressions, e.g.

zu Hause
at home

im Grunde genommen
basically

im Laufe der Zeit
in the course of time

Nouns of all three genders must add an **n** in the dative plural if the plural form does not already end in **-n**, e.g.

in den Zimmern (< pl. **Zimmer**)
in the rooms

unter den Bäumen (< pl. **Bäume**)
under the trees

von den Mädchen (< pl. **Mädchen**, i.e. plural already ends in **n**)
from the girls

4.2 Other uses of the nominative case

A noun used in isolation (i.e. not as part of a sentence) is assumed to be in the nominative case, e.g.

Ein toller Film, nicht?
A great film, don't you think?

If an isolated noun is in fact the object of an otherwise unuttered sentence, as in abbreviated answers to questions, the accusative or dative may be required, e.g.

A: Was liest du? B: Einen Roman.
A: What are you reading. B: A novel.

A: Wem hast du das Geld gegeben? B: Dem Sohn.
A: Who did you give the money to? B: The son.

People are addressed in the nominative case, e.g.

Was ist passiert, mein lieber Freund?
What (has) happened, my dear friend?

Complements of the following so-called copula verbs are in the nominative case; copula verbs take the nom. case both before and after them: **bleiben** (to remain, stay), **scheinen** (to seem, appear), **sein** (to be) and **werden** (to become), e.g.

Er ist ein sehr guter Lehrer.
He is a very good teacher.

Er wird ein ausgezeichneter Athlet.
He's becoming an excellent athlete.

Er scheint ein ausgezeichneter Athlet zu sein.
He seems to be an excellent athlete.

4.3 Other uses of the accusative case

Expressions such as **guten Morgen, guten Tag** and **gute Nacht** are in the accusative case as they are theoretical contractions of something like **Ich wünsche dir einen guten Morgen.** Similarly with **guten Appetit** (bon appétit), **herzlichen Glückwunsch** (congratulations) and **(recht) vielen Dank** (thanks very much).

The date at the top of a letter stands in the accusative case, although this is not always evident, depending on the format applied, e.g.

den 8. (achten) September 2006 or **8. September 2006**
8th September 2006

Many adverbial expressions denoting a particular point in time or a period of time take the acc. case (see 4.4 and 9.4 for expressions of time in the gen. case), e.g.

Sie kommt erst nächsten Montag zurück.
She won't be back till next Monday.

Ich habe den ganzen Tag auf dich gewartet.
I waited all day for you.

For prepositions that take the acc. case see 12.1 and 12.3.

4.4 The genitive case

The genitive case usually indicates possession and very often equates to the use of 's and s' in English or to 'of', e.g.

die Kinder meines Lehrers
my teacher's children

die Spitze dieses Berges
the top of this mountain ('this mountain's top' sounds strange as it is inanimate)

The ending **-s** occurs in German too as a sign of possession but it is limited to personal names and no apostrophe is used with it, e.g.

Ottos Schwester/Marias neue Küche/Thomas Manns Romane
Otto's sister/Maria's new kitchen/Thomas Mann's novels

Forms like **Frau Emsbergers Hund** (Mrs Emsberger's dog) and **Herrn Müllers Büro** (Mr Müller's office) are also possible.

An expression such as 'my aunt's dog' cannot be expressed in this way in German but must be rephrased as 'the dog of my aunt' where 'of my aunt' is in the genitive case, i.e. **der Hund meiner Tante.**

In more formal sounding German the **-s** ending is applied to the names of towns and countries but in everyday German is replaced by **von**, e.g.

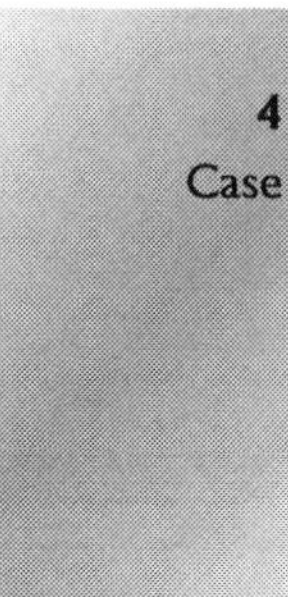

die Hauptstadt Deutschlands/Deutschlands Hauptstadt/die Hauptstadt von Deutschland
Germany's capital city/the capital city of Germany

in der Nähe Berlins/in der Nähe von Berlin
near (lit. in the vicinity of) Berlin

The adverbial expression **eines Tages** (one day) takes the gen. case (see 4.3 and 9.4 for expressions of time in the acc. case). The adverbial expressions **morgens/vormittags** (in the morning), **nachmittags** (in the afternoon), **abends** (in the evening), **nachts** (during the night), as well as **tagsüber** (during the day), have all been derived from genitive forms but are no longer seen as such; compare 'of a morning/evening' etc. in English.

For prepositions that take the gen. case see 12.4.

The genitive of the interrogative pronoun 'who' is 'whose' or **wessen** in German (see 7.5) and the genitive of 'whose' as a relative pronoun is **dessen** or **deren** (see 7.6).

4.5 Other uses of the dative case

Envelopes addressed to men, where the title used is **Herr**, require the dative of **Herr** to be used because what is implied is 'To Mr. X', e.g. **Herrn Joachim Polenz** (see n-nouns 6.1.1.h).

A considerable number of commonly used verbs take an indirect object, i.e. dative object, where in English the same verbs take a direct object (see 10.4.4 for use of these verbs in the passive), e.g.

danken (to thank s.o.)

Ich danke dir/Ihnen.
Thank you. (a stylistic variant of **danke schön**)

helfen (to help s.o.)

Die Krankenschwester hat dem Patienten nicht geholfen.
The nurse did not help the patient.

Other common verbs that take a dative object are:

antworten (to answer s.o.)
begegnen (to bump into s.o.)
beiwohnen (to be present at)
danken (to thank)

dienen (to serve s.o.)
folgen (to follow)
gehorchen (to obey)
gehören (to belong to)
glauben (to believe s.o.)
gleichen (to resemble)
gratulieren (to congratulate)
helfen (to help)
imponieren (to impress)
kündigen (to fire, sack)
nachlaufen (to run after)
nützen (to be of use to s.o.)
passen (to suit)
schaden (to be harmful to, to damage)
schmeicheln (to flatter)
trauen (to trust)
vertrauen (to have trust in)
wehtun (to hurt)
widersprechen (to contradict)
zustimmen (to agree with s.t.)

For prepositions that take the dat. case see 12.2 and 12.3.

4.6 Nouns in apposition

Look at the following sentence:

Ludwig Schmollgruber, früherer Direktor dieser Schule, ist heute in einem Autounfall umgekommen.
Ludwig Schmollgruber, this school's former headmaster, died today in a car accident.

The expression **früherer Direktor dieser Schule** is said to stand in apposition to **Ludwig Schmollgruber**; it offers, between commas, additional information about the noun that precedes it. This is significant in German as a noun standing in apposition to another must be in the same case as the noun to which it refers, e.g.

Ich habe Ludwig Schmollgruber, den früheren Direktor dieser Schule, gekannt.
I knew Ludwig Schmollgruber, this school's former headmaster.

Ich hatte es Herrn Schmollgruber, dem früheren Direktor dieser Schule, schon zigmal gesagt.
I had told Mr Schmollgruber, this school's former headmaster, umpteen times.

4.7 Order of cases in paradigms

So many aspects of German grammar are presented in the form of paradigms, as for example the following paradigm for the definite article:

	M	*F*	*N*	*Pl*
N	**der**	**die**	**das**	**die**
A	**den**	**die**	**das**	**die**
G	**des**	**der**	**des**	**der**
D	**dem**	**der**	**dem**	**den**

Not all books use this order of the cases when setting out such paradigms. NAGD is the traditional order in the Anglo-Saxon world and the one adhered to here. In Germany, where there is a long tradition of learning Latin and Greek at school, the order NGDA is traditionally used, as this is the order most usual in the learning of classical languages. This order is also the explanation for the cases commonly being called in German **der erste, zweite, dritte** and **vierte Fall** respectively, e.g. **Direktor steht im dritten Fall** – **Direktor** is in the dative case (in the last example in 4.6). Some textbooks for beginners adopt the order NADG, which is the order in which you normally learn the cases, as the genitive is usually regarded as the most difficult case to learn as well as being the least common.

Some textbooks also apply the order MNF to genders instead of the usual MFN when setting out paradigms like the above. This can be very confusing so be on the lookout for variation in this respect from book to book.

Chapter 5

Articles and other determiners

Articles is the collective name for the definite and the indefinite article. The definite article in English is 'the' and the indefinite article is 'a/an'; compare 'the man', a particular or definite man, and 'a man', meaning any man, not a particular one. These articles vary in German according to gender, number and case, as illustrated in 5.1.

Not only articles but other words too can stand in front of nouns and these also vary according to gender, number and case, e.g. **dieser** (this/these), **jeder** (each/every), **jener** (that/those), **mancher** (many a), **solcher** (such), **welcher** (which), as well as all the possessive pronouns (e.g. **mein**, **dein**, **sein**, **ihr**, **unser**, **euer**, **Ihr/ihr**). All these words, together with the articles, are referred to collectively as determiners. Depending on the determiner before the noun, any adjective that follows it will also be subject to a variety of endings (see 8.1.1 to 8.1.3), the variation in ending of the determiner and a following adjective being perhaps the most difficult aspect of German to master. Tricky and all as this might be to learn and apply, there is an underlying logic and system to it all. You need to persevere until the penny drops.

5.1 The definite article

	M	*F*	*N*	*Pl*
N	**der**	**die**	**das**	**die**
A	**den**	**die**	**das**	**die**
G	**des**	**der**	**des**	**der**
D	**dem**	**der**	**dem**	**den**

The definite article in English, 'the', could not be simpler whereas the German equivalents are considerably more complicated. Whenever you utter the word 'the' in German you have to ask yourself firstly whether the following noun is masculine, feminine, neuter or plural and secondly whether that noun is the subject (nom.), direct object (acc.) or indirect object (dat.) or shows possession (gen.); only then can you decide which of the sixteen words above is appropriate for the context. To say there are sixteen forms is of course a slight exaggeration, as several of the forms occur more than once; this is possible because context always makes it clear what is intended. Let's take **den**, for example:

> **Die Frau hat den Mann in der Stadt getroffen.** (masculine acc.)
> The woman met the man in the city.
>
> **Der Schulleiter hat den Eltern einen Brief geschickt.** (plural dat.)
> The headmaster sent the parents a letter.

As you should learn every new German noun together with its definite article, you will know from the outset that a noun is masculine, feminine or neuter, which is more or less a matter of rote learning, and thus all you have to think about is what case is required in a given context. If you understand the general make-up of a sentence, i.e. who is doing what to whom, deciding on the appropriate case is easy.

The **der/die/das** paradigm given here fulfils several functions in German, all of which are clear from the context, but the variety of meanings it can have can be confusing to the beginner. In addition to rendering the definite article, it can also translate 'that/those' (see 5.1.1), 'he/she/it' (see 7.1.5), as well as render the relative pronoun (see 7.6).

5.1.1 *Use of the definite article*

Although generally speaking the definite article is used in German as in English, there are a number of cases where it is required in German but not in English. Some cases are situations where its use can be defined, others are individual idioms.

a) It is always used before a large variety of abstract nouns:

die Geschichte	history
der Himmel	heaven
die Hölle	hell
das Leben	life

die Liebe	love
der Mensch	mankind
die moderne Kunst	modern art
die Natur	nature
der Tod	death

Die Natur ist zu bewundern.
Nature is to be admired.

der längste Krieg in der Geschichte
the longest war in history

So ist das Leben.
Such is life.

b) It is always used before names of towns and countries when they are preceded by an adjective:

das schöne Berlin
beautiful Berlin

im damaligen Deutschland
in Germany at that time

c) It is always used before seasons:

Der Frühling ist die schönste Jahreszeit.
Spring is the nicest season.

Sie war im Winter in Australien.
She was in Australia in winter.

d) It is always used with meals after prepositions:

nach/vor dem Abendessen
after/before dinner

beim/zum Frühstück
at/for breakfast

e) It is always used before the names of streets:

Ich wohne in der Friedrichstraße.
I live in Friedrich Street.

Es ist im Langenkampsweg passiert.
It happened in Langenkamp Road.

f) The names of just a few countries require the definite article (compare 'the Ukraine', 'the Sudan'):

masculine	*feminine*	*plural*
der Irak	**die Schweiz**	**die Niederlande**
der Iran	**die Slowakei**	**die Philippinen**
der Libanon	**die Türkei**	**die Vereinigten Staaten/die USA**
der Sudan	**die Ukraine**	

Use the appropriate case of the definite article where a preposition is involved, e.g.

Er wohnt schon seit Jahren in der Türkei/im Irak.
He has been living in Turkey/Iraq for years.

Wir fliegen morgen in die Vereinigten Staaten.
We are flying to the United States tomorrow.

The same applies to the name of a few regions:

das Elsass (Alsace)
der Kosovo
die Lombardei (Lombardy)
die Normandie
die Toskana (Tuscany)

g) It is used in various idioms together with prepositions where the article is not required in English, e.g.

in die Stadt/in der Stadt	to town/in town
in die Kirche/in der Kirche	to church/in church
in die Schule/in der Schule	to school/at school
Die Schule beginnt um...	School begins at...
im Gefängnis	in jail
an der Universität	at university
in der Praxis	in practice
über/unter dem Meeresspiegel	above/below sea level

aus dem Deutschen übersetzen	to translate from German
ins Deutsche übersetzen	to translate into German
im zweiten Gang	in second gear
mit dem Auto/Zug/Flugzeug etc.	by car/train/plane etc.
mit der Hand	by hand
das nächste Mal	next time

5.2 Other determiners inflected like der/die/das

A context may require you to refer to 'this man', rather than 'the man', or alternatively 'that man' (**jener Mann**), 'every man' (**jeder Mann**) or 'which man' (**welcher Mann**). Each of these words is a determiner which takes the same endings as **der/die/das**. Here are the paradigms for **dieser** and **welcher**, for example:

	M	*F*	*N*	*Pl*
N	**dieser**	**diese**	**dieses**	**diese**
A	**diesen**	**diese**	**dieses**	**diese**
G	**dieses**	**dieser**	**dieses**	**dieser**
D	**diesem**	**dieser**	**diesem**	**diesen**

	M	*F*	*N*	*Pl*
N	**welcher**	**welche**	**welches**	**welche**
A	**welchen**	**welche**	**welches**	**welche**
G	**welches**	**welcher**	**welches**	**welcher**
D	**welchem**	**welcher**	**welchem**	**welchen**

Even in English 'this' changes to 'these' before a plural noun and 'that' to 'those', which gives you some taste for what German is doing here, e.g. **dieses Haus** (this house) > **diese Häuser** (these houses).

Jener (that/those) is a word seldom encountered in speech or even in natural writing. There are two more usual ways of expressing 'that/those' in German. The first way is by using **der/die/das** but with emphasis, e.g.

> **Den Namen kenne ich nicht.** (commonly starting with the emphasized word)
> I don't know that name.

Wir wohnen in d e m Haus. (spacing can indicate stress in written German)
We live in <u>that</u> house.

The second way of expressing 'that/those' is simply by using **dieser** and dispensing with the distinction we make in English between 'this' and 'that':

Diesen Namen kenne ich nicht.
Wir wohnen in diesem Haus.

There are two other determiners which take the endings of **der/die/das** but these are most frequently encountered in the plural, i.e. **mancher** (some, many a), **solcher** (such), e.g.

Manche Leute mögen es so.
Some people (= many a person) like it like that.

Solche Leute kann ich nicht ausstehen.
I can't stand such people/people like that.

The most frequent way of expressing 'such a' is **solch ein**, where **solch** is invariable and **ein** is declined (see 5.3).

5.3 The indefinite article

	M	*F*	*N*
N	**ein**	**eine**	**ein**
A	**einen**	**eine**	**ein**
G	**eines**	**einer**	**eines**
D	**einem**	**einer**	**einem**

The indefinite article in English, 'a' or 'an', is very simple. The German equivalent, **ein**, not only means 'a/an' but also 'one'. The numeral 'one', when counting, is **eins**, e.g. **eins, zwei, drei** (see 13.1), but when followed by a noun **ein** in both senses takes all the above endings, the distinction in meaning between 'one' and 'a/an' being made by stressing the former, and the ending being determined by the gender and case of the noun, e.g.

Sie hat nur e i n e n Sohn.
She has only <u>one</u> son.

Sie hat einen Sohn.
She has a son.

There is of course no fourth column with plural forms in the above paradigm, unlike for **der/die/das**, because by definition 'a/an' cannot be followed by a plural noun.

5.3.1 *Omission of the indefinite article*

The indefinite article is sometimes omitted in German where it is used in English.

a) It is usually omitted after the preposition **als**, e.g.

Er hat seine Untertasse als Aschenbecher benutzt.
He used his saucer as an ashtray.

b) It is commonly omitted after the preposition **ohne** (see 12.1), e.g.

Er ist ohne Hut in dieser Hitze spazieren gegangen.
He has gone for a stroll in this heat without a hat.

c) It is omitted before professions after copula verbs (see 4.2) but is always inserted when the profession is preceded by an adjective:

Er ist Lehrer.
He is a teacher.

Er ist ein sehr guter Lehrer.
He is a very good teacher.

Er ist Vater geworden.
He has become a father.

d) It is omitted before nationalities after copula verbs (see 4.2) but is always inserted when the nationality is preceded by an adjective:

Er ist Deutscher/Berliner.
He is a German/Berliner.

Er ist ein waschechter Deutscher/Berliner.
He is a genuine German/Berliner.

e) It is omitted in various standard expressions:

Das ist schade.	That's a pity.
Kopfschmerzen haben	to have a headache
Auge um Auge	an eye for an eye
Es ist Viertel vor/nach zwei.	It is a quarter to/past two.

5.4 Other determiners inflected like ein

There are a number of determiners that take the same endings as **ein**, namely **kein** (no, not a/any) and the possessive adjectives **mein**, **dein**, **sein**, **ihr**, **unser**, **euer** and **ihr**, several of which sound like **ein**, as you can see, e.g.

	M	*F*	*N*	*Pl*
N	**mein**	**meine**	**mein**	**meine**
A	**meinen**	**meine**	**mein**	**meine**
G	**meines**	**meiner**	**meines**	**meiner**
D	**meinem**	**meiner**	**meinem**	**meinen**

The paradigm for these deteminers has a fourth, plural column which is not present in the **ein** paradigm (see 5.3).

5.5 Indefinite pronouns used as determiners (see 7.7.1 and 8.1.4)

When followed by a plural noun the pronouns **alle** (all), **andere** (other), **einige** (some), **mehrere** (several), **viele** (many), **verschiedene** (various/different) and **wenige** (few) are used as determiners which are inflected for case, e.g.

N	**alle/viele Städte**	all/many cities
A	**alle/viele Städte**	
G	**aller/vieler Städte**	
D	**allen/vielen Städten**	

Chapter 6

Nouns

6.1 Gender of nouns

All German nouns belong to one of three genders: masculine, feminine or neuter. It is imperative you learn nouns together with the appropriate definite article (i.e. **der**, **die** or **das**, see 5.1), as the ramifications of belonging to one of these three genders pervade German. Without knowing the gender of a noun you will not, for example, be able to correctly say 'the table/door/house', 'a table/door/house', 'a big table/door/house', 'this table/door/house', 'which table/door/house', or 'his table/door/house' as 'the', 'a', 'big', 'that', 'this', 'which' and 'his' will most likely vary as 'table' is masculine, 'door' is feminine and 'house' is neuter, e.g.

der Tisch/die Tür/das Haus

ein Tisch/eine Tür/ein Haus

ein großer Tisch/eine große Tür/ein großes Haus

dieser Tisch/diese Tür/dieses Haus

welcher Tisch/welche Tür/welches Haus

sein Tisch/seine Tür/sein Haus

You will even be faced by nouns not preceded by a determiner like **der/die/das**, which indicate the gender of the noun, but where you simply need to know intuitively what gender the noun is, e.g. **frische Milch** (fresh milk) and **kaltes Bier** (cold beer), where the knowledge that **Milch** is feminine and **Bier** is neuter determines the ending on the preceding adjective.

Learning the gender of each noun is one of the most difficult aspects of learning German but one you will have to master. There are a few rules that will give you some assistance in learning the gender of a noun but they only cover a minority of nouns.

A small minority of German nouns are neuter, possibly no more than 10 per cent, so if you have no idea of the gender of a noun and are forced to guess, it would not be wise to opt for neuter. Feminine nouns, as the rules given below will indicate, are often recognizable as feminine due to their ending. Nouns that end in -**e** are overwhelmingly feminine. So few neuter nouns end in -**e** that they can be rote learnt, e.g. **das Auge** (eye), **das Ende** (end), **das Interesse** (interest). Masculine nouns that end in -**e** are weak nouns (also called n-nouns, see 6.1.1.h) and nearly all of them refer to masculine beings and thus their masculine gender is obvious, e.g. **der Russe** (Russian). Otherwise you can assume that any noun ending in -**e** is feminine, e.g. **die Decke** (ceiling), **die Katze** (cat), **die Tapete** (wallpaper).

Sometimes the meaning of a noun serves as an aid to gender. The word for a 'painter', **der Maler**, must be masculine as it refers to a male being. The word for a 'bear', **der Bär**, is also masculine as it refers to a large, strong animal, whereas a 'mouse' is **die Maus**; but this does not help much as the word for a 'horse' is **das Pferd**. But there is a sub-rule here that can help: if there is a separate word for the male and female of a given animal, e.g. 'stallion' and 'mare', those words will be masculine and feminine respectively but the generic word, 'horse', will often be neuter, e.g. **das Huhn/der Hahn/die Henne** (chicken/rooster/hen), **das Schwein/der Eber/die Sau** (pig/boar/sow). But this rule has its limits too as a 'duck' is **die Ente** and a 'goose' is **die Gans**, but that is because, as in English, the name of the female of the species is the generic term for the species.

Sometimes gender is determined by the form of the word; certain endings will always be masculine, feminine or neuter, e.g. **die Gelegenheit** (opportunity) and **die Geschwindigkeit** (speed) because all nouns that end in **-heit** or **-keit** are feminine (see below).

The rules for gender that follow are far from ideal but they are as good as it gets.

When nouns are joined together to form a compound noun (see 2.4 and 6.8) the gender of the new word is the same as that of the last element in the compound, e.g. **die Zeit** + **der Plan** > **der Zeitplan** (schedule), **das Haus** + **die Tür** > **die Haustür** (front door).

6.1.1 *Rules for masculine gender*

Nouns in the following categories are masculine:

a) All professions and nationalities that refer to male beings, e.g. **der Bäcker** (baker), **der Lehrer** (teacher), **der Philosoph** (philosopher), **der Amerikaner** (American), **der Deutsche** (German).
b) The names of large wild animals, e.g. **der Elefant** (elephant), **der Löwe** (lion), **der Tiger** (tiger). Large domestic animals are often neuter but the male of the species, where a separate word exists, is masculine, e.g. **der Enterich** (drake), **der Hengst** (stallion), **der Stier** (bull).
c) The four seasons, e.g. **der Frühling, der Sommer, der Herbst, der Winter**.
d) The days of the week, e.g. **der Sonnabend, der Sonntag, der Montag** etc.
e) The months of the year, e.g. **der Januar, der Februar, der März** etc.
f) All nouns derived from verbs beginning with an inseparable prefix where the **-en** of the infinitive has been dropped, e.g. **der Besuch** (visit, <**besuchen** 'to visit'), **der Versuch** (attempt, <**versuchen** 'to try').
g) The names of many rivers (those that aren't masculine are feminine, never neuter), e.g. **der Inn, der Lech, der Main, der Rhein** (Rhine); **der Amazonas** (Amazon), **der Ganges, der Nil** (Nile).
h) **Weak masculine nouns or n-nouns**
Nearly all the following nouns denote masculine beings but don't end in **-e**, but, like those that do end in **-e**, all are weak masculine nouns and also take **-en** in the singular in all cases but the nominative. All nouns ending in **-arch, -ant, -anz, -ent, -enz, -ist, -it, -krat, -nom, -ot** and **-soph** belong here.

der Agent	**der Despot**	**der Idiot**	**der Mensch**
der Akrobat	**der Diplomat**	**der Journalist**	**der Monarch**
der Analphabet	**der Dozent**	**der Kaffer***	**der Musikant**
der Architekt	**der Elefant**	**der Kakerlak**	**der Nachbar***
der Asiat	**der Favorit**	**der Kamerad**	**der Nachfahr**
der Astronom	**der Fink**	**der Kandidat**	**der Narr**
der Bandit	**der Fotograf**	**der Katholik**	**der Obelisk**
der Bär	**der Fürst**	**der Klient**	**der Päderast**
der Bauer*	**der Geck**	**der Kommandant**	**der Patriarch**
der Bayer*	**der Graf**	**der Konsonant**	**der Patriot**
der Bürokrat	**der Gymnasiast**	**der Kosak**	**der Philosoph**
der Chaot	**der Held**	**der Kosmonaut**	**der Pilot**
der Christ	**der Herr***	**der Leopard**	**der Pirat**
der Demokrat	**der Hirt**	**der Mandant**	**der Polizist**

der Präfekt	**der Regent**	**der Student**	**der Urahn**
der Präsident	**der Rekrut**	**der Tor**	**der Veteran**
der Prinz	**der Soldat**	**der Transvestit**	**der Vorfahr**
der Prophet	**der Spatz**	**der Tyrann**	**der Zar**
der Rebell	**der Steinmetz**	**der Ungar***	**der Zypriot**

* **Herr** takes **-n** in the singular but **-en** in the plural, whereas **Bauer, Bayer, Kaffer, Nachbar** and **Ungar** take **-n** in both the singular and the plural.

There are a few weak masculine nouns, all loanwords with a stressed ending, that don't designate living beings:

der Automat, Diamant, Paragraph, Planet, Quotient, Satellit

The following masculine nouns in **-e** take **-ens** in the genitive but otherwise behave like other weak masculine nouns, taking **-en** in all cases except the nom. in the singular, as well as the plural. These are the only weak nouns ending in **-e** that do not refer to masculine beings:

der Buchstabe	**der Funke**	**der Glaube**	**der Wille**
der Drache	**der Gedanke**	**der Name**	

6.1.2 *Rules for feminine gender*

Nouns in the following categories are feminine:

a) All nouns ending in **-in**, which is added to the masculine form of professions and nationalities to render the female of the species, e.g. **die Lehrerin, die Philosophin, die Amerikanerin.**
b) All nouns ending in **-heit** and **-keit**, all of which express abstract concepts, e.g. **die Gelegenheit** (opportunity), **die Gemütlichkeit** (cosiness).
c) All nouns ending in **-ung**, e.g. **die Übung** (exercise), **die Zeitung** (newspaper).
d) All nouns of French origin ending in **-ie**, **-ik**, **-ion**, e.g. **die Biologie, die Musik, die Station.**
e) Those rivers that are not masculine (see 6.1.1.g) are feminine, never neuter, e.g. **die Donau** (Danube), **die Elbe, die Isar, die Oder, die Weser; die Seine, die Themse** (Thames).

6.1.3 *Rules for neuter gender*

Nouns in the following categories are neuter:

a) All diminutives ending in **-chen** and **-lein** regardless of the gender of the orginal noun, e.g. **das Hündchen** (< **der Hund** 'puppy'), **das Püppchen** (< **die Puppe** 'little doll').
b) All nouns derived from infinitives, e.g. **das Essen** (eating/food), **das Kochen** (cooking), **das Lesen** (reading).
c) The names of all cities and countries (except the very few notable masculine and feminine ones, see 5.1.1.f) are neuter. You are not normally aware of this, e.g.

Er wohnt in Warschau/Polen.
He lives in Warsaw/Poland.

But if the name of a town or country is qualified in some way, usually by an adjective, the definite article must be used and that must be neuter, e.g.

das wunderschöne Venedig
wonderful Venice

im damaligen Deutschland
in Germany at that time

das Rom von heute/von Cäsar
the Rome of today/of Caesar

6.2 Pluralization of nouns

Deciding on how to pluralize a German noun is a bothersome aspect of the language, as plurals can be formed in any one of nine ways, i.e. by adding **¨**, **-e**, **¨e**, **-er**, **¨er**, **-n**, **-en**, **-s** or by simply doing nothing to the noun. There is a direct connection between the gender of a noun and the way it forms its plural – only certain endings apply to certain genders. Some generalizations apply, even if there are many exceptions to these rules, e.g.

a) A monosyllabic masculine noun forms its plural by adding **¨e** (**Baum** > **Bäume**), although some add just **-e** (**Schuh** > **Schuhe**).
b) A feminine noun takes **-en** (**Tür** > **Türen**), but some take **¨e** (**Stadt** > **Städte**).

c) A monosyllabic neuter noun takes ¨-er (**Haus** > **Häuser**), but some take -e (**Jahr** > **Jahre**).

Nearly all German nouns belong to one of the following five groups. Learn the following by heart and you will seldom have to deal with exceptions to these rules. The system applied below is as follows. Each group starts with the rule, e.g. **do not change in the plural.** Then follow the definitions of the nouns that belong in that group and then the common exceptions to the rule are listed. The lists of exceptions are not complete, but they do contain by far the most common nouns you are likely to encounter. In some instances the lists contain not the exceptions to the rule, but the nouns to which the rule in question applies, as the number of nouns concerned is finite. A little time spent now getting this under your belt will save you a great deal of floundering later.

6.2.1 GROUP 1: *do not change in the plural*

1 Masculine and neuter nouns ending in **-el**, **-en** and **-er**, e.g. **der Beutel, der Balken, das Fenster**
2 Diminutives in **-chen** and **-lein**, e.g. **das Männchen, das Büchlein**
3 Neuter nouns beginning with **Ge-** and ending in **-e**, e.g. **Gebäude**
4 Two feminine nouns, **die Mutter** and **die Tochter**, which become **Mütter** and **Töchter**

These masculine nouns do not take an ending but do take an Umlaut in the plural:

der Acker	**der Faden**	**der Laden**	**der Schaden**
der Apfel	**der Garten**	**der Mangel**	**der Schnabel**
der Boden	**der Graben**	**der Mantel**	**der Vater**
der Bogen	**der Hammer**	**der Nagel**	**der Vogel**
der Bruder	**der Kasten**	**der Ofen**	Also: **das Kloster**

6.2.2 GROUP 2: *add ¨-e or -e (if the vowel is not umlautable)*

1 Masculine nouns of one syllable (as well as a few bisyllabic nouns), e.g. **Baum, Stuhl**
2 Some neuter nouns of one syllable (listed here); none take an Umlaut except **das Floß**
3 Some feminine nouns of one syllable (listed here)
4 Masculine and neuter nouns ending in **-ich**, **-ig**, **-ing**, **-nis**, **-sal**, e.g **der König, der Jüngling, das Gefängnis** (NB: Those ending in **-nis** go **-nisse** in the plural)

5 Masculine and neuter nouns beginning with Ge- and ending in a stressed syllable, e.g. **das Gebet** (see Group 3 for some neuter exceptions)

These masculine nouns do not take an Umlaut in the plural:

der Arm	**der Flur**	**der Mond**	**der Ruf**	**der Tag**
der Besuch	**der Hund**	**der Ort**	**der Schuh**	
der Dom	**der Monat**	**der Punkt**	**der Stoff**	

These neuter nouns do not take an Umlaut (no neuter nouns in Group 2 do except **das Floß**):

das Bein	**das Haar**	**das Pult**	**das Schwein**	**das Tier**	**das Wort***
das Boot	**das Jahr**	**das Schaf**	**das Spiel**	**das Tor**	
das Ding	**das Pferd**	**das Schiff**	**das Stück**	**das Werk**	

*Also found in Group 3 but with a different meaning, i.e. **Worte** is a collective referring to what someone said, e.g. **Gottes Worte** (the words of God).

These are the most common feminine nouns in this group but there are more:

die Angst	**die Gans**	**die Luft**	**die Nuss**	**die Wurst**
die Axt	**die Hand**	**die Lust**	**die Schnur**	
die Bank	**die Haut**	**die Macht**	**die Stadt**	
die Braut	**die Kraft**	**die Maus**	**die Sucht**	
die Faust	**die Kuh**	**die Nacht**	**die Wand**	
die Frucht	**die Kunst**	**die Not**	**die Werkstatt**	

6.2.3 *GROUP 3: add ¨er or -er (if the vowel is not umlautable)*

1 A few masculine nouns (listed here)
2 Some neuter nouns (listed here)
3 Masculine and neuter nouns ending in **-tum**, e.g. **der Reichtum**, **das Altertum**

These are the masculine nouns that don't end in **-tum**:

der Geist	**der Mann**	**der Strauch**
der Gott	**der Mund**	**der Wald**
der Leib	**der Rand**	**der Wurm**

This is a sample of the neuter nouns but there are more:

das Amt	**das Feld**	**das Haus**	**das Loch**
das Bad	**das Gehalt**	**das Huhn**	**das Maul**
das Band	**das Geld**	**das Kalb**	**das Nest**
das Bild	**das Gesicht**	**das Kind**	**das Rad**
das Buch	**das Gespenst**	**das Lamm**	**das Schloss**
das Dach	**das Glas**	**das Land**	**das Tal**
das Dorf	**das Glied**	**das Licht**	**das Volk**
das Ei	**das Grab**	**das Lied**	**das Wort***

* Also found in Group 2 but with a different meaning, i.e. **Wörter** refers to indiviudal words, not words as a collective, e.g. **das Wörterbuch** (dictionary).

6.2.4 *GROUP 4: add -n or -en*

1 Most feminine nouns (i.e. all those not listed in Group 2)
2 Weak masculine nouns, also called n-nouns (i.e. all those ending in **-e** plus those listed here, see 6.1.1.h)
3 A few neuter nouns (listed here)

These masculine nouns are weak although they do not end in **-e**:

der Bär	**der Graf**	**der Präsident**
der Bauer	**der Held**	**der Prinz**
der Dozent	**der Herr**	**der Soldat**
der Elefant	**der Kamerad**	**der Spatz**
der Fink	**der Mensch**	**der Student**
der Fürst	**der Nachbar**	**der Vorfahr**

These are the few neuter nouns in this group:

das Auge	**das Hemd**	**das Interesse**
das Bett	**das Herz**	**das Ohr**
das Ende	**das Insekt**	

6.2.5 *GROUP 5: add -s*

1 Foreign words ending in **-a**, **-i**, **-o** and **-u**, e.g. **das Sofa**, **das Taxi**, **das Auto**, **das Känguru**
2 English loanwords ending in **-y**, e.g. **das Baby**, **das Hobby**, **das Handy**
3 Several English and French loanwords: **der Park**, **der Scheck**, **die Bar**, **die Band**, **das Hotel**, **das Modem**, **das Restaurant**

6.3 Diminutization of nouns

There are two ways of forming the diminutive in German, by adding either -**chen** or -**lein** to a noun while umlauting the vowel in the root syllable if it can take an Umlaut, e.g. **das Haus** > **das Häuschen, der Tisch** > **das Tischlein**. These days -**lein** tends to sound a little poetic or archaic. In practice -**chen** is much more commonly used than -**lein**, so stick to -**chen** yourself. All diminutized nouns, whatever their original gender, become neuter once they take either of these endings.

Although in theory any (usually only) monosyllabic noun can be diminutized in either of these ways, it is best not to use diminutives you have not seen or heard before; they are seldom necessary. If you want to say 'a small card', for example, that can be just as well expressed by **eine kleine Karte** as by **ein (kleines) Kärtchen**.

Although the diminutized form generally expresses a smaller example of whatever the noun is, there are numerous recognized diminutive forms that render a new item of vocabulary, e.g. a **Fräulein** is not a small **Frau** but an unmarried woman, **Mädchen** (diminutive of archaic **die Maid** 'maiden') is the usual word for girl, and a **Brötchen** is a breadroll, not a small loaf of bread. 'Male' and 'female' of animals are rendered by the words **Männchen** and **Weibchen**, which theoretically can also mean 'little man' and 'little woman', but the latter is a good example of the added semantic connotations that can occur when a noun is diminutized and why you should be careful with diminutives because **Weibchen** can also mean 'the little woman' (i.e. the wife) or a 'dumb broad'. The young of animals are often diminutive forms, e.g. **Kätzchen** (kitten), **Wölfchen** (wolf cub).

In southern German the endings -**l**, -**el**, -**erl** and -**ele** are commonly heard and occasionally written, e.g. **das Mäde(r)l, das Backhendl** (= **Backhähnchen** 'roast chicken'), **das Dirndl(kleid)** (traditional female costume in the south). In Switzerland the ending -**li** is used in spoken German, e.g. **das Müesli** (muesli), **das Maidli** (girl), **das Tischli** (table).

Using a diminutive ending does not prevent you from also using an adjective like **klein** (small) or **winzig** (tiny) with the noun in question if you want to impart how minute something is, e.g.

> **Meine Tante hat ein kleines Ferienhäuschen auf Helgoland.**
> My aunt has a really small holiday house on Heligoland.

Diminutives are particularly common in fairytales, whose titles frequently contain a diminutive too, e.g. **Aschenbrödel/Aschenputtel** (Cinderella),

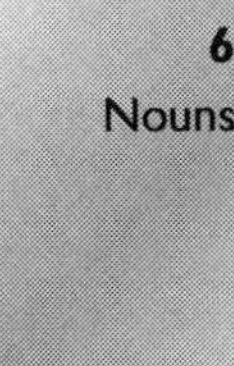

Dornröschen (Sleeping Beauty), **Hänsel und Gretel** (Hansel and Gretel), **Rotkäppchen** (Little Red Riding Hood), **Rumpelstilzchen** (Rumpelstiltskin).

6.4 Names of towns

6.4.1 *Names of German towns*

The names of a few well-known German-speaking towns differ in German from English. Where the stress differs from English below, ' precedes the stressed syllable:

Basel	Bâle
Hameln	Hamlin
Han'nover	Hanover
'Koblenz	Coblence
Köln	Cologne
München	Munich
Nürnberg	Nuremberg
Wien	Vienna
Zürich	Zurich

6.4.2 *Names of foreign towns*

The names of many cities throughout the world differ in German from English; these are the most important; sometimes the difference is merely one of spelling. Some are spelt as in English, and are thus not given here, but are pronounced differently in German, e.g. **Pa'ris, Stockholm** (pron. shtockholm).

Ant'werpen	Antwerp	**Brügge**	Bruges
A'then	Athens	**Brüssel**	Brussels
Bagdad	Baghdad	**Bukarest**	Bucharest
Belgrad	Belgrade	**Damaskus**	Damascus
Breslau	Wroclaw	**Danzig**	Gdansk

Den Haag	The Hague	**Nizza**	Nice
Flo'renz	Florence	**Ost'ende**	Ostend
Genf	Geneva	**Peking**	Beijing
Kairo	Cairo	**Piräus**	Pireus
Kalkutta	Calcutta	**Pjöngjang**	Pyongyang
Kanton	Canton	**Prag**	Prague
Kapstadt	Cape Town	**Pressburg**	Bratislava
Karatschi	Karachi	**Rangun**	Rangoon
Khartum	Khartoum	**Reval**	Talinn
Kiew	Kiev	**Riad**	Riyadh
Königsberg	Kaliningrad	**Rom**	Rome
Kopenhagen	Copenhagen	**Sankt Petersburg**	Saint P.
Laibach	Ljubljana	**Sevilla**	Seville
Lissabon	Lisbon	**Singapur**	Singapore
Löwen	Louvain	**Straßburg**	Strasbourg
Lüttich	Liège	**'Tanger**	Tangiers
Lu'zern	Lucerne	**Teheran**	Tehran
Mailand	Milan	**'Tiflis**	Tbilisi
Mexiko-Stadt	M. City	**Tokio**	Tokyo
Moskau	Moscow	**Tripolis**	Tripoli
Ne'apel	Naples	**Ve'nedig**	Venice
Neu-Delhi	New Delhi	**Warschau**	Warsaw
Nimwegen	Nijmegen	**Wilna**	Vilnius

6.4.3 *Inhabitants of towns*

The male inhabitant of a town is derived by adding **-er** to the name, e.g. **Berlin** > **der Berliner**, and the female inhabitant is derived by adding **-in** to this, e.g. **die Berlinerin**. The plurals are **die Berliner** and **die Berlinerinnen** respectively. The adjectival form of such place names also ends in -**er** and is indeclinable, e.g. **der Kölner Dom, der Münchner Hauptbahnhof.**

6.5 Names of countries (see Appendix 1)

6.5.1 *Inhabitants of countries*

Nationalities are derived from the names of countries, as in English, e.g. **Norwegen/der Norweger** (Norway/the Norwegian). All nationalities follow one of two patterns – they either end in -**er** or -**e**. Male inhabitants ending in -**er** do not change in the plural and the females add -**in** with a plural in -**innen**, e.g. **England** (England), **der Engländer** (the Englishman), **die Engländer** (the Englishmen/the English [m. & f.]), **die Engländerin** (the English woman), **die Engländerinnen** (the English women/the English [f.]). Male inhabitants ending in -**e** are n-nouns, as are **Ungar** and **Zypriot**; the female equivalent ends in -**in** and is of course not weak, e.g. **Schweden** (Sweden), **der Schwede** (the Swede), **die Schweden** (the Swedes), **die Schwedin** (the Swedish woman), **die Schwedinnen** (the Swedish women).

There is only one exception to these two patterns for the deriving of nationality, namely 'the German'. **Der Deutsche** is an adjectival noun, the female equivalent consequently being **die Deutsche** (see 6.7). The difference between **der Deutsche** and **der Schwede**, as illustrated here, does not immediately meet the eye, but put the indefinite article in front of them and you see the difference, e.g. **ein Schwede** but **ein Deutscher**. The same happens with **viele**, for example: **viele Schweden** (many Swedes) but **viele Deutsche** (many Germans); **viele Schwedinnen** (many Swedish women) but **viele Deutsche [Frauen]** (many German women).

6.6 Feminizing agents

German, unlike English, is inherently sexist because of the existence of grammatical gender. You cannot get around the fact in German that **Maler** (painter) is masculine, whereas its English equivalent can refer to a person of either sex who paints. The female form of professions, like that of nationalities (see 6.5.1), must be derived from the male form. To do so you simply add -**in** to the male form, e.g. **der Maler** > **die Malerin, der Journalist** > **die Journalistin, der Sekretär** > **die Sekretärin**. Where the male form is an n-noun ending in -**e**, the -**e** is replaced by -**in**, e.g. **der Beamte** >

die Beamtin (civil servant). There are a few traditionally female professions where this has led to alternative forms, e.g. **die Krankenschwester** (nurse [f.]), **der Krankenpfleger** (nurse [m.]), which of course can give rise to **die Krankenpflegerin**.

If referring to a mixed group of males and females of a given profession or nationality, the masculine form traditionally prevails, e.g.

> **Alle Lehrer an dieser Schule kriegen nächsten Montag frei.**
> All teachers at this school are getting next Monday off.

> **Alle Polen kaufen gern in Deutschland ein.**
> All Poles like shopping in Germany.

In this politically correct age it is most usual when addressing mixed groups of a given profession to use both the male and female forms and to mention the females first, e.g.

> **Liebe Lehrerinnen und Lehrer** (at the beginning of a speech)
> Dear teachers

In writing, the following inclusive form is used with professions: **LehrerInnen**. The above introduction to a speech might well have been written **Liebe LehrerInnen** in a letter, but if read aloud this must be read as **Liebe Lehrerinnen und Lehrer**.

See indefinite pronouns (7.7) for a further example of masculine forms predominating in German due to grammatical gender.

6.7 Adjectival nouns

An adjectival noun is a noun formed from an adjective. This is done first and foremost with adjectives referring to male and female beings. You can express, for example, 'a blind man' in one of two ways, either as **ein blinder Mann** or as **ein Blinder**, where the adjective is capitalized and the noun is understood. Likewise with 'a blind woman', i.e. **eine blinde Frau** or **eine Blinde**. And in the plural 'blind people' can be expressed as **Blinde**, where 'people' is understood. But being in fact adjectives where the following noun is implied, these adjectival nouns are inflected like adjectives, which means that all the above examples may change when preceded by the definite article, e.g. **der Blinde** (the blind man), **die Blinde** (the blind woman), **die Blinden** (the blind). In the plural we do something similar in English, i.e. the blind, the poor, the living etc. Such nouns are derived from a limited number of adjectives on the whole. Quite a number of such adjectives are derived from past participles (marked with an asterisk) and some from present participles (marked with two asterisks); here is a representative list:

der/die Alte	the old man/woman/person
der/die Arme	the poor man/woman/person
der/die Angeklagte*	the accused
der/die Angestellte*	the employee
der/die Anwesende**	the person present, bystander
der/die Arbeitslose	the unemployed man/woman/person
der Beamte[1]	the official
der/die Bekannte*	the acquaintance
der/die Deutsche[2]	the German
der/die Erwachsene*	the adult/grown-up
der/die Fremde	the stranger
der/die Gefangene*	the prisoner
der/die Kranke	the sick man/woman/person (patient)
der/die Reiche	the rich man/woman/person
der/die Reisende**	the traveller
der/die Schuldige	the guilty man/woman/person
der/die Tote	the dead man/woman/person
der/die Verwandte*	the relative

Notes:

1 The feminine of this word is not an adjectival noun but a normal noun ending in **-in**, e.g. **die Beamtin** (female official).

2 Of all nationalities only 'the German' is expressed by an adjectival noun (see 6.5.1).

6.7.1 *Neuter adjectival nouns*

There is another small category of adjectival nouns that are neuter. These do not refer to people, like those above, but usually refer to abstract concepts, e.g. **das Gute/Schlechte/Blöde daran** (the good/bad/stupid thing about it). Such neuter adjectival nouns commonly follow the impersonal pronouns **alles, etwas, nichts, viel** and **wenig**, weak adjectival endings (see 8.1.1) being used after **alles** and strong adjectival endings (see 8.1.3) after all the others, e.g.

Ich habe schon alles Mögliche probiert.
I've already tried everything possible.

Auf wiedersehen. Alles Gute.
Goodbye. All the best.

Das ist nichts Neues/etwas Besonderes.
That's nothing new/something special.

Er hatte viel/wenig Positives zu berichten.
He had a lot of/few positive things to report.

Such forms occasionally occur in other contexts too, e.g. **Gehacktes** (minced meat). The ending varies according to the determiner in front of it because, remember, it has the meaning of a noun but the form of an adjective, e.g.

Dieses Gehackte riecht nicht gut./Ich muss noch Gehacktes fürs Abendessen kaufen.
This mince doesn't smell right./I still have to buy mince for dinner.

6.8 Compound nouns

As mentioned under 2.4, German does not hyphenate compound nouns but is happy to join the words together, even though this may lead to what seem like ridiculously long words, e.g. **Balkonsonnenbader** (balcony sunbather), **Hupverbotsbeachter** (someone who observes the prohibition on tooting). When nouns are joined together in this way, they take the gender of the final element, e.g. **die Küche** (kitchen), **der Tisch** (table), **der Küchentisch** (kitchen table).

The above examples also illustrate a complication in forming such compounds for which it is unfortunately not possible to formulate prescriptive rules. **Balkonsonnenbader** is formed from the nouns **Balkon** +

Sonne + **Bader, Küchentisch** from **Küche** + **Tisch** and **Hupverbotsbeachter** from **Hup** + **Verbot** + **Beachter.** Note the medial **n** in the first two and the medial **s** in the last example. These sounds are inserted in countless such compounds. Native speakers can hear where they are required but it is very difficult to formulate rules that will be of help to non-native speakers. About the only thing that can be said with a reasonable degree of certainty is that if a word ends in **-e**, it will take an **n** when another word is joined to it, as illustrated in the two examples above. As for where **s** is required in compounds, only this can be said: when a noun ends in **-heit/-keit** or **-ung**, an **s** must be inserted, e.g. **Gelegenheitsarbeit** (casual work), **Zeitungszar** (media baron). On rare occasions it is **-es-** that is inserted, e.g. **Jahreszeit** (season), **Meeresspiegel** (sea level). Otherwise, as far as **s** is concerned, you will simply have to observe and copy.

For compounds like **der Rotwein** (red wine), where German prefixes the adjective to the noun rather than inflecting it as an attributive adjective, see 8.1.5.1.

6.9 **Nouns in apposition** (see 4.6)

Chapter 7

Pronouns

As pronouns by definition stand in for nouns and nouns are subject to case (see 4.1), so are pronouns. The following sorts of pronouns occur in both English and German: personal pronouns (e.g. I, me), possessive pronouns (e.g. my/mine), reflexive pronouns (e.g. myself), demonstrative pronouns (e.g. this, that), relative pronouns (e.g. the man who/that ...), interrogative pronouns (e.g. who, which, what), indefinite pronouns (e.g. someone, several). Each category of pronoun has its own complexities and they are looked at individually in this chapter.

7.1 Personal pronouns

Personal pronouns consist of subject pronouns (nominative case), object pronouns (accusative case) and indirect object pronouns (dative case). This is the full paradigm of forms, but the three categories are dealt with separately below.

N	**ich**	**du**	**er**	**sie**	**es**	**wir**	**ihr**	**Sie**	**sie**
A	**mich**	**dich**	**ihn**	**sie**	**es**	**uns**	**euch**	**Sie**	**sie**
D	**mir**	**dir**	**ihm**	**ihr**	**ihm**	**uns**	**euch**	**Ihnen**	**ihnen**

7.1.1 *Subject or nominative pronouns*

The subject pronouns are:

ich (I), **du** (you), **er** (he), **sie** (she), **es** (it), **wir** (we), **ihr** (you), **Sie** (you), **sie** (they)

Ich is referred to as the first person singular, **du** as the second person singular (familiar), **er/sie/es** as the third persons singular, **wir** as the first person plural, **ihr** as the second person plural (familiar), **Sie** as the second person singular and plural (polite) and **sie** as the third person plural.

7.1.1.1 Second person subject pronouns

Sie meaning 'you' (polite) is derived historically from **sie** meaning 'they' (it is akin to the so-called royal 'we'). It is capitalized to distinguish it from **sie** in writing. No distinction between the two is made in speech where intonation and context always make the distinction clear, e.g. **Wohnen Sie schon lange in Deutschland?** (Have you lived in Germany long?). Theoretically, in speech this could mean 'Have they lived in Germany long?' but the circumstances of the conversation would make it obvious what is intended.

You will notice that German has three words for 'you', **du**, **ihr** and **Sie**. English is peculiar in having just one word. **Du** is used when addressing children, animals, relatives and close friends, i.e. people whom you normally address by their first or given name. God is also addressed as **du** in prayer. **Du** is regarded as the familiar form of address.

The plural of **du** is **ihr**, e.g.

> **Gehst du jetzt nach Hause, Peter?**
> Are you going home now, Peter?
>
> **Geht ihr jetzt nach Hause?**
> Are you (more than one person) going home now?

In colloquial English you often hear things like 'you all', 'youse', 'you guys' or 'the two/three of you' where the speaker is attempting to fill the void of a plural form of 'you' in the language. These are all expressed by **ihr** or **Sie** (see below) in German.

When addressing strangers or acquaintances with whom you are not (yet) on Christian name terms, **Sie**, which is used for both singular and plural, is the appropriate form; it is regarded as the polite or non-familiar form of address, e.g.

> **Gehen Sie jetzt nach Hause, Frau Meyer?**
> Are you going home now, Mrs Meyer?

Normally the use of a given name and **du** go hand in hand, but there can be situations, for example in the workplace, where you know someone well as a colleague but do not regard the person as a close friend, so you might use a combination of the given name and **Sie**, e.g.

Sylvia, wären Sie bitte so nett, mir hiermit zu helfen?
Sylvia, would you be so kind as to help me with this please?

The point at which a friendship changes from a **Sie** to a **du** basis is a culturally significant moment. As an English speaker you will find it difficult to judge when the appropriate time has come to suggest to an acquaintance that you feel the friendship has progressed to this point, so leave it up to the German to make the move, especially if s/he is significantly older than you. The ice may be broken by the person saying something like, **Sag mal du zu mir!** (Call me du) or **Ich heiße übrigens Gerhard** (By the way, my name is Gert; in other words, use my first name from now on and thus also stop using the **Sie** form).

There are gradations of familiarity which can require the one form of address or the other. The above description will cover the majority of situations you are likely to find yourself in, but, for example, if you were in conversation with someone you didn't know, and were thus using the **Sie** form, and the conversation turned nasty and abusive, the politeness of **Sie** might well be dropped and **du** resorted to in combination with suitable expletives, e.g.

Du Schwein/Arschloch!
You pig/arsehole!

These are subtleties of the use of **du**, **ihr** and **Sie** which you will become more comfortable with after some exposure to the living language. Even Germans can be a bit unsure of the appropriate form of address in certain situations. If you have already learnt another European language in which such distinctions are made, you will find the concept very similar, if not identical, in German.

7.1.1.2 Use of **man** to render 'you'

Be careful when rendering a 'you' that does not refer directly to the person you are talking to, but means in fact 'one'; in such a situation German uses 'one', i.e. **man** (see 7.7.2 and 10.4.7), e.g.

Wenn man weniger isst, nimmt man nicht zu.
If you eat less you don't put on weight.

Compare the following that is addressed directly to someone:

Wenn du weniger essen würdest, würdest du nicht zunehmen.
If you ate less, you would not put on weight.

7.1.1.3 Use of subject pronouns where English uses object pronouns

In contexts like 'Who's that at the door?' where the most natural sounding answer in English is 'Me', an object pronoun, German requires a subject or nominative pronoun, i.e. **ich**. The alternative 'It's me' (as no one really ever says 'It is I', as purists might insist) is in German **Ich bin es**; likewise 'It's him/us/them' etc. is **Er ist es./Wir sind es./Sie sind es** etc.

Similarly, in comparatives of the sort 'He is taller than me', which is everyday English for the puristic 'He is taller than I (am)/you (are)', German can only express it in the latter way, i.e. **Er ist größer als ich/du**. Likewise, 'He is just as tall as me/you', **Er ist genau so groß wie ich/du**.

In English, object pronouns are colloquially used in the following idiom, but in German only subject pronouns are possible:

Wenn ich du/er wäre, ...
If I were you/him ... (= If I were he ...)

Where a pronoun is uttered in isolation in response to a question, you have to imagine the unuttered sentence of which it is theoretically part and use the appropriate case form, e.g.

A: Wer hat ihm geholfen? B: Ich.
A: Who helped him? B: Me (= I [did]).

A: Wem hat er das Geld gegeben? B: Mir.
A: Who did he give the money to? B: Me.

7.1.1.4 The use of subject pronouns with the six persons of the verb

When conjugating a verb in German (see 10.1.1), you derive the six persons of the verb from the infinitive; the present tense of **machen**, for example, looks like this:

ich mache	**wir machen**
du machst	**ihr macht**
er macht	**sie machen**

In so doing, it is understood that **sie macht** and **es macht**, both being third persons, will follow the **er** form, and **Sie machen** will follow the **sie** (plural) form, so that although there are in fact nine persons of the verb if you include **sie**, **es** and **Sie**, for the sake of brevity only six are usually given.

Remember that 'it' as a third person subject pronoun is not necessarily simply **es**; it may be **er** or **sie** if relating back to a masculine or feminine noun respectively, e.g.

A: Was hast du mit dem Hammer gemacht? B: Er liegt auf dem Tisch.
A: What have you done with the hammer? B: It is on the table.

A: Mach die Tür bitte zu! B: Sie ist schon zu.
A: Please shut the door. B: It's already shut.

7.1.1.5 **Es/dies/das** as subject pronouns referring to nouns of all three genders and plurals

Although 'it' with reference to a preceding noun usually agrees in gender with that noun (i.e. 'it' is rendered by either **er**, **sie** or **es**, see 7.1.1.4), only **es** is used when the verb that follows is **sein** and the predicate of the clause (i.e. that part which follows the verb) contains a noun or an adjective used as a noun, e.g.

Siehst du diesen Tisch? Es ist ein uralter Tisch./Es ist ein uralter.
See this table? It is a really old table./It's a really old one.

Ich trinke Limonade. Es ist herrliche Limonade./Es ist eine herrliche.
I'm drinking a soft drink. It is a delicious soft drink./It's a delicious one.

Er hat ein Auto. Es ist ein neues Auto./Es ist ein neues.
He's got a car. It is a new car. It is a new one.

But if the predicate of the clause contains an adjective, then **er**, **sie** or **es** must be used, depending on the gender of the noun to which the 'it' refers, e.g.

Siehst du diesen Tisch? Er ist uralt.
See this table? It is really old.

Ich trinke Limonade. Sie ist herrlich.
I'm drinking a soft drink. It is delicious.

Er hat ein Auto. Es ist neu.
He has got a car. It is new.

But further still, this use of **es** is not limited to the above. It is also used with reference to plural antecedents, thereby rendering 'they' and being followed by a plural verb, **sind**, e.g.

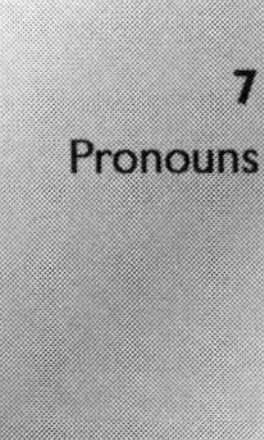

Wir haben beide einen neuen Wagen.
We have both got a new car.

Es sind ganz teure Wagen./Es sind ganz teure.
They are quite expensive cars./They are quite expensive ones.

Sie sind ganz teuer.
They are quite expensive.

In a similar way **dies** (this/these) and **das** (that/those) are also used, e.g.

Diese Leute kenne ich sehr gut.
I know these people very well.

Dies/das sind sehr nette Leute.
These/those are very nice people.

Compare:

Es sind sehr nette Leute.
They are very nice people.

Note too **Das/dies ist sein Vater** (That/this is his father) where **das** and **dies** are used regardless of the gender of the noun that follows the verb.

The above use of **es** instead of **er/sie** (he/she) or **sie** (they) also extends to people, but in this case the use of **es** instead of **er/sie** or **sie** is optional, although in the singular **er/sie** are more usual than **es**, but in the plural **es** is more usual than **sie**, e.g.

Seine Mutter lebt noch. Es/sie ist eine alte Frau. (**sie** more usual)
His mother is still alive. She is an old lady.

Siehst du die Kinder dort? Es/sie sind meine Kinder. (**es** more usual)
See those kids there? They're my kids.

For those who have learnt French, this use of **es** described here is identical to that of **ce** versus **il** or **elle** in French.

Note: See 10.4.5 and 10.4.6 for use of **es** as a dummy subject.

7.1.2 *Object or accusative pronouns*

When English makes a distinction between subject and object forms of the personal pronouns, it is in fact employing case, e.g. 'I/me', 'you/you', 'he/him', 'she/her', 'it/it', 'we/us', 'you/you', 'they/them'. To say 'I see him', and not 'I see he', is to make a grammatical distinction between a subject and an object form of the pronoun or, in other words, to employ case. English is inconsistent here since in the case of 'you' and 'it' no such distinction is made. Compare the German, where not all persons make a distinction either, but context always makes the distinction clear as it does in English, e.g.

ich/mich, du/dich, er/ihn, sie/sie, es/es, wir/uns, ihr/euch, Sie/Sie, sie/sie

Sie hat mich in der Stadt getroffen.
She met me in town.

Ich habe sie in der Stadt getroffen.
I met her in town.

7.1.2.1 Use of object pronouns with certain prepositions

These accusative forms of the personal pronouns are also used after certain prepositions (see 12.1 and 12.3).

7.1.3 *Indirect object or dative pronouns*

English makes no distinction between direct and indirect object pronouns. In other words, the paradigm of personal pronouns is only two-tiered, i.e.

I	you	he	she	it	we	you	they
me	you	him	her	it	us	you	them

But in German the paradigm is three-tiered as German distinguishes between 'I', 'me' and 'to me' etc., where 'to me' is referred to as the indirect object or the dative, i.e.

N	**ich**	**du**	**er**	**sie**	**es**	**wir**	**ihr**	**Sie**	**sie**
A	**mich**	**dich**	**ihn**	**sie**	**es**	**uns**	**euch**	**Sie**	**sie**
D	**mir**	**dir**	**ihm**	**ihr**	**ihm**	**uns**	**euch**	**Ihnen**	**ihnen**

Er hat mich im Kino gesehen.
He saw me in the cinema.

Er hat mir fünf Euro gegeben.
He gave me five euros.

Rephrasing the second sentence as 'He gave five euros to me' reveals the 'me' in the second sentence as in fact meaning 'to me', which is an indirect

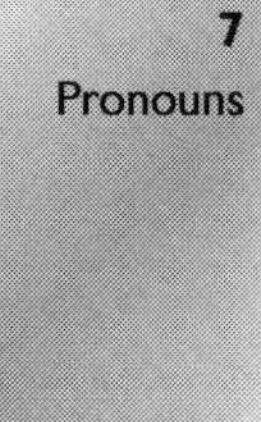

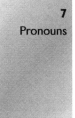

object and thus requires the dative form of the appropriate pronoun. Compare:

Sie hat ihm einen Brief geschickt.
She sent him a letter. (= She sent a letter to him.) (dative), *but*

Sie hat ihn nach Hause geschickt.
She sent him home. (accusative)

7.1.3.1 Use of indirect object pronouns with certain prepositions

These dative forms of the personal pronouns are also used after certain prepositions (see 12.2 and 12.3).

7.1.4 *Prepositional adverbs (i.e. **da(r)-** + preposition and **hier-** + preposition)*

The subject and object pronouns of the third person singular and plural are as follows:

	M	*F*	*N*	*Pl*
A	**ihn**	**sie**	**es**	**sie**
D	**ihm**	**ihr**	**ihm**	**ihnen**

When 'it' and 'them' with reference to things, as opposed to people, are preceded by a preposition, the above pronominal forms cannot be used; in other words **in es, auf es** etc. are not possible at all, and **in ihn, auf ihm** etc. and **in sie, auf ihr** etc. are only possible if referring to a person. German uses the so-called prepositional adverb in such cases, formed by combining **da** (there, an adverb) with the preposition in question, e.g. **damit** (with it/them), **dahinter** (behind it/them). When the preposition begins with a vowel, an **r** is inserted to aid pronunciation, e.g. **darauf** (on it/them), **darin** (in it/them), e.g.

Ich habe Knoblauch mit diesem Messer geschnitten, also kann ich das Brot nicht damit schneiden.
I have cut garlic with this knife so I can't cut the bread with it.

Sie konnte ihre Brille nicht finden, denn sie saß darauf.
She couldn't find her glasses because she was sitting on them.

Unsere Nachbarn sind in vielen Ländern gewesen und wollen jetzt ein Buch darüber schreiben.
Our neighbours have been in lots of countries and now want to write a book about them/about it.

The forms with an **r** in them very commonly drop the vowel in **dar-** in colloquial speech, e.g. **drauf, dran, drüber**.

The topic of the prepositional adverb does not end there, however. Forms like **damit, darin, darauf** etc. do not just render 'with it/them', 'in it/them', 'on it/them' etc. but also translate 'with that/those', 'in that/those, 'on that/those' etc., e.g.

> **Damit kann man keine Brötchen schneiden.**
> You can't cut breadrolls with that/those.

And just as the adverb **da** (there) replaces the pronouns 'that/those' in such cases, so too does the adverb **hier** (here) replace **dies** (this/these), where the pronouns 'this/these' follow a preposition, e.g.

> **Wie soll ich um gottes Willen hiermit das Brot schneiden?**
> How am I meant to cut the bread with this/these for heaven's sake?

> **Setz dich hierauf!**
> Sit on this.

The only prepositions which cannot be combined with **da-** and **hier-** are those that take the genitive (see 12.4) as well as **außer, gegenüber, ohne** and **seit**.

To understand how these constructions work in German, compare the use of similar constructions with 'there/here' + preposition in archaic English, e.g. 'He's cut the breadrolls therewith', which can stand for either 'with it' in the case of one knife or 'with them' in the case of several knives. A very similar construction occurs with **wo(r)-** (see 7.5 and 7.6.3).

7.1.5 *Pronominal use of articles and other determiners*

Articles, both definite and indefinite, as well as other determiners followed by nouns are dealt with under 5.5, 7.7.1 and 8.1.4. But all these words can also be used as pronouns, in which case the noun to which they refer is not mentioned but understood, and thus the gender and case of the implied noun must be observed.

The **der/die/das** paradigm (see 5.1), in addition to translating 'the', can also be used to translate 'he/she/it' in the nom., acc. and dat., especially when there is some emphasis, in which case they normally stand at the beginning of their clause; this is particularly common in spoken German, e.g.

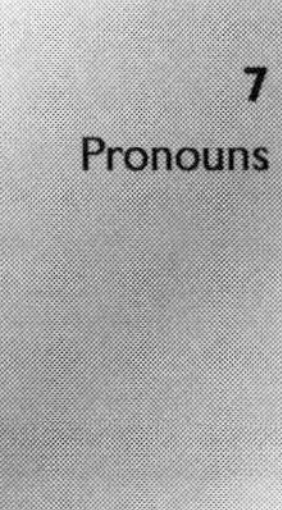

A: Kennst du Johann Müller? B: Ja, den kenne ich sehr gut.
A: Do you know Johann Müller? B: Yes, I know him very well.

A: Sind die Mayers verreist? B: Ja, die sind zur Zeit in Sizilien.
A: Are the Mayers away? B: Yes, they are in Sicily at the moment.

7.2 Possessives

The following constitute the possessives in English:

my, your, his, her, its, our, your, their

Because these words stand in front of nouns they are, strictly speaking, possessive adjectives, not possessive pronouns, but derived from them are the true possessive pronouns – they are pronouns because they can stand alone replacing a noun; in English these are:

mine, yours, his, hers, its, ours, yours, theirs

The distinction between the two sets of forms is as follows:

'This is my book./This is mine.' or 'My book is blue./Mine is blue.'
'That is his dog./This is his.' or 'His dog is brown./His is brown.'

In expressing these forms in German, you need to take note of both gender and case.

7.2.1 *The possessive adjectives*

mein (my), **dein** (your), **sein** (his), **ihr** (her), **sein** (its), **unser** (our), **euer** (your), **Ihr** (your), **ihr** (their)

The endings of these possessive adjectives are exactly the same as those for **ein** (see 5.3 and 5.4), except that these also have plural endings of course (i.e. 'my books' is possible whereas 'a books' is not); the plural endings are identical to those of **der/die/das**, i.e.

	M	*F*	*N*	*Pl*
N	**mein**	**meine**	**mein**	**meine**
A	**meinen**	**meine**	**mein**	**meine**
G	**meines**	**meiner**	**meines**	**meiner**
D	**meinem**	**meiner**	**meinem**	**meinen**

You must apply these endings to all the possessive adjectives given above, e.g.

Er kennt unseren Vater nicht.
He doesn't know our father.

Ich habe den Namen ihres Lehrers vergessen.
I have forgotten her/their teacher's name.

Just as context usually makes it clear whether **sie** means 'she' or 'they' (see 7.1.1), whether **ihr** means 'her' or 'their' is normally revealed by context too.

7.2.2 *Possessive pronouns*

The paradigm of the possessive pronoun differs from that of the possessive adjective given in 7.2.1 as follows – the three differences are underlined:

	M	*F*	*N*	*Pl*
N	**meiner**	**meine**	**mein(e)s**	**meine**
A	**meinen**	**meine**	**mein(e)s**	**meine**
G	**meines**	**meiner**	**meines**	**meiner**
D	**meinem**	**meiner**	**meinem**	**meinen**

Note how the two paradigms alternate:

Dies ist mein Buch./Dies ist mein(e)s.
This is my book./This is mine.

Mein Buch ist blau./Mein(e)s ist blau.
My book is blue./Mine is blue.

Das ist sein Hund./Das ist seiner.
That is his dog./This is his.

Sein Hund ist braun./Seiner ist braun.
His dog is brown./His is brown.

Ich habe heute Morgen deinen Hund im Park hier gegenüber gesehen, aber meinen habe ich noch nicht finden können.
I saw your dog in the park opposite this morning but I still haven't been able to find mine.

In speech it is usual to drop the **e** from the ending of the nom. and acc. neuter forms, which is also not uncommon in less formal writing.

A phrase such as 'a friend of mine' uses the independent possessive in English, but the dative personal pronoun in German, e.g. **ein Freund von mir**; compare **einer meiner Freunde** (one of my friends).

7.2.2.1 Alternative forms of the possessive pronoun

In elevated style two alternative paradigms of the possessive pronoun occur which you will merely need to recognize, but will never need to use. Firstly there is the **der meinige/deinige/seinige/ihrige/unserige/eurige/ihrige** paradigm where the forms in **-ige** are regarded as adjectives and thus take the endings of an adjective after the definite article (see 8.1), e.g.

	M	*F*	*N*	*Pl*
N	**der meinige**	**die meinige**	**das meinige**	**die meinigen**
A	**den meinigen**	**die meinige**	**das meinige**	**die meinigen**
G	**des meinigen**	**der meinigen**	**des meinigen**	**der meinigen**
D	**dem meinigen**	**der meinigen**	**dem meinigen**	**den meinigen**

Seine ganzen Verwandten sind nach Australien ausgewandert, aber die ihrigen wohnen alle noch in der Bundesrepublik.
All of his relatives have migrated to Australia but hers still all live in Germany.

The following paradigm exists as an alternative to the above but it too is limited to formal contexts and merely needs to be recognized, not used:

	M	*F*	*N*	*Pl*
N	**der meine**	**die meine**	**das meine**	**die meinen**
A	**den meinen**	**die meine**	**das meine**	**die meinen**
G	**des meinen**	**der meinen**	**des meinen**	**der meinen**
D	**dem meinen**	**der meinen**	**dem meinen**	**den meinen**

Similarly **der deine/seine/ihre/unsere/eure/Ihre/ihre**, e.g.

Ihre vier Kinder sind alle Mädchen, die seinen aber alle Jungen.
Her four children are all girls but his are all boys.

7.3 Reflexive pronouns

Reflexive pronouns are used primarily with certain verbs when the doers of those verbs are regarded as performing the action on themselves, e.g. **sich waschen** (to wash [oneself], see 7.3.1), where the reflexive 'oneself' is superfluous in English but obligatory in German. The verb **sich waschen** is called a reflexive verb and it is conjugated as follows with each person employing the reflexive pronoun after it:

ich wasche mich	**wir waschen uns**
du wäschst dich	**ihr wascht euch**
er wäscht sich	**sie waschen sich**

All forms are identical to accusative pronouns except for the third person singular and plural where **sich** means 'himself', 'herself', 'itself', 'oneself' and 'themselves'. The non-familiar second person singular and plural form is of course **Sie waschen sich** where **sich** means 'yourself/ yourselves'.

There is an emphatic form of the reflexive pronoun which consists of the above forms followed by **selbst**, i.e. **mich selbst, dich selbst, sich selbst** etc. You need to be careful here as these forms closely resemble the unemphatic reflexive forms in English, i.e. 'myself', 'yourself' etc., but in German these emphatic forms are only used when a contrast is made between performing the action on someone else and on yourself, e.g.

> **Er rasiert jeden Morgen seinen Opa, bevor er sich selbst rasiert.**
> He shaves his granddad every morning before he shaves himself.

The use of 'himself' here in English, rather than omitting the reflexive altogether, shows that there is an emphasis, which means that **selbst** must be employed in German. Compare:

> **Er rasiert sich nicht jeden Tag.**
> He doesn't shave every day. (reflexive superfluous in English)

> **Er hat sich in Italien sehr amüsiert.**
> He enjoyed himself a great deal in Italy. (reflexive obligatory in English)

7.3.1 *Dative reflexive pronouns*

There are also dative forms of the reflexive pronouns, i.e. **mir, dir, sich, uns, euch, sich.** As you can see, these differ only slightly from the accusative forms in 7.3, i.e. **mich, dich, sich, uns, euch, sich**. In fact only the first and second persons singular differ. These dative forms are used in two instances.

Firstly, when using an optionally reflexive verb, i.e. a verb like **waschen** or **rasieren**, which expresses actions that can be performed on others (in which case they are used as normal transitive verbs and require no reflexive pronoun), the dative form of the reflexive pronoun is required if the verb has a direct object, e.g.

> **Ich wasche mich jeden Tag.** (no object mentioned)
> I wash every day.

Ich wasche mir die Hände mindestens zehnmal am Tag. (die **Hände** = object)
I wash my hands at least ten times a day.

But it is only with **ich** and **du** as subjects of the verb that a distinction is made. Look at the same two sentences with **er** as their subject:

Er wäscht sich jeden Tag.
He washes every day.

Er wäscht sich die Hände mindestens zehnmal am Tag.
He washes his hands at least ten times a day.

The second use of the dative of the reflexive is dealt with under 7.3.2.

7.3.2 *Reflexive pronouns used independently of verbs*

It is possible for reflexive pronouns to be used after a limited number of prepositions referring back to the subject of the sentence, e.g.

Ich war außer mir vor Angst./Er war außer sich vor Angst.
I was beside myself with fear./He was beside himself with fear.

Ich habe kein Taschentuch bei mir./Er hat kein Geld bei sich.
I haven't got a handkerchief on me./He hasn't got any money on him.

7.3.3 *Use of* selbst/selber *to render English reflexives*

Where an English reflexive pronoun (i.e. myself, yourself, himself/herself/itself, ourselves, yourselves, themselves) is used independently of a reflexive verb and expresses an emphatic 'myself' etc., German does not use reflexive pronouns but rather **selbst** or **selber** – the two are synonymous and interchangeable, e.g.

A: Soll ich dir helfen? B: Danke, ich kann es selbst/selber machen.
A: Shall I help you? B: No thanks, I can do it myself.

Er hat den Brief selber geschrieben.
He wrote the letter himself.

7.4 Demonstrative pronouns

Demonstrative pronouns, which are identical in form to demonstrative adjectives, are dealt with under articles and other determiners (see 5.1 and 5.2).

7.5 Interrogative pronouns

These pronouns are used when asking questions. They must not be confused with 'who/whose/whom' as relative pronouns (see 7.6). 'Whom', which is more usually 'who' in spoken English, is a vestige of the accusative/dative, a distinction which is of course still made in German, e.g.

Wer wohnt in diesem Haus?
Who lives in this house?

Wen hast du im Park gesehen?
Who(m) did you see in the park?

Wessen Tochter ist sie?
Whose daughter is she?

Wem hat er den Brief gegeben?
Who(m) did he give the letter to?/To whom did he give the letter?

N	**wer**	who
A	**wen**	who(m)
G	**wessen**	whose
D	**wem**	(to) who(m)

Although **wessen** literally means 'whose', when asking about possession it is more usual in German to use **gehören** + dat. (to belong to) if context permits it, e.g.

Wem gehört diese Handtasche?
Whose handbag is this? (lit. Who does this handbag belong to?)

Use of these interrogative pronouns is not limited to direct questions but also applies to indirect questions, in which case the pronouns act like subordinating conjunctions and relative pronouns by sending the finite verb in their clause to the end of that clause, e.g.

Er fragte mich, wer in diesem Haus wohnt.
He asked me who lives in this house.

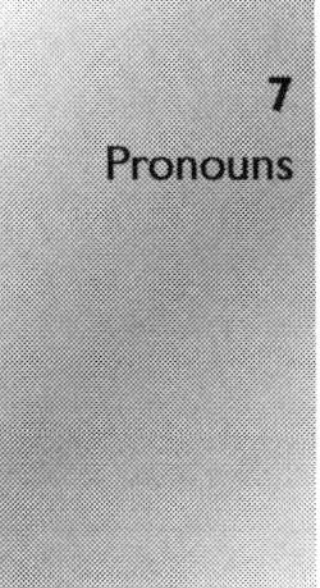

Ich weiß nicht, wem diese Handtasche gehört.
I don't know who this handbag belongs to/whose handbag this is.

Was (what) is also an interrogative pronoun, e.g.

Was hat sie in der Hand?
What has she got in her hand?

Ich habe keine Ahnung, was sie in der Hand hat.
I have no idea what she has in her hand.

Was, unlike English 'what', cannot be used in combination with a preposition, which in English is usually placed at the end of the clause. Where this occurs in English, German uses an adverbial construction with **wo(r)-**, the **r** being inserted when the preposition begins with a vowel. In so doing, prepositions are not left dangling at the end of a sentence in German as is so often the case in English, e.g.

Womit spielen die Kinder?
What are the kids playing with?

Worauf wartest du?
What are you waiting for?

These constructions have parallels in archaic English (compare **da-** under 7.1.4), e.g. 'Wherefore was he not helped?', 'Whereon lieth the snow?'

See 7.6.3 for the use of **wo(r)-** as a relative pronoun.

7.6 Relative pronouns

	M	*F*	*N*	*Pl*
N	**der**	**die**	**das**	**die**
A	**den**	**die**	**das**	**die**
G	**dessen**	**deren**	**dessen**	**deren**
D	**dem**	**der**	**dem**	**denen**

A relative pronoun introduces a subordinate clause, called a relative clause, that relates back to a noun just mentioned (the antecedent) in order to add extra information about that noun; it is commonly embedded in a main clause, which is shown in German by placing commas both before and after it, while the use of commas with relative clauses in English is inconsistent, e.g.

Der Mann, der nebenan wohnt, hat die Absicht nach Amerika auszuwandern.
The man who lives next-door is intending to emigrate to America.

In the above example the word order in the main clause, i.e. **Der Mann hat die Absicht nach Amerika auszuwandern**, remains untouched by the insertion of the relative clause, **der nebenan wohnt**. The finite verb in the main clause remains in second position, as it would without the addition of a relative clause, whereas the verb in the relative clause is in final position, unlike English, but in accordance with it being a form of subordinate clause (see 11.2).

The gender of the relative pronoun is determined by that of the noun which it relates back to, while its case is determined by the grammatical role it is playing in the relative clause. In the above example **der** has been selected from the paradigm as **Mann** is masculine and the relative pronoun **der** is the subject of **wohnt**. But look at the following examples where other case forms occur:

Mein Nachbar, den ich sehr gern habe, ist Deutscher.
My neighbour, who(m) I like a great deal, is a German.

Das ist die Ärztin, deren Sohn in meiner Klasse ist.
That is the doctor whose son is in my class.

There are several complications in English with regard to relative pronouns that do not exist in German. The relative in English can be either 'who' or 'which', depending on whether the antecedent is personal or not, or even 'that' for both personal and non-personal antecedents. In fact, the relative pronoun is commonly even omitted in English, though only when it is not the subject of its clause, but it can never be omitted in German. All the following English examples can only be rendered in one way in German:

Das ist nicht der Mann, den ich gestern Abend in der Stadt gesehen habe.
That is not the man who(m) I saw in town last night.
That is not the man that I saw in town last night.
That is not the man I saw in town last night.

The same applies to non-personal antecedents:

Dies ist der Tisch, den wir renoviert haben.
This is the table which we renovated.
This is the table that we renovated.
This is the table we renovated.

You must be careful with omitted 'thats' in English. Often an omitted 'that' is the subordinating conjunction **dass** (see 11.2), not a relative pronoun, but in German omission is not possible in either case, e.g. 'He said (that) he'd do it.' (see 10.3.1.1 for omission of **dass** with indirect speech).

7.6.1 Relative pronouns preceded by prepositions

Prepositions commonly precede relative pronouns in German, thereby determining the case of that pronoun. It can be difficult to recognize when this is the case as colloquial English normally places the preposition at the end of the clause instead of before the relative pronoun – which is however done in more formal English – and to complicate the issue even further, English commonly drops the relative pronoun altogether despite the presence of a preposition. In German you must always place the preposition before the appropriate relative pronoun at the beginning of the clause and place the finite verb at the end, e.g.

Ich habe den Stuhl, auf dem du jetzt sitzt, erst heute Nachmittag repariert.
I repaired the chair you're now sitting on only this afternoon.
I only repaired the chair which/that you're now sitting on this afternoon.
I only repaired the chair on which you're now sitting this afternoon.

Die Leute, von denen wir dieses Haus gekauft haben, wohnen jetzt in Stade.
The people we bought this house from now live in Stade.
The people who/that we bought this house from now live in Stade.
The people from whom we bought this house now live in Stade.

Note that 'whose' is commonly avoided in English these days when the antecedent is non-personal, a contorted construction with 'of which' being preferred, but in German use of **dessen** and **deren** is purely dependent on the gender of the antecedent and whether it is personal or non-personal is irrelevant, e.g.

Die Häuser, deren Dächer im Sturm weggeweht sind, werden sofort repariert.
The houses whose roofs blew away in the storm will be repaired immediately.
The houses of which the roofs blew away in the storm will be repaired immediately.

It is stylistically preferable in German not to separate a relative pronoun from its antecedent, although this is sometimes possible – the problem does not arise in English as past participles and infinitives are not sent to the end of their clause, e.g.

Mein Sohn hat das Fahrrad verkauft, das ich ihm zum Geburtstag geschenkt habe.
Mein Sohn hat das Fahrrad, das ich ihm zum Geburtstag geschenkt habe, verkauft. (avoid this although it is possible)
My son has sold the bicycle which I gave him for his birthday.

7.6.2 *Wo as a relative pronoun relating back to place and time*

Wo, which literally means 'where' (see 11.2), is used in spoken German to replace a preposition + a relative pronoun with reference to a place, but this alternation has a parallel in English too, e.g.

Die Stadt, wo er jahrelang als Kind gewohnt hat, hat er nie wieder besucht.
He never again visited the city where he lived as a child.

Die Stadt, in der er jahrelang als Kind gewohnt hat, hat er nie wieder besucht.
He never again visited the city in which he lived as a child.

But this use of **wo** does not stop here in German, unlike English. In German it can even be used, once again more in spoken than written German, to relate back to an expression of time, e.g.

Wir leben jetzt in einer Zeit, wo die Luftverschmutzung immer schlechter wird.
We are now living in a time in which air pollution is getting worse and worse.

In more formal German this would be expressed with a relative pronoun, e.g.

Wir leben jetzt in einer Zeit, in der die Luftverschmutzung immer schlechter wird.

7.6.3 *Was and wo(r)- as relative pronouns*

'Which' is used in English to relate back to indefinite antecedents that are not nouns with a given gender but indefinite pronouns, and may even be entire clauses. In German **was** is used in such cases, e.g.

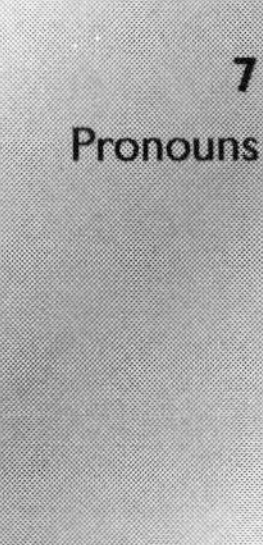

Nicht alles, was er sagt, ist wahr, weißt du?
Not everything (that) he says is true, you know.

Die Inflationsrate ist im letzten Jahr gestiegen, was gar nicht gut für die Wirtschaft ist.
The inflation rate has risen over the last year which is not at all good for the economy. (The antecedent is the whole first clause, i.e. the fact that the inflation rate has risen.)

The relative pronoun **was** above cannot be used in combination with a preposition. Where English uses 'that' or 'which' to refer to an indefinite antecedent in combination with a preposition, German uses **wo(r)** + the appropriate preposition, e.g.

Das ist etwas, worauf wir sehr lange gewartet haben.
That is something that/which we waited a very long time for.
That is something we waited a very long time for.
That is something for which we waited a very long time.

7.6.4 *Use of participles in extended adjectival phrases in lieu of relative clauses*

In slightly more formal style, and very often in journalese, you might find an avoidance of relative clauses by placing the information usually contained in the relative clause before the noun it refers to, in an extended adjectival phrase. Such phrases always contain a past or present participle (see 10.6), and are only translatable into English by converting them back into relative clauses which often contain a passive (see 10.4), e.g.

Gestern wurde auf der Ausstellung ein neu <u>entwickeltes</u> Modell vorgestellt. (past participle)
Gestern wurde auf der Ausstellung ein Modell vorgestellt, das neu entwickelt worden ist. (relative clause in passive)
A model was presented at the exhibition yesterday that has been newly developed.

Ich las eine Kritik über das kürzlich <u>veröffentlichte</u> Buch. (past participle)
Ich las eine Kritik über das Buch, das kürzlich veröffentlicht worden war. (relative clause in passive)
I read a review of the book which had recently been published.

Sie sah ein in entgegengesetzter Richtung fahrendes Auto. (present participle)
Sie sah ein Auto, das in entgegengesetzter Richtung fuhr. (relative clause)
She saw a car which was driving in the opposite direction.

Es handelte sich da um eine nicht zu vermeidende Schwierigkeit. (present participle)
Es handelte sich da um eine Schwierigkeit, die nicht zu vermeiden war. (relative clause, see 10.4.7.c)
It was a matter of a difficulty which could not be avoided.

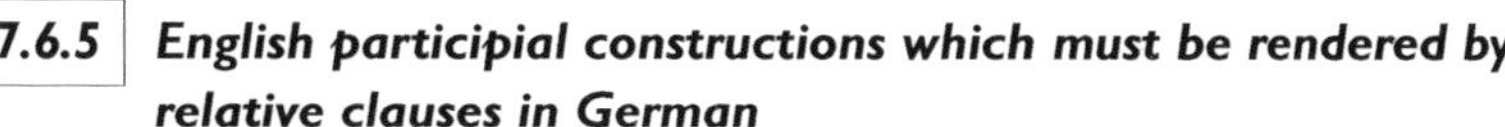

7.6.5 *English participial constructions which must be rendered by relative clauses in German*

Under 7.6.4 examples are given of German participial constructions which are rendered by relative clauses in English. There are, however, participial (both past and present) constructions in English which must be rendered by relative clauses in German, e.g.

Diese Häuser, die in den fünfziger Jahren gebaut worden sind, sind von minderwertiger Qualität.
These houses built in the fifties are of inferior quality.

This could also be rendered by an adjectival phrase placed before the noun:

Diese in den fünfziger Jahren gebauten Häuser sind von minderwertiger Qualität.

Der Mann, der in der Ecke des Wartezimmers die Zeitung liest, ist sehr krank.
The man reading the paper in the corner of the waiting room is very sick.

7.7 Indefinite pronouns

a) Indefinite pronouns like **jeder(mann)** (everybody), **jemand** (somebody) and **niemand** (nobody), although they refer to any person of either gender, require the use of masculine forms of the possessive. The current use of 'their' in English to avoid an unwieldy 'his/her' is not possible in German, e.g.

Jeder wollte seine Meinung äußern.
Everyone wanted to air their opinion.

Niemand hat seinen Hund mitnehmen dürfen.
No one was allowed to take their dog with them.

b) 'Everyone, everybody'

The most usual word is **jeder**, but it is sometimes found in the fuller form **jedermann**, e.g.

Das weiß doch jeder.
Everyone/everybody knows that.

c) 'Someone, somebody; anyone, anybody; no one, nobody'

The subtle distinction between 'someone' and 'anyone' does not exist in German; both are rendered by **jemand**, and when 'anyone' is used together with a negative in English, German simply uses **niemand** (nobody) (see 14.2.h), e.g.

Hast du jemand gesehen?
Did you see anyone/anybody?

Ja, ich habe jemand gesehen.
Yes, I saw someone/somebody.

Nein, ich habe niemand gesehen.
No, I didn't see anyone/anybody. (i.e. I saw nobody/no one.)

'Anyone' that means 'absolutely anyone' is, however, rendered by **jeder**, e.g.

Sie redet mit jedem.
She talks to anyone. (= everyone; see point b above)

Jemand and **niemand** also have case forms, although the acc. and dat. forms are only used in more formal style, e.g.

N	**jemand**	**niemand**
A	**jemanden**	**niemanden**
G	**jemands**	**niemands**
D	**jemandem**	**niemandem**

Die Polizei hat noch mit niemandem gesprochen.
The police have not yet spoken to anyone.

Ich habe jemands Mütze im Schuppen gefunden.
I found somebody's cap in the shed.

'Somebody/someone else' is **jemand anders**.

d) 'Something, anything, nothing' (see 14.2.h)

The situation here is similar to that above: 'something/anything' are rendered by **etwas**, or more colloquially by **was**; 'nothing' is **nichts** or in the spoken language **nix**, e.g.

Hast du etwas/was gekauft?
Did you buy anything?

Ja, ich habe etwas/was gekauft.
Yes, I bought something.

Nein, ich habe nichts gekauft.
No, I didn't buy anything. (i.e. I bought nothing.)

For **etwas** and **nichts** followed by an adjective see 6.7.1.

Be warned that **etwas** is also an adverb meaning 'somewhat', but context always makes this clear as the adjective that follows is not inflected, e.g.

Ich finde den Anzug etwas teuer.
I find the suit somewhat expensive.

e) 'Whoever, whatever'

Wer ... auch and **was ... auch** translate the above but be careful with the syntax that they require, as **auch** is placed later in the clause and note the lack of inversion of subject and verb in the second clause of the second example.

Wer am Theaterstück auch teilnehmen will, ist meinetwegen herzlich willkommen.
Whoever wants to take part in the play is welcome as far as I'm concerned.

Was er auch schon beigetragen hat, er kann noch mehr für die Sache tun.
Whatever he has already contributed, he can do even more for the cause.

Wo(hin) ... auch (wherever) and **wann ... auch** (whenever), although not pronouns but adverbs, are used in similar constructions.

7.7.1 *Indefinite pronouns also used as determiners*

a) Other aspects of these indefinite pronouns are dealt with under determiners (see 5.5) and adjectives (see 8.1.4) but here their pronominal functions are dealt with.

When the following words are used independently, i.e. when they are not followed by a noun, but a noun can be inferred, they are pronouns: **alle** (all), **andere** (other), **beide** (both), **einige** (some), **mehrere** (several), **viele** (many), **verschiedene** (various/different) and **wenige** (few). The inferred noun is by necessity plural and these pronouns are inflected for case, e.g.

Alle (Anwesenden/Gäste) werden gebeten, den Saal zu verlassen. (nom.)
All (present/guests) are requested to leave the room.

Einige (Schüler) machen den Ausflug, aber andere nicht. (nom.)
Some (pupils) are going on the excursion but others aren't.

Die Namen mehrerer (Teilnehmer) habe ich schon vergessen. (gen.)
I have already forgotten the names of several (participants).

In diesem Land ist Alkohol zollfrei, aber in vielen (Ländern) ist das nicht der Fall. (dat.)
In this country alcohol is duty-free but in many that is not the case.

Welche (some, a few) and **die meisten** (most of) can also be used pronominally, e.g.

A: Ich muss Äpfel kaufen. B: Brauchst du nicht. Ich hab' schon welche gekauft.
A: I must buy apples. B: You don't need to. I've already bought some/a few.

Die Bewohner mussten das Gebäude verlassen, aber die meisten wollten es nicht.
The residents had to leave the building but most (of them) didn't want to.

Another indefinite pronoun worthy of mention here is **ein paar** (some, a few), which contrasts with **ein Paar** (a pair of), e.g.

Ich habe heute ein Paar Sandalen am Strand gefunden.
I found a pair of sandals on the beach today.

A: Hat er überhaupt Freunde? B: Ja, er hat ein paar (neue Freunde gemacht).
A: Has he got any friends at all? B: Yes, he has a few (has made a few new friends).

b) **Beide** (both)

Beide, in addition to being used as both an indefinite pronoun and a determiner like all the above, can also be used as an adjective after other determiners, e.g.

A: Wer will also mitkommen, Julia oder Felix? B: Beide möchten mitgehen.
A: Who wants to come with me, Julia or Felix? B: Both want to go with you.

Beide Bücher/die beiden Bücher waren teuer.
Both (the) books were expensive.

This adjectival use of **beide** is also a way of rendering 'two', e.g.

Die beiden Brüder sind früh gestorben.
The two brothers died young.

There is also a neuter inflected form, **beides**, which is used pronominally with reference to objects, e.g.

A: Was möchtest du zum Geburtstag – eine Kamera oder einen Videorecorder? B: Beides.
A: What would you like for your birthday – a camera or a videorecorder? B: Both.

7.7.2 ***The indefinite pronoun*** *man (see 7.1.1.2 and 10.4.7)*

Man means 'one', but whereas this pronoun generally sounds rather formal in English, it is an everyday word in German, e.g.

Man muss vorsichtig sein.
One must be careful. (= You must be careful.)

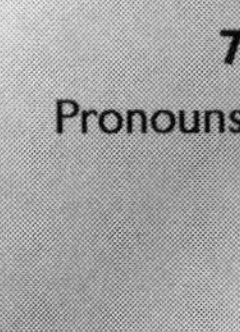

There are several tricks to watch out for when using **man**. It has case forms and the possessive 'one's' is expressed by **sein**, e.g.

N	**man**
A	**einen**
D	**einem**

Wenn es einem schlecht geht, findet man oft, dass einen seine Freunde vergessen haben.
When one is having a hard time one often finds that one's friends have forgotten one.

The appropriate reflexive pronoun to use when **man** is the subject of a reflexive verb is **sich**, e.g.

Man befindet sich hier in einer Traumwelt.
One finds oneself in a dreamworld here.

When you learn a reflexive verb in its infinitive form (e.g. **sich amüsieren**), this translates in fact as 'to enjoy onself' (see 7.3).

Generally speaking, spoken English prefers to use 'you' instead of 'one'. Colloquially German has the possibility of using **du** in the same way, but not because it is felt that **man** sounds too formal (see 7.1.1.2), e.g.

Du musst in Kairo aufpassen, dass du nicht beraubt wirst.
You have to be careful in Cairo that you don't get robbed.

Man muss in Kairo aufpassen, dass man nicht beraubt wird.
One has to be careful in Cairo that one doesn't get robbed.

See 10.4.7 for how **man** is used to avoid the passive.

Chapter 8

Adjectives

As you will see below, an intricate system of adjectival endings prevails in German. It is perhaps the best example of German as an inflectional language. The following paradigms show how adjectives are inflected or declined and are thus often referred to as adjectival inflections or declensions.

Adjectives are used both predicatively and attributively, as in English. A predicate (also called predicative) adjective is one that does not stand in front of a noun, i.e. it is not used attributively like one standing in front of a noun, e.g. 'His car is red' (a predicate adjective), but 'his red car' (an attributive adjective). Predicate adjectives are invariable, i.e. they do not take endings, thus **Sein Auto ist rot**. But attributive adjectives must agree in gender, number and case with the noun they precede, thus **sein rotes Auto** (neuter, singular, nominative). And here lies another bothersome aspect of German which takes some mastering.

There are three paradigms or sets of adjectival endings that need to be learnt in order to know exactly what the correct ending is for an attributive adjective standing in front of a German noun. There are

1 the endings used after **der/die/das** (also called weak endings)
2 the endings used after **ein/eine/ein** (also called mixed endings) and
3 the unpreceded adjectival endings (also called strong endings).

8.1 Rules for inflection

8.1.1 The *der/die/das* (weak) endings:

	M	F	N	Pl
N	**-e**	**-e**	**-e**	**-en**
A	**-en**	**-e**	**-e**	**-en**
G	**-en**	**-en**	**-en**	**-en**
D	**-en**	**-en**	**-en**	**-en**

This set of endings consists of merely an **-e** or an **-en**. There is a reason for this. They are used after **der/die/das** and other determiners (see 5.2) that take the same endings as **der/die/das** themselves, i.e. **dieser, jeder, jener, solcher, welcher.** As the determiners themselves have endings that clearly indicate gender, number and case, there is little need for the adjectives that follow them to repeat this information and thus German makes do with either **-e** or **-en**, e.g. nom. case **dieser arme Mann, welche alte Frau, jedes brave Kind**; dat. case **diesem armen Mann, welcher alten Frau, jedem braven Kind. Solcher** is generally only found before a plural noun in natural sounding German, i.e. **solche guten Leute** (such good people). (See last paragraph in 5.2.)

8.1.2 The *ein/eine/ein* (mixed) endings:

	M	F	N	Pl
N	**-er**	**-e**	**-es**	**-en**
A	**-en**	**-e**	**-es**	**-en**
G	**-en**	**-en**	**-en**	**-en**
D	**-en**	**-en**	**-en**	**-en**

This set of endings is not quite so bland as the first, at least in the nom. and acc., but in the other cases and the plural the endings are identical to each other and to those applying in the set above. Again, there is a reason for this. Look at **ein guter Mann** and **ein gutes Kind** and compare this with **der gute Mann** and **das gute Kind.** The determiner **ein** here, unlike **der** and **das,** makes no distinction between the genders – only the adjective here tells you what the gender of the noun is. But in the genitive and dative cases, there is no difference between the endings in sets 1 and 2 as the determiners, both **der/die/das** and **ein/eine/ein**, indicate the gender and case, i.e. **dem/einem guten Mann, der/einer guten Frau, dem/einem guten Kind.**

The endings in this paradigm are applied after all the possessive adjectives (i.e. **mein, dein, sein/ihr/sein, unser, euer, Ihr, ihr** – see 7.2.1) as well as after

kein. Of course you cannot get a plural noun after **ein**, but you can after all the other determiners in this group and thus there is a fourth column above, i.e. **keine alten Leute**. A person's name with a gen. **-s** ending (see 4.4) standing before the adjective fulfils the same function as a possessive adjective and thus these endings are required, e.g. **Karls nagelneues Auto** (Karl's brand new car).

The black lines drawn between the accusative and the genitive endings in sets 1 and 2 are intended to emphasize that below these lines, including the plural, these two sets of endings are identical. This greatly reduces what you need to learn by heart. It is only in the nominative and accusative that you have to be careful if a determiner precedes a noun, because in the other two cases and in the plural there is only one possible ending, i.e. **-en**.

Remember this: a German noun with a determiner and an adjective in front of it can only grunt (rrr!) or hiss (sss!) once, i.e. **der gute Mann/ein guter Mann** and **das gute Kind/ein gutes Kind**. In other words **der guter Mann** and **das gutes Kind** are not possible – the system is more economical than this.

8.1.3 *The unpreceded adjectival (strong) endings*

	M	*F*	*N*	*Pl*
N	**-er**	**-e**	**-es**	**-e**
A	**-en**	**-e**	**-es**	**-e**
G	**-en**	**-er**	**-en**	**-er**
D	**-em**	**-er**	**-em**	**-en**

These endings closely resemble the endings of **der/die/das** themselves. But there is a reason for this. These are the endings that apply when nothing (i.e. no determiner) precedes the noun and thus you only have the adjective to indicate the gender, number and case, e.g. **teurer Wein, frische Milch, kaltes Bier, gute Leute**. The full diversity of endings is needed here to convey these necessary grammatical relationships. But note that the masculine and neuter genitive endings are **-en**, not **-es**, which you would expect if this paradigm were exactly parallel to that of **der/die/das** (gen. **des/der/des**). To emphasize this apparent discrepancy, the **-en** endings in the genitive, where **-es** might be expected, have had their **n** underlined in the paradigm above. The ending **-es** in the genitive has been dispensed with here as the noun shows the case, because all masculine and neuter nouns end in **-(e)s** in the genitive singular (see 4.1), e.g. **Anfang nächsten Monats** (at the beginning of next month), **Ende letzten Jahres** (at the end of last year). This is another example of the

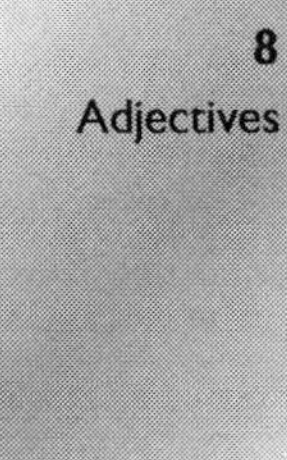

economy of the system of adjectival inflection; two indicators of the genitive are considered superfluous in this instance.

8.1.4 *Adjectival endings after indefinite pronouns*

Alle (all), **einige** (some), **mehrere** (several), **verschiedene** (various), **viele** (many) and **wenige** (few), in addition to being used as pronouns (see 7.7), can stand in front of plural nouns with an adjective between the two. The endings required after **alle** are the same as for the plural of **der/die/das** and those required after the others are the same as for unpreceded adjectives, i.e. the ending on the pronouns is identical to the ending on the adjective, e.g.

N	**alle guten Leute**	*N*	**viele gute Leute**
A	**alle guten Leute**	*A*	**viele gute Leute**
G	**aller guten Leute**	*G*	**vieler guter Leute**
D	**allen guten Leuten**	*D*	**vielen guten Leuten**

The reason for this distinction in endings between **alle** and the other pronouns is that **alle** refers to a definite number and the others to an indefinite number.

8.1.5 *Indeclinable adjectives*

There is a handful of common adjectives borrowed from other languages that cannot take the endings given under 8.1.1 to 8.1.3, e.g. **beige, lila** (mauve), **orange, purpur** (purple). These adjectives can be used both attributively and predicatively but if used before a noun they often combine in writing with **-farben**, which can take the usual endings, e.g.

Ihre Bluse ist lila. Ihre lila/lilafarbene Bluse.
Her blouse is mauve. Her mauve blouse.

8.1.5.1 Adjectives which are prefixed to the noun

There is a considerable number of compound nouns in German where the adjective is not inflected before the noun but actually joined to it as the compound is regarded as a concept. You can do nothing more than note them as you come across them, e.g. **Rotwein** not **roter Wein** (red wine), **Weißbrot** not **weißes Brot** (white bread). Likewise **die Fremdsprache** (foreign language), **die Privatschule** (private school), **der Blauwal** (blue whale), **der Neubau** (new building), **der Nahverkehr** (local traffic), **das Sauerkraut.**

Sometimes the first part of such compound nouns is a noun in German but an adjective in English, e.g. **der Hauptbahnhof** (central/main station), **der Politikwissenschaftler** (political scientist), **mein Lieblingsbuch** (my favourite book).

8.2 Comparative of adjectives and adverbs

As German does not distinguish between adjectives and adverbs in predicative position (see 9.1), what is said here with regard to adjectives applies equally to adverbs.

The comparative form of the adjective, i.e. when stating that something is 'bigger' or 'smaller' etc. than something else, is formed in German as in English, i.e. by the addition of **-er** to the adjective, e.g.

klein > **kleiner** small > smaller

billig > **billiger** cheap > cheaper

When adding the **-er** ending, the vowel of the adjective is usually umlauted, if it can be, i.e. if it is an **a**, **o** or **u**, e.g.

warm > **wärmer** warm > warmer

groß > **größer** big > bigger

klug > **klüger** clever > cleverer

Adjectives containing **au** never umlaut, e.g.

grau > **grauer** grey > greyer

schlau> **schlauer** smart > smarter

There is a substantial number of additional adjectives that do not umlaut despite containing an umlautable vowel, e.g.

brav, bunt, dunkel, falsch, flach, froh, hohl, kahl, klar, knapp, lahm, morsch, nackt, platt, plump, rasch, roh, rund, sanft, satt, schlank, stolz, stumm, stumpf, toll, voll, wahr, zahm

In the case of the following adjectives usage varies:

bang, blass, glatt, dumm, fromm, gesund, krumm, nass, schmal, zart

There are just a few adjectives/adverbs that have an irregular comparative, e.g.

gern > **lieber** — like > prefer

gut > **besser** — good > better

hoch > **höher** — high > higher

nah > **näher** — close/near > closer/nearer

viel > **mehr** — much > more

Note the following. When an English adjective/adverb contains more than two syllables, and sometimes even if it has only two syllables, we prefer to form its comparative by means of 'more' rather than adding **-er**; however long the word is in German, add **-er** to the end of it, e.g.

interessant > **interessanter** — interesting > more interesting

oft > **öfter** — often > more often/oftener

Adjectives that end in **-e** simply add **-r**, e.g.

müde > **müder** — tired > more tired

Adjectives that end in unstressed **-el** and **-er** drop that e when adding the **-er** ending, e.g.

dunkel > **dunkler** — dark > darker

teuer > **teurer** — expensive > more expensive

8.2.1 Common constructions that incorporate the comparative

We'll take **groß**, meaning 'big', 'large' or 'tall', to illustrate how the following phrases that compare two things work – you can substitute any adjective or adverb.

Er ist (genau) so groß wie ich.
He is (just) as tall as I/me.

Er ist nicht so groß wie ich.
He is not as tall as I/me.

Er ist größer als ich.
He is taller than I/me.

Er wird immer größer.
He's getting taller and taller.

In colloquial English we often use an object pronoun in expressions such as these (i.e. 'me'), whereas formal grammar demands a subject pronoun (i.e. 'I'). No such confusion exists in German where the **ich** is seen to be a contraction of **... ich bin** and thus only a subject pronoun is possible.

When **je ... desto** (the ... the) is used in a full sentence, as in the second example below, note that the first clause has subordinate word order (i.e. the verb is placed at the end of that clause) and the second clause undergoes inversion of subject and verb, e.g.

je größer desto besser
the taller the better

Je reicher er wird, desto geiziger wird er.
The richer he gets, the more miserly he becomes.

8.3 Superlative of adjectives and adverbs

8.3.1 *The superlative of the adjective* (see also 8.3.2)

The superlative of the adjective is formed by adding -st, as is usually the case in English too, and umlauting the preceding vowel where appropriate, e.g.

billig > **der/die/das billigste**	cheap > the cheapest
gesund > **die/die/das gesündeste**	healthy > the healthiest
groß > **der/die/das größte**	big > the biggest
klein > **der/die/das kleinste**	small > the smallest

Adjectives ending in **-d**, **-t** or any s-sound (i.e. **-s**, **-ss**, **-ß**, **-sch** or **-z**) insert an **e** before adding **-st**, e.g.

hübsch > **Elke ist das hübscheste Mädchen in der Klasse.**
pretty > Elke is the prettiest girl in the class.

The same applies to the adjective **neu** (new), i.e. **der neueste/am neuesten.**

Adjectives of more than two syllables in English employ 'most' instead of the ending '-st', but this is not the case in German where **-st** can be added to an adjective whatever the number of syllables it contains, e.g.

langweilig > der langweiligste Film
boring > the most boring film

interessant > das interessanteste Buch
interesting > the most interesting book

8.3.2 *The superlative of the adverb*

The superlative of the adverb differs from that of the adjective explained above. It is formed as follows:

langsam > am langsamsten	slowly > slowest
schnell > am schnellsten	fast > fastest

There are several irregular adverbial superlatives, e.g.

gern > am liebsten	like > like most of all (see **gern/ lieber** above)
gut > am besten	well > best
hoch > am höchsten	high > highest
nah > am nächsten	close/near > closest/nearest
viel > am meisten	much > most of all

This is how they are used in practice:

Er ist am schnellsten/langsamsten gelaufen.
He ran (the) fastest/(the) slowest.

Wer ist am höchsten gesprungen?
Who jumped (the) highest?

It can sometimes be difficult to ascertain whether an English superlative is the superlative of the adjective or the adverb. The test is to ask yourself if 'the' before the superlative can be omitted and still sound correct, in which case you are dealing with the superlative of the adverb and thus an **am ...-sten** form is required; if it can't be omitted, you are dealing with the superlative of the adjective and a **der/die/das ...-ste** form is required, e.g.

Wer hat am besten gesungen?/Wer war am besten?
Who sang (the) best?/Who was (the) best?

Wer war der beste (Sänger)?
Who was the best (singer)?

Although this distinction can be a little tricky to determine in English, German offers you an easy way out. The **am ...-sten** form is very commonly used as the superlative of the adjective, as well as of the adverb, and thus it is seldom necessary to make any distinction if you stick to the **am ...-sten** form, e.g.

Wer war der beste/schnellste/klügste? or
Wer war am besten/schnellsten/klügsten?
Who was the best/fastest/cleverest?

In forms like **der beste/schnellste/klügste** the adjective is not capitalized, despite the fact that it would seem to be functioning as a noun; it is felt here that the noun is implied.

8.4 Predicate adjectives followed by a prepositional object

As in English, there is a large number of adjectives used predicatively that are followed by a fixed preposition, but whose preposition is often different from that used in English and thus these have to be learnt one by one. Here is a list of the most common. The adjective can either precede or follow a noun, although preceding it is more usual, whereas it nearly always follows a pronoun, e.g.

Der Iran ist sehr reich an Öl.
Iran is very rich in oil.

Er ist in sie verliebt.
He is in love with her.

In the following list the required grammatical case is given with all two-way prepositions but it should be noted that **auf** and **über** following such adjectives always govern the accusative, never the dative (see 12.3).

abhängig von	dependent on
allergisch gegen	allergic to
anders als (an adverb)	different from

arm an (+ dat.)	poor in (e.g. minerals)
aufgeregt über (+ acc.)	excited about
aufmerksam auf (+ acc.)	aware of
bedeckt mit	covered in/with
begeistert von/über (+ acc.)	enthusiastic about
bekannt wegen	(well-)known for
bereit zu	ready for
berühmt um	famous for
besessen von	obsessed with
besorgt um	worried/anxious about
bewusst (+ gen.)	aware of
böse auf (+ acc.)	angry with, mad at
charakteristisch für	characteristic of
dankbar für	grateful for
durstig nach	thirsty for
eifersüchtig auf (+ acc.)	jealous of
empfindlich gegen	sensitive to
empört über (+ acc.)	indignant about
enttäuscht von	disappointed in/with s.o.
erstaunt über (+ acc.)	amazed at
fähig zu	capable of
freundlich zu	friendly towards
gespannt auf (+ acc.)	curious about
gewöhnt an (+ acc.)	used to
gierig nach	greedy for
glücklich über (+ acc.)	happy about
gut in (+ dat.)	good at (e.g. languages)

gut zu	nice to
hungrig nach	hungry for
interessiert an (+ dat.)	interested in
neidisch auf (+ acc.)	envious of
neugierig auf (+ acc.)	curious about
optimistisch über (+ acc.)	optimistic about
parallel mit	parallel to
pessimistisch über (+ acc.)	pessimistic about
reich an (+ dat.)	rich in (e.g. minerals)
schlecht in (+ dat.)	bad at (e.g. languages)
schuldig (+ gen.)	guilty of
schwach in (+ dat.)	weak at (e.g. mathematics)
sicher vor (+ acc.)	safe from
stolz auf (+ acc.)	proud of
traurig über (+ acc.)	sad about
typisch für	typical of
überzeugt von	convinced of
umgeben von	surrounded by
unabhängig von	independent of
verantwortlich für	responsible for
verglichen mit	compared to/with
verheiratet mit	married to
verliebt in (+ acc.)	in love with
verwandt mit	related to
voll (mit)	full of
wütend auf (+ acc.)	furious with
zufrieden mit	pleased/satisfied with

Chapter 9

Adverbs

Adverbs are those words which give information about the when, where, why and how of the action (i.e. the verb) of the sentence, but they can also qualify adjectives (e.g. 'very good') as well as other adverbs (e.g. 'quite slowly'). They can be individual words or complete phrases. The approach adopted here is to look at the simplest adverbs, i.e. those derived from adjectives, and then to list the most common adverbs of time and place (see Time-Manner-Place rule under 9.4.1) as well as interrogative adverbs. Otherwise mastering adverbs is really chiefly a matter of extending your vocabulary.

9.1 Adverbs that are also adjectives

The adverb and adjective are identical in German, i.e. German does not have any equivalent of the English '-ly', e.g.

Er ist sehr langsam. Er fährt sehr langsam.
He is very slow. He drives very slowly.

Adverbs, unlike adjectives, do not inflect, which is why in the following sentences **furchtbar, schrecklich, scheußlich, typisch** and **wahnsinnig** have no ending but **nett, teuer, bitter** and **deutsch** do:

eine furchtbar nette Frau	an awfully nice woman
ein schrecklich teures Auto	a terribly expensive car
ein scheußlich bitterer Geschmack	a horribly bitter taste
ein typisch deutsches Gericht	a typically German dish
ein wahnsinnig interessantes Buch	an awfully interesting book

Compare the following, where both are adjectives qualifying **Geschmack** and thus both take an ending:

ein scheußlicher, bitterer Geschmack a horrible, bitter taste

9.2 Comparative and superlative of adverbs

As German makes no distinction between adjectives and adverbs, generally speaking adverbs form their comparative and superlative in the same way as adjectives and this is dealt with under adjectives (see 8.2 and 8.3.2).

9.3 Intensifying adverbs

There is a variety of intensifying adverbs, as indeed there is in English too, which are used to qualify other adverbs and adjectives. The following adverbs are very commonly used to intensify adjectives and other adverbs:

außergewöhnlich	exceptionally
äußerst	extremely
besonders	especially, particularly
enorm	enormously
furchtbar	frightfully, awfully
höchst	highly
scheußlich	horribly
schrecklich	terribly, awfully
sehr	very
wahnsinnig	madly

9.3.1 How to render 'especially'

Take care with translating English 'especially'. When it is used as an adjectival or adverbial intensifier, **besonders** is the appropriate word, e.g.

Es war besonders interessant.
It was especially (particularly) interesting.

But when it stands alone not qualifying an adjective or adverb, i.e. in contexts where 'especially' can be substituted by 'above all', the expression **vor allem** is required, e.g.

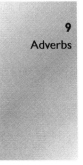

Vor allem wenn es regnet.
Especially when it rains.

vor allem im Sommer
especially in (the) summer

9.4 Adverbs of time

Adverbial expressions of specific time such as 'last week', 'next year', 'this weekend', 'every day', of which there are many, are always expressed in the accusative case. This is only obvious, however, with masculine nouns. The determiners and adjectival endings in the nom. and acc. in such cases are identical for feminine and neuter nouns, e.g. **letzte Woche** (f.), **nächstes Jahr** (n.), **dieses Wochenende** (n.), **jeden Tag** (m.), **nächsten Mittwoch** (m.).

Warte bitte einen Augenblick!
Please wait a moment.

If the adverbial expression of time contains a preposition, the preposition determines the case, e.g. **am nächsten Tag** (the next day, dat.), **um Mitternacht** (at midnight, acc.).

A very limited number of adverbial expressions of indefinite or habitual time take the genitive case, e.g. **eines Tages** (one day), **eines Montags** (one Monday) and even **eines Nachts** (one night), despite the fact that it is feminine. Even expressions such as **morgens** (in the morning[s]) and **montags** (on Mondays) are derived from genitives too (see 9.4.7).

9.4.1 *The Time-Manner-Place rule (TMP)*

It is good style in German to begin clauses with adverbs of time. It is particularly advisable to do this when there are also adverbs of manner and place in the same clause. German insists on the order Time, Manner, Place whereas English usually has the reverse order, e.g.

P M T
He goes to school by bus every day.

T M P
Er fährt jeden Tag mit dem Bus zur Schule.

By beginning clauses with time in German, you then need only concentrate on putting manner and place in the correct order, e.g.

Jeden Tag fährt er mit dem Bus zur Schule.

Notice that if you begin the clause with time, inversion of subject and verb takes place.

Only statements can of course begin with time, never questions, where the verb must be in first position, e.g.

Kommst du morgen mit dem Zug oder mit der Straßenbahn?
Are you coming by train or tram tomorrow?

9.4.2 *Two expressions of time in one clause*

When there are two expressions of time in a clause, the general always precedes the particular:

Ich stehe jeden Morgen um sechs Uhr auf.
Jeden Morgen stehe ich um sechs Uhr auf.
I get up at six o'clock every morning.

Er liest immer bis Mitternacht.
He always reads till midnight.

9.4.3 *Adverbs of time cannot precede the finite verb*

Note that in the previous English sentence the adverb of time occurs between the subject and the finite verb. This is very common in English but is impossible in German because of the necessity for the verb always to stand in second position, e.g.

Er ruft seine Mutter selten/oft an.
He seldom/often rings his mother.

Er hat mir das Geld nie zurückbezahlt.
He never paid me back the money.

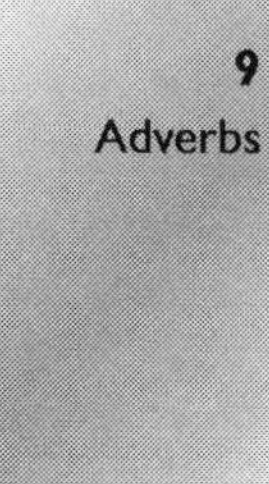

9.4.4 *Word order of adverbs of time and object*

When an expression of time occurs in a sentence with a nominal direct object, it precedes the object, not however when the object is pronominal, e.g.

Ihr müsst heute Abend dieses Kapitel lesen.
You must read this chapter tonight. (nominal object)

Ihr müsst es heute Abend lesen.
You must read it tonight. (pronominal object)

Ich habe ihm gestern das Geld gegeben.
I gave him the money yesterday. (both a pronominal and nominal object)

This problem can be avoided by beginning with time:

Heute Abend müsst ihr dieses Kapitel lesen.
Gestern habe ich ihm das Geld gegeben.

9.4.5 *Word order with adverbs of time in coordinate clauses*

The coordinating conjunctions **aber**, **denn**, **oder**, **sondern** and **und** do not affect the word order (see 11.1). Thus in the following example **morgen** is taken as the first idea in the new clause and consequently inversion of subject and verb takes place:

Gestern ist er nach Moskau geflogen, aber morgen kommt er zurück.
Yesterday he flew to Moscow but he is coming back tomorrow.

A stylistic variant of the above, not placing time at the beginning of each clause, is:

Er ist gestern nach Moskau geflogen, aber (er) kommt morgen zurück.

(If **er** is not repeated, no comma should be inserted before **aber**.)

9.4.6 *How to translate 'for' in expressions of time*

Whether 'for' in expressions of time is translated, and if so how, depends on the tense of the statement. With reference to the future **auf** + acc. and **für** are interchangeable, e.g.

(Auf/für) wie lange gehst du? Ich gehe auf/für zwei Wochen dahin.
How long are you going for? I'm going there for two weeks.

With reference to past time 'for' is not translated, e.g.

Ich bin zwei Wochen da gewesen.
I was there for two weeks.

Er hat zehn Jahre in Schottland gewohnt.
He lived in Scotland for ten years.

But when an action began in the past and has continued into the present, in which case English uses the perfect tense and German uses the present tense, German uses either **schon** or **seit** to render 'for' (see 10.1.5.3), e.g.

Er wohnt schon zehn Jahre in Schottland.
Er wohnt seit zehn Jahren in Schottland.
He has been living in Scotland for ten years.

Schon, being an adverb itself, is followed by an adverbial expression of time in the accusative case, but **seit**, being a preposition, puts the adverbial expression that follows it in the dative case. Both **schon** and **seit** are commonly used together to render 'for' in such expressions too, e.g.

Er wohnt schon seit zehn Jahren in Schottland.

9.4.7 *Common adverbial expressions of time*

Days of the week (die Wochentage) (see 13.8)

on Sundays	**sonntags** or **an Sonntagen** etc.
on Mondays	**montags**
on Tuesdays	**dienstags**
on Wednesdays	**mittwochs**
on Thursdays	**donnerstags**
on Fridays	**freitags**
on Saturdays	**samstags, sonnabends**
on Sunday (past and coming)	**am Sonntag**

the Sunday after	**am folgenden Sonntag**
Sunday morning, afternoon, evening/night	**Sonntagmorgen, -nachmittag, -abend**
on Sunday evenings	**am Sonntagabend, an Sonntagabenden**
by Sunday	**bis Sonntag**
next Sunday	**nächsten Sonntag**
last Sunday	**letzten Sonntag**
from Sunday (on)	**ab Sonntag/von Sonntag an**
on Sundays and holidays	**an Sonn- und Feiertagen**

Yesterday, today, tomorrow etc.

According to the pre-1998 spelling (see 2.5) compound expressions such as **gestern Morgen** were written **gestern morgen**. This has now changed to reflect the fact that **Morgen** is a noun and should thus be capitalized, whereas **gestern** is an adverb and is not capitalized.

yesterday	**gestern**
yesterday morning	**gestern Morgen**
yesterday afternoon	**gestern Nachmittag**
yesterday evening or (more usually) last night	**gestern Abend**
the day before yesterday	**vorgestern**
the morning of the day before yesterday*	**vorgestern Morgen**
the evening of the day before yesterday*	**vorgestern Abend**

(*In such cases in English we would be more likely to say 'Wednesday morning/night' if today were Friday, for example.)

today	**heute**
from today on	**ab heute**

this morning/afternoon	**heute Morgen/Nachmittag**
tonight, this evening	**heute Abend**
tonight (after midnight)	**heute Nacht**
last night (after midnight)	**heute Nacht**
in a week's time	**heute in 8 Tagen**
in a fortnight's time	**heute in 14 Tagen**
tomorrow	**morgen**
tomorrow morning	**morgen früh** (not **morgen Morgen**)
tomorrow afternoon	**morgen Nachmittag**
tomorrow evening/night	**morgen Abend**
the day after tomorrow	**übermorgen**

Periods of the day (die Tageszeiten)

in the morning(s)	**morgens, am Morgen**
in the afternoon(s)	**nachmittags, am Nachmittag**
in the evening(s)	**abends, am Abend**
at night	**nachts, in der Nacht**
during the day	**tagsüber**
late in the evening	**spät abends, spät am Abend**
at nine in the evening	**abends um neun**
early in the morning	**früh morgens**
at lunchtime/midday	**zu Mittag**
at one o'clock in the morning/a.m.	**um ein Uhr nachts**
at five o'clock in the morning/a.m.	**um fünf Uhr morgens/vormittags**

Weekend (das Wochenende)

this/next weekend	**dieses/nächstes Wochenende**

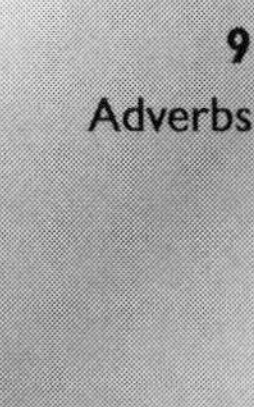

last weekend	**letztes Wochenende**
at/on the weekend	**am Wochenende**

Seasons (die Jahreszeiten)

the summer, winter, autumn, spring	**der Sommer, Winter, Herbst, Frühling**
in summer etc.	**im Sommer**
next summer etc.	**nächsten Sommer**
last summer etc.	**letzten Sommer**
this summer etc.	**diesen Sommer**

Now

now	**jetzt**
from now on	**ab jetzt, von nun an**
until now, up to now	**bis jetzt**
nowadays	**heutzutage**
now and then	**ab und zu**
at the present time, currently	**zur Zeit**

Hour

for hours	**stundenlang**
two hours ago	**vor zwei Stunden**
in two hours' time	**in zwei Stunden**

Day

one day, morning, evening	**eines Tages, Morgens, Abends**
that day, morning, evening	**an dem Tag, Morgen, Abend**
the next day	**am nächsten Tag**
the day after	**am Tag danach**
the day before	**am Tag davor/am vorigen Tag**

all day, evening	**den ganzen Tag, Abend**
all night	**die ganze Nacht**
for days	**tagelang**
one of these days	**irgendwann, eines Tages**
(on) the same day	**am selben Tag**
once/twice a day	**einmal/zweimal am Tag**
daily, every day	**täglich, jeden Tag**
the day after (that)	**am Tag danach, am nächsten Tag**
the day before	**am vorigen Tag**

Week

this week	**diese Woche**
next week	**nächste Woche**
last week	**letzte Woche**
in a week, in a week's time	**in einer Woche**
in a fortnight, in a fortnight's time	**in zwei Wochen, in vierzehn Tagen**
within a week	**innerhalb einer Woche**
a week ago	**vor einer Woche**
a fortnight ago	**vor vierzehn Tagen**
Friday week, a week from Friday	**Freitag in einer Woche**
during the week	**während der Woche**
on weekdays	**wochentags, an Wochentagen**
at the beginning of next week	**Anfang nächster Woche**
at the end of last week	**Ende letzter Woche**
all week (long)	**die ganze Woche hindurch**
from next week on	**ab nächster Woche**
once/twice a week	**einmal/zweimal in der Woche einmal/zweimal pro Woche**

Month (see 13.8)

this month	**diesen Monat**
next month	**nächsten Monat**
last month	**letzten Monat**
from next month (on)	**ab nächstem Monat**
in a month's time	**in einem Monat**
within a month	**innerhalb eines Monats**
a month ago	**vor einem Monat**
for months	**monatelang**
once/twice a month	**einmal/zweimal im Monat**
at the beginning of January	**Anfang Januar**
in the middle of January	**Mitte Januar**
at the end of January	**Ende Januar**
in January	**im Januar**

Year

this year	**dieses Jahr**
from this year (on)	**ab diesem Jahr**
next year	**nächstes Jahr**
last year	**letztes Jahr**
in two years' time	**in zwei Jahren**
two years ago	**vor zwei Jahren**
years ago	**vor Jahren, Jahre her**
throughout the year	**das ganze Jahr hindurch**
once a year	**einmal im Jahr**
in the (nineteen) sixties	**in den sechziger Jahren**

Holidays (Feiertage)

on public holidays	**an Feiertagen**
Ascension Day	**Himmelfahrt**
All Hallows/All Saints' Day	**Allerheiligen**
(at) Christmas	**(zu) Weihnachten**
Christmas Day	**erster Weihnachtstag**
Boxing Day	**zweiter Weihnachtstag**
New Year's Eve	**Sylvester**
(at) Easter	**(zu) Ostern**
(at) Whitsun(tide)/Pentecost	**(zu) Pfingsten**
October 3rd	**Tag der deutschen Einheit**

Time

at the same time	**zur gleichen Zeit, gleichzeitig**
some time ago, after some time	**vor/nach einiger Zeit**
a little while	**ein Weilchen**
a moment	**einen Augenblick**
at the moment	**zur Zeit**
all the time	**die ganze Zeit**
for a long time	**lange**
on time	**rechtzeitig**
at all times/any time	**zu jeder Zeit, jederzeit**
once, one time	**einmal**
twice, three times etc.	**zweimal, dreimal**
a few/several times	**ein paar Mal**
last time	**das letzte Mal**
next time	**das nächste Mal**
this time	**diesmal**

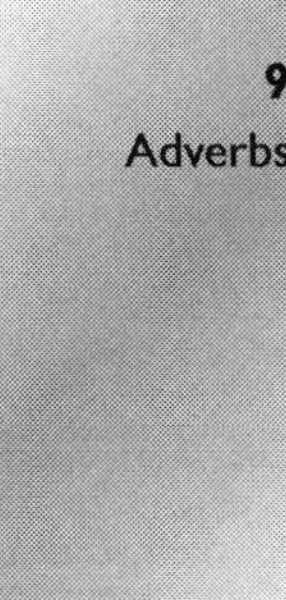

twice a day	**zweimal am Tag**
in the course of time	**im Laufe der Zeit**
in the long run	**auf die Dauer**

General expressions of time

always	**immer**
still	**noch, immer noch, noch stets**
not yet	**noch nicht**
still not	**immer noch nicht**
for good	**für immer**
seldom	**selten**
ever	**je, jemals**
never	**nie, niemals, noch nie** (see 14.2.g)
mostly	**meistens**
sometimes	**manchmal**
now and again/then	**ab und zu**
meanwhile	**inzwischen, mittlerweile**
often, more often	**oft, öfter**
once in a while, from time to time	**öfters**
usually	**gewöhnlich**
recently	**vor kurzem, kürzlich**
recently, the other day	**neulich** (not as recent as **vor kurzem**)
lately	**in letzter Zeit**
at the latest	**spätestens**
at the earliest	**frühestens**
late	**zu spät**
these days	**heutzutage**

in (the) future	**in Zukunft, künftig**
henceforth, from now on	**von nun an**
from then on	**von da an**
high time	**höchste Zeit**
for the time being, provisionally	**vorläufig**
temporarily	**vorübergehend**
since, since then	**seitdem, seither** (lit.)
immediately	**sofort**
presently, in a moment	**gleich**
soon, quickly	**bald**
soon afterwards	**bald danach**
as soon as possible	**so bald wie möglich**

9.4.8 *Adverbs of time with alternative translations in German*

Afterwards

afterwards, after that	**dann, danach, nachher**

Again

again	**wieder**
(yet) again	**schon wieder**
again and again	**immer wieder**

Before

before, earlier, formerly, previously	**früher**
(as) (never) before	**(wie) (nie) zuvor**
before that	**davor, vorher**

Finally

finally	**zum Schluss, schließlich, letztens**
finally, at last	**endlich**
eventually	**schließlich**

Firstly

firstly	**zuerst**
first (as in 'Show me the letter first')	**zuerst**
for the first time	**zum ersten Mal**
firstly (secondly, thirdly etc.)	**erstens (zweitens, drittens** etc.)
at first	**anfangs, am Anfang**

Then

then	**dann**
then, at that time (in the past)	**damals**

9.5 Adverbs of place and direction

You will notice in several of the groups of adverbs below that there is a form with and without the preposition **nach**. In English there is usually only one word to express both place and motion towards a place but in the latter case these German adverbs of direction express motion towards a place by means of **nach**.

He lives here.	**Er wohnt hier.**
How often does he come here?	**Wie oft kommt er hierher?** (see 9.7.3)
He works there.	**Er arbeitet da/dort.**
How does he get there?	**Wie fährt er dahin/dorthin?** (see 9.7.3)
She's sitting outside.	**Sie sitzt draußen.**

She went outside.	**Sie ging nach draußen.** (see 9.7.3)
She sleeps upstairs/downstairs.	**Sie schläft oben/unten.**
She went upstairs/downstairs.	**Sie ging nach oben/unten.** (see 9.7.3)
(to) here	**hierher** (see 9.7.3)
(to) there	**dahin, dorthin** (see 9.7.3)
next-door	**nebenan**
on this/these	**hierauf** (see 7.1.4)
in this/these	**hierin**

Similarly:

on that/those	**darauf** (see 7.1.4)
in that/those	**darin**
on the left, (turn) left	**links**
on the right, (turn) right	**rechts**
to the left	**nach links**
to the right	**nach rechts**
in the middle	**in der Mitte**
straight ahead	**geradeaus**
in/at the front	**vorn(e)**
in/at the back	**hinten**
(go) to the front	**nach vorne**
(go) to the back	**nach hinten**
upstairs	**oben**
downstairs	**unten**
(to) upstairs	**nach oben** (see 9.7.3 for **hinauf**)
(to) downstairs	**nach unten**
inside	**drinnen**

outside	**draußen**
(to) inside	**nach drinnen**
(to) outside	**nach draußen** (see 9.7.3 for **hinaus**)
home	**nach Hause/heim**
at home	**zu Hause/daheim**
away	**weg**
far away	**weit weg**
underway, on the way	**unterwegs**
uphill	**bergauf**
downhill	**bergab**
everywhere	**überall**
somewhere	**irgendwo**
nowhere	**nirgendwo, nirgends**

9.6 Adverbs of manner and degree

Adverbs of manner and degree are too numerous and diverse to list, e.g. **mit dem Zug** (by train), **glücklicherweise** (fortunately), **mit lauter Stimme** (in a loud voice), etc. You are advised to consult a good dictionary for such expressions.

9.7 Interrogative adverbs

Interrogative adverbs are those words that introduce questions asking when, where, how and why etc. (see also Interrogative pronouns under 7.5). For interrogative adverbs in indirect questions see 11.2.

why	**warum**
when	**wann**
how	**wie**
where	**wo**

where ... (to)	**wohin, wo ... hin** (see 9.7.2)
where ... from	**woher, wo ... her** (see 9.7.2)

9.7.1 *Wie* ***occasionally renders English 'what'***

Wie ist Ihr Name? or **Wie heißen Sie?**
What is your name?

Otherwise **wie** means 'how' and, like 'how' in English, it is often followed by other adverbs, e.g.

(for) how long	**wie lange**
how much	**wie viel**
how many	**wie viele**
how often	**wie oft**
how far	**wie weit**

Wie viel hast du für deinen neuen Porsche bezahlt?
How much did you pay for your new Porsche?

Note the following idiomatic ways of asking the date (see 13.8):

Der wievielte ist heute? or **Den wievielten haben wir heute?**
What is the date today?

9.7.2 *Wo, wohin, woher*

Whenever **wo** occurs in a question with a verb of motion designating direction to or from a place, German must use the compounds **wohin** or **woher** respectively (compare the use of 'whither' and 'whence' in archaic English), but two word orders are possible, e.g.

Wo wohnen Sie?
Where do you live?

Wohin gehen Sie? or **Wo gehen Sie hin?**
Where are you going? (= whither)

Woher kommen Sie? or **Wo kommen Sie her?**
Where do you come from? (= whence)

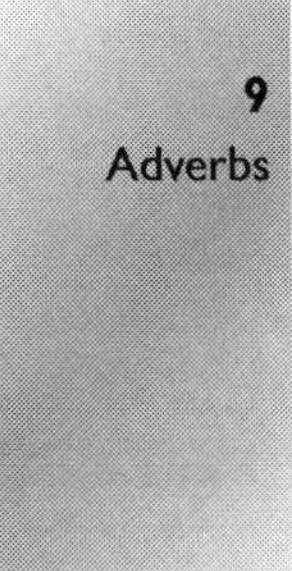

9.7.3 *Hin **and** her*

Hin and **her** are adverbs that indicate direction away from and towards the speaker respectively. They are most commonly used together with prepositions to form separable prefixes of separable verbs to emphasize movement (see 10.9.1): **herab, herauf, heraus, hinein, hinüber, hinunter**, e.g.

> **Bring die Stühle bitte herein!**
> Please bring the chairs in.
>
> **Er ging die Treppe hinauf.**
> He went up the stairs.

In spoken German both **hin** and **her** used in combination with such prepositional prefixes (see 10.9.1.a) are pronounced simply as **r**, e.g.

> **Geh rauf! (< Geh hinauf), Komm runter! (< Komm herunter), Raus! (< Hinaus)**
> Go upstairs, Come down(stairs), Get out.

The prefixes do not always indicate literal but rather figurative movement, e.g.

> **Was habt ihr herausgefunden?**
> What did you find out?

Hin and **her** can act as separable verbal prefixes on their own (see 10.9.1.b), e.g.

> **Wie hast du das hingekriegt?**
> How did you manage that?
>
> **Gib das her!**
> Hand it over.

Hin und her is an adverbial expression in itself meaning 'to and fro' or 'back and forth'.

Chapter 10

Verbs

German verbs, just like English verbs, all have tenses which indicate the time of the action being performed, whether it is being performed now, was being performed at some point in the past or will be performed at some point in the future. Every tense in English has a parallel tense in German but it should be noted that one of the most important respects in which these two languages differ from each other is the way in which they use certain tenses, e.g. see the use of the future (10.1.2) and perfect tenses (10.1.5.3).

German, like English, has both regular and irregular verbs. Many grammars of German refer to regular verbs as 'weak' verbs, but these terms are synonymous. A regular verb in German is one that uses variations of the ending **-te** in the past (compare an English verb that adds '-ed', e.g. worked) and forms its past participle by adding **-t**, e.g. **ich wohnte** – 'I lived', **ich habe gewohnt** – 'I have lived'. An irregular verb, also commonly called a strong verb, does not take an ending in the past tenses but usually changes the vowel of the stem in both English and German in the past tenses, e.g. **ich fand** (I found), **ich habe gefunden** (I have found). Technically you can make a distinction between an irregular and a strong verb, but in general usage these two terms are treated as synonymous.

All verbs are learnt in their infinitive form, i.e. the form that has not yet defined who is performing the action of the verb, e.g. **kaufen** = 'to buy'. Once you employ a verb in a sentence, naming the doer of that verb, you turn that verb into a finite verb and the ending it takes depends on its subject, i.e. **ich kaufe** = 'I buy', **du kaufst** = 'you buy' etc. In German there is a greater variety of such endings than in English.

10.1 Formation of tenses

10.1.1 *The present tense*

The stem of a verb is what is left when the **-en** of the infinitive is removed, i.e. **trinken** > **trink-**, **wohnen** > **wohn-**, **finden** > **find-**, **kaufen** > **kauf-**. The present tense of most verbs is formed by adding endings to this stem. What follows is the conjugation of a typical regular verb, **wohnen** (to live), in the present tense.

ich wohne
du wohnst
er wohnt
wir wohnen
ihr wohnt
sie wohnen

In this chapter all verbs will be given as above, i.e. showing six persons of the verb, those being the first, second and third person singular and the first, second and third person plural. A form like **er wohnt** also represents what is required when the subject is **sie** (she) and **es** (it). The same applies to **sie wohnen** (they live), which also represents **Sie wohnen** (you live).

A form like **er wohnt** can be translated in three different ways in English, i.e. 'he lives', 'he is living' or 'he does live', depending on context. This is a complexity of English which does not exist in German, e.g.

Wo wohnt dein Bruder heutzutage?
Where is your brother living these days?

Er wohnt in Amerika.
He lives/is living in America. (see 10.7)

The same applies to a question. Although we say in English 'He lives in Germany', when you ask a question you have to say 'Where does he live?', whereas German simply inverts the subject and verb saying 'Where lives he?', i.e. **Wo wohnt er?** Similarly with 'He is living in Germany', where the question form in English is 'Is he still living in Germany?', i.e. **Wohnt er noch in Deutschland?**

In spoken German it is very common to drop the **-e** of the first person, which, if ever done in writing, should be indicated by the use of an apostrophe, though this is not always observed, e.g.

Ich komm' schon.
I'm coming.

Was mach ich jetzt?
What am I going to do now?

When the stem of a verb ends in **-t** or **-d**, an **e** is inserted between the stem and an **-st** or a **-t** ending, e.g. **arbeiten** (to work) and **finden** (to find):

ich arbeite	**ich finde**
du arbeitest	**du findest**
er arbeitet	**er findet**
wir arbeiten	**wir finden**
ihr arbeitet	**ihr findet**
sie arbeiten	**sie finden**

Verbs whose stem ends in a consonant + **n** or **m** also insert an **e** before the endings **-st** and **-t** in order to make them easier to pronounce, e.g. **öffnen** (to open) and **widmen** (to devote):

ich öffne	**ich widme**
du öffnest	**du widmest**
er öffnet	**er widmet**
wir öffnen	**wir widmen**
ihr öffnet	**ihr widmet**
sie öffnen	**sie widmen**

When the stem of a verb ends in **-s**, **-ss**, **-ß**, **-tz** or **-z**, the ending used for the second person singular is just **-t**, not **-st** as you would expect, which means that the second and third persons look the same, e.g. **heißen** (to be called) > **du/er heißt**, **reisen** (to travel) > **du/er reist** and **sitzen** (to sit) > **du/er sitzt**.

A few verbs end in **-eln** or **-ern**, thus not **-en** as is usually the case. The first person of those ending in **-eln** drops this **e** when adding the **e**-ending of the first person singular, but those in **-ern** do not, e.g. **lächeln** (to smile) and **wandern** (to hike, go walking):

ich lächle (not **lächele**)	**ich wandere** (not **wandre**)
du lächelst	**du wanderst**
er lächelt	**er wandert**
wir lächeln	**wir wandern**
ihr lächelt	**ihr wandert**
sie lächeln	**sie wandern**

10.1.1.1 The present tense of irregular verbs

The real indicator of whether a verb is regular or irregular is how it behaves in the past tenses (see 10.1.4.2). Many verbs that are irregular in the past are regular in the present, e.g. **kommen** which is conjugated in the present like **wohnen** in 10.1.1, but whose past tense is **ich kam**, indicating that it is in fact an irregular verb.

But there are many common irregular verbs that show one of several irregularities in the present tense as well. These are dealt with here. The irregularities usually apply only to the second and third persons singular. One thing is certain with respect to irregular verbs: if a verb is irregular in any of the following ways in the present tense, it is most certainly irregular in the past tenses and will thus be found in the list of irregular verbs under 10.12.1.

Some, but not all, irregular verbs whose stem contains an **e** change that **e** to **i** in the second and third persons singular, e.g. **geben** (to give) and **essen** (to eat):

ich gebe	**ich esse**
du gibst	**du isst**
er gibt	**er isst**
wir geben	**wir essen**
ihr gebt	**ihr esst**
sie geben	**sie essen**

Nearly all verbs that do this are very common and are thus easily learnt. Here is a list of the most common: **helfen** (to help), **nehmen** (to take), **sprechen** (to speak), **sterben** (to die), **treffen** (to meet), **treten** (to tread, step), **vergessen** (to forget), **werfen** (to throw).

Just **nehmen** (to take) and **treten** (to tread) show further idiosyncrasies of spelling in the second and third persons singular:

ich nehme	**ich trete**
du nimmst	**du trittst**
er nimmt	**er tritt**
wir nehmen	**wir treten**
ihr nehmt	**ihr tretet**
sie nehmen	**sie treten**

A much smaller number of verbs change the **e** to **ie** in the second and third persons singular, e.g. **lesen** (to read) and **sehen** (to see):

ich lese	**ich sehe**
du liest	**du siehst**
er liest	**er sieht**
wir lesen	**wir sehen**
ihr lest	**ihr seht**
sie lesen	**sie sehen**

The following verbs do the same: **empfehlen** (to recommend), **geschehen** (to happen), **stehlen** (to steal).

A sizeable number of irregular verbs whose stem contains an **a** add an Umlaut to the **a** in the second and third persons singular in the present tense; there are also a couple with **au** in their stem that do likewise, as well as one with **o** that takes an Umlaut, e.g. **schlafen** (to sleep), **laufen** (to run) and **stoßen** (to shove):

ich schlafe	**ich laufe**	**ich stoße**
du schläfst	**du läufst**	**du stößt**
er schläft	**er läuft**	**er stößt**
wir schlafen	**wir laufen**	**wir stoßen**
ihr schlaft	**ihr lauft**	**ihr stoßt**
sie schlafen	**sie laufen**	**sie stoßen**

Here is a list of the most common verbs that do this: **braten** (to roast), **fahren** (to drive, travel), **fallen** (to fall), **fangen** (to catch), **halten** (to hold, stop), **laden** (to load), **lassen** (to leave), **raten** (to guess, advise), **saufen** (to booze), **tragen** (to carry), **wachsen** (to grow), **waschen** (to wash). Of these verbs just **halten, laden** and **raten** have exceptional endings in the second and third persons singular because their stems end in **-t** or **-d**, and thus an **e** might otherwise have been expected before the **-st** ending of the second person and an **e** + **t** in the third person, i.e.

ich halte	**ich lade**	**ich rate**
du hältst	**du lädst**	**du rätst**
er hält	**er lädt**	**er rät**
wir halten	**wir laden**	**wir raten**
ihr haltet	**ihr ladet**	**ihr ratet**
sie halten	**sie laden**	**sie raten**

The verb **tun** (to do) is only irregular in the present in that it ends in **-n**, not **-en**, but to conjugate it you simply remove the **-n** and add the usual endings, as with **wohnen** above, e.g.

ich tue
du tust
er tut
wir tun
ihr tut
sie tun

The verb **haben** (to have) shows irregularities in the second and third persons singular that are peculiar to it alone:

ich habe
du hast
er hat
wir haben
ihr habt
sie haben

The verb **werden** (to become, get) also shows irregularities in the second and third persons singular that are peculiar to it alone:

ich werde
du wirst
er wird
wir werden
ihr werdet
sie werden

The verb **sein** (to be), the most irregular verb in both English and German, is conjugated like no other verb in the present tense; compare the English equivalents of the following forms:

ich bin	I am
du bist	you are
er ist	he is
wir sind	we are
ihr seid	you are
sie sind	they are

The above irregularities in the forming of the present tense of German verbs tend to occur overwhelmingly in very commonly used verbs, which is what ultimately makes remembering them easy – you will simply be confronted with these 'exceptions' so frequently that they will cease to look exceptional.

10.1.2 *The future tense*

Although most German grammars will tell you that the future tense in German is expressed by **werden** + infinitive, which is comparable to English 'will' + infinitive, in reality the situation is not quite so simple, as the present tense is commonly used in German to express the future (see 10.1.2.2). Other than in those cases described under 10.1.2.2, **werden** is what you will require to express 'will'. It is conjugated as follows:

ich werde
du wirst
er wird
wir werden
ihr werdet
sie werden

Was wirst du in dem Fall machen?
What will you do in that case?

Das wird nicht helfen.
That won't help.

English, in addition to 'will' and the present tense, often uses 'to go' to express the future. German does not do this. In such cases you must choose between **werden** and the present tense according to the rules given here and in 10.1.2.2, e.g.

Er wird an der Universität Bremen studieren.
He's going to study at the University of Bremen.

Ich mähe morgen den Rasen.
I'm going to mow the lawn tomorrow.

10.1.2.1 Other uses of werden

a) **Werden**, like 'will', is also used in requests, where it is interchangeable with **würde** (would), which sounds even politer, e.g.

Wirst du mir bitte helfen?
Will you please help me?

Würdest du mir bitte helfen?
Would you please help me?

b) **Werden** is commonly used in combination with **wohl** to render 'will probably' where this means 'is most likely to', e.g.

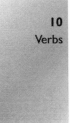

Otto wird wohl im Wirtshaus sein.
Otto will be in the pub./Otto is sure to be in the pub.

See too the use of **werden** in the future perfect tense 10.1.7.

c) **Werden** is a somewhat overworked verb in German. It has three distinctly different functions but its meaning is always clear from the context:

i) First and foremost it is a normal verb meaning 'to become' or 'to get' (in the sense of 'to become'), e.g.

Mein Sohn ist Soldat geworden.
My son has become a soldier.

Es wird im Januar sehr früh dunkel.
It gets dark very early in January.

ii) It is used as an auxiliary verb to render 'to be' in the passive in German (see 10.4).

iii) It is used as an auxiliary verb to render 'will' in the future tense.

10.1.2.2 Use of the present tense to express the future

It is important to note that German uses the present tense to express the future when future time is clearly indicated in some other way, i.e. most usually by an adverbial expression of time; as the second example below illustrates, this convention occurs in English too but is less common in English than in German, e.g.

Das tu' ich morgen.
I'll do it tomorrow.

Er kommt nächste Woche zurück.
He'll be returning next week./He's coming back next week.

10.1.3 The imperative

The imperative is the command form of the verb, i.e. that form used when issuing an order to someone to 'stand up', 'sit down', 'come in' etc. Because this is said to someone you are directly addressing, in other words it is short for 'you stand up' etc., and because German has three words for you, each with its own verb form, there are three ways of issuing commands in German. The verb 'to stand/get up' is **aufstehen** and the three ways of saying 'stand/get up' are

Steh auf!
Steht auf!
Stehen Sie auf!

The first is said to someone you are on **du** terms with (see 7.1.1.1), the second is said to two or more people you are on **du** terms with and the third is said to one or more people you are still on **Sie** terms with (see 7.1.1.1). If issuing a command to a group of people, some of whom you address individually as **du** and others as **Sie**, you need to make a diplomatic choice; if those you know well clearly outnumber those you don't, you might opt for the second form, but if not, you might prefer to play it safe and opt for the third form. What is quite common in all situations, both familiar and polite, is simply to use the infinitive as a non-personal imperative form, e.g.

Bitte, aufstehen!
Please stand/get up.

This form is commonly used for impersonal public signs, e.g.

(Bitte) nicht rauchen!
(Please) don't smoke.

It is most usual, although not always consistently observed (particularly when the sentence is longer), to use an exclamation mark after imperatives in German.

Irregular verbs that change the **e** of their stem to **i** or **ie** in the present tense (see 10.1.1.1) also apply that change in the **du** form of the imperative, e.g.

Gib es ihm!
Give it to him.

Lies es mir bitte vor!
Please read it out to me.

Irregular verbs that change the **a** of their stem to ä in the present tense (see 10.1.1.1) do not apply that change in the **du** form of the imperative, e.g.

Fahr nicht so schnell!
Don't drive so fast.

The **du** form of the imperative of all verbs, except those that change **e** to **i** or **ie**, can end in **-e** but this is most usually dropped in spoken German, except when the stem ends in **-t**, **-d** or **-ig**, e.g.

Komme/komm sofort!
Come immediately.

Antworte mir!
Answer me.

Lade das nicht runter!
Don't download that.

Entschuldige!
Excuse me.

The imperative of **sein** (to be) is totally irregular and is particularly common, e.g.

Sei nicht böse!
Seid nicht böse!
Seien Sie nicht böse!
Don't be angry.

When adding **bitte** (please) to a command, it can go in one of three places in German whereas in English it can only go at the beginning or the end; the third option is the most common in German, e.g.

Bitte, komm nicht zu spät nach Hause!
Komm nicht zu spät nach Hause, bitte!
Komm bitte nicht zu spät nach Hause!
Please don't come home late.

There is also a first person plural of the imperative used, as is English 'Let's …', to express a suggestion to do something. In German this is identical to the **wir** question form of the verb, but the intonation in speech and the exclamation mark in writing clearly distinguish this form from the question, e.g.

Gehen wir jetzt nach Hause!
Let's go home now.

Compare:

> **Gehen wir jetzt nach Hause?**
> Are we going home now?

The first person plural of the imperative is just as commonly expressed as

> **Lass uns jetzt nach Hause gehen!**

10.1.4 The imperfect tense

The imperfect tense is sometimes referred to as the preterite or the simple past tense, contrasting with the perfect or compound past tense.

The difference between a regular and an irregular verb really comes to the fore in the past tenses. Verbs like **kommen** and **finden**, and many others, don't differ from regular verbs in the present, but they certainly do in the past (i.e. **kam, fand**). All English irregular verbs are regular in the present, their irregularity only showing itself in the past, e.g. 'came', 'found'.

10.1.4.1 The imperfect tense of regular verbs

The indicator of a regular verb in English is the ending '-ed' in the past, while the equivalent of this in German is **-te**, **-test**, **-te**, **-ten**, **-tet** or **-ten**, depending on the person of the verb, e.g.

wohnen (to live)	**reden** (to talk)	**arbeiten** (to work)
ich wohnte	**ich redete**	**ich arbeitete**
du wohntest	**du redetest**	**du arbeitetest**
er wohnte	**er redete**	**er arbeitete**
wir wohnten	**wir redeten**	**wir arbeiteten**
ihr wohntet	**ihr redetet**	**ihr arbeitet**
sie wohnten	**sie redeten**	**sie arbeiteten**

The endings all require an **e** before them when the stem of the verb ends in **-d** or **-t**, as illustrated by **reden** and **arbeiten**.

Parallel with what is the case in the present tense (10.1.1), a form like **er wohnte** translates 'he lived', 'he was living' and 'he did live', depending on context, and thus a question such as **Wo wohnte er damals?** can be translated as either 'Where was he living/did he live at that time?' (see 10.1.5.3

for uses of the perfect tense). In fact an imperfect form like **er wohnte** can even render English 'used to live', e.g. **Da wohnte er früher** (He used to live there).

10.1.4.2 The imperfect tense of irregular verbs

An irregular verb is any verb that does not form its past tense by adding **-te**, **-test**, **-te**, **-ten**, **-tet** or **-ten** in the imperfect. The most common form of irregularity in the imperfect is the changing of the vowel in the stem of the verb (called Ablaut or vowel gradation), exactly as in English where we say 'came' (not 'comed'), found (not 'finded') etc. There are seven patterns (or Ablautreihen) of the so-called strong verb; it is usual to list them as follows, where the fourth column contains the past participle (called Partizip II in German) of the verbs in question (see perfect tense 10.1.5). Group 1, verbs with **ei** in the infinitive, contains two patterns, as does group 7 where the past participle contains the same vowel as the infinitive, i.e. **a**:

	infinitive	*present*	*imperfect*	*past participle*
1	**schreiben**	**schreibt**	**schrieb**	**geschrieben**
	beißen	**beißt**	**biss**	**gebissen**
2	**fliegen**	**fliegt**	**flog**	**geflogen**
3	**trinken**	**trinkt**	**trank**	**getrunken**
4	**sprechen**	**spricht**	**sprach**	**gesprochen**
5	**geben**	**gibt**	**gab**	**gegeben**
6	**fahren**	**fährt**	**fuhr**	**gefahren**
7	**schlafen**	**schläft**	**schlief**	**geschlafen**
	fangen	**fängt**	**fing**	**gefangen**

The full conjugation of an irregular verb in the imperfect looks like this – note that the first and third persons singular are identical:

ich schrieb I wrote/was writing/did write
du schriebst
er schrieb
wir schrieben
ihr schriebt
sie schrieben

If the stem of the imperfect ends in **-d** or **-t**, an **e** must be inserted between the stem and the ending in the second person singular and plural, as illustrated here by **finden** (group 3) and **halten** (group 7):

ich fand	I found	**ich hielt**	I held
du fandest		**du hieltest**	
er fand		**er hielt**	
wir fanden		**wir hielten**	
ihr fandet		**ihr hieltet**	
sie fanden		**sie hielten**	

If the stem of the imperfect ends in **-s**, an **e** must be inserted between the stem and the ending in the second person singular, as illustrated here by **lesen** (group 5):

ich las	I read
du lasest	
er las	
wir lasen	
ihr last	
sie lasen	

You cannot tell from an infinitive whether a verb is regular or irregular. **Reisen** (to travel) and **greifen** (to grab) both contain an **ei**, just as **sagen** (to say) and **tragen** (to carry, wear) both contain an **a** and **kaufen** and **laufen** an **au** – nothing here tells you that the former in each case is a regular verb and the latter a strong verb. **Reisen** (to travel), **sagen** (to say) and **kaufen** (to buy) are regular verbs and have a past in **-te** etc. whereas **greifen** is a group 1 irregular verb that has a past like **beißen, tragen** is a group 6 irregular verb that has a past like **fahren** and **laufen** is a group 7 irregular verb that has a past like **schlafen**, i.e. **griff, trug** and **lief**. You simply have to learn whether a verb is regular or irregular and, if irregular, in which way it is irregular, but the number of irregular verbs is quite finite.

10.1.4.3 Use of the imperfect tense

Although there are many similarities between English and German in the way in which the imperfect tense is formed, the two languages differ markedly from each other in the way in which they use this tense. The imperfect of most verbs is not nearly as frequently used in speech as the perfect is (see 10.1.5.3). Where it is used most is in relating a narrative of past events in writing. Let's assume you're reading the story of Little Red Riding Hood, which might start like this:

Eines Tages ging Rotkäppchen in den Wald. Sie wollte zu ihrer Großmutter gehen und pflückte unterwegs Blumen für

sie. Plötzlich sprang von hinter einem Baum ein Wolf hervor, der sie erschreckte. Er war groß und stark und hatte Hunger …

Although it is not at all impossible for the imperfect to be used in this way in speech too, if Little Red Riding Hood were telling the tale herself to someone, it would be more usual for her to use the perfect tense. But there is one notable exception to the tendency to use the perfect tense in speech instead of the imperfect. Although you should be careful to be consistent in your use of tense and not mix the two (i.e. don't say **Plötzlich ist von hinter einem Baum ein Wolf hervorgesprungen, der sie erschreckte** or **Plötzlich sprang von hinter einem Baum ein Wolf hervor, der sie erschreckt hat**), it is most usual in spoken German to use the imperfect of **sein**, **haben**, **werden** and all modals while putting all other verbs in the perfect, in which case the following oral version of the above narrative (and thus it is in the first person) is permissible too, despite reverting to the imperfect of **wollen**, **sein** and **haben**:

Ich bin eines Tages in den Wald gegangen. Ich wollte zu meiner Großmutter gehen und habe unterwegs Blumen für sie gepflückt. Plötzlich ist von hinter einem Baum ein Wolf hervorgesprungen, der mich erschreckt hat. Er war groß und stark und hatte Hunger …

You are more likely to hear the imperfect being used in the speech of northern Germans than southern Germans, as the imperfect has died out in all southern dialects and thus this use of the perfect in dialect is often reflected in the standard German of southern Germans, even being applied to auxiliary verbs.

Getting used to consistently using the perfect instead of the imperfect in speech is not easy for English speakers as the two tenses are not interchangeable in English. English has a rule that if the time of an event that occurred in the past is mentioned, then the imperfect must be used, but if the time is omitted, the perfect is required, e.g.

He returned from Hamburg yesterday.
He has returned from Hamburg.
He has returned from Hamburg yesterday. (not grammatical)

This distinction is not made in German, e.g.

Er kam gestern von Hamburg zurück. (written narrative form)
Er ist gestern von Hamburg zurückgekommen. (most usual spoken form)
Er ist von Hamburg zurückgekommen.

The final sentence can be translated either as 'He has returned from Hamburg' or as 'He returned from Hamburg', depending on the context.

This is the golden rule for choosing the correct past tense to use in German to render a given past tense form in English: an English perfect is always rendered by a perfect in German, whereas an English imperfect can be rendered either by an imperfect or a perfect in German, but more usually the latter in speech, except where **sein**, **haben**, **werden** and the modals are involved, in which case you can choose which tense you use, though these days the imperfect is more common in such cases. For example:

> **Sie hat seinen Namen vergessen.** (perfect)
> She has forgotten his name. (perfect)
>
> **Sie vergaß seinen Namen.** (imperfect – more usual in a written narrative)
> **Sie hat seinen Namen vergessen.** (perfect – more usual in speech)
> She forgot his name. (imperfect)
>
> **Er war furchtbar schüchtern.** (imperfect – usual in both speech and writing)
> **Er ist furchtbar schüchtern gewesen.** (perfect – possible in speech)
> He was terribly shy. (imperfect)

On the one hand, what is expected of us here in German is easier than English as you can generally simply stick to using the perfect in all situations and you will never be wrong. On the other hand, the perfect is a much more complicated tense to form in German than in English as you not only have to keep in mind whether a verb requires **haben** or **sein** in its perfect tense (see 10.1.5.2), but you have to suspend the past participle till the end of the clause and thus have extra issues of word order to address. Nevertheless, this is a matter you have to come to terms with very early in the learning of German if your German is ever to sound natural. If asked, for example, how you say 'I saw him in town yesterday' get used to making your immediate response this: **Ich habe ihn gestern in der Stadt gesehen** and not **Ich sah ihn gestern in der Stadt**, even though the latter is not strictly speaking incorrect.

This preference for the perfect over the imperfect applies equally to the passive voice in spoken German, a fact which is frequently overlooked by non-natives (see 10.4).

10.1.5 The perfect tense

The perfect tense is sometimes referred to as the present perfect or the compound past tense, contrasting with the imperfect or simple past tense. In English it is formed by combining a finite form of the verb 'to have' with the past participle, e.g. 'He has played' or alternatively 'He has been playing'. German is similar in the way in which it forms this tense, e.g. **Er hat gespielt**, where it is immediately obvious the two English forms, where the second is the progressive form, are both rendered by the one form in German. There is a parallel here in the present and imperfect in English (see 10.1.1 and 10.1.4.1). There are two complications in forming the perfect tense in German: firstly you need to derive the correct form of the past participle from the infinitive of the verb concerned, and secondly you need to decide whether the auxiliary verb it is to be used in conjunction with is **haben**, as in English, or **sein**, an option which no longer exists in English.

10.1.5.1 Deriving the past participle of a verb from its infinitive

To derive the past participle of a regular verb, you take the stem and add **ge-** to the beginning and **-t** to the end of it, e.g.

> **spielen** > **gespielt** (played), **kaufen** > **gekauft** (bought), **loben** > **gelobt** (praised)

Where the stem ends in **-d**, **-t** or a consonant + **n**, you must add **-et**, e.g.

> **reden** > **geredet** (talked), **beten** > **gebetet** (prayed), **regnen** > **geregnet** (rained)

The past participles of all strong verbs, those belonging to groups 1 to 7 (see 10.1.4.2), start with **ge-** and, like many English irregular verbs, end in **-en**, and the vowel of the stem depends on which group of strong verbs the verb in question belongs to, e.g.

> **schreiben** > **geschrieben** (written), **stehlen** > **gestohlen** (stolen), **kommen** > **gekommen** (come)

Any verb that starts with one of the following unstressed inseparable prefixes, whether regular or irregular, does not add **ge-**, which would add a second unstressed prefix and thus is avoided, e.g.

> **be-**, **emp-**, **ent-**, **er-**, **ge-**, **miss-**, **ver-**, **zer-**

regular verbs:

bezahlen > **bezahlt** (paid), **erreichen** > **erreicht** (reached)

irregular verbs:

empfehlen > **empfohlen** (recommended), **verstehen** > **verstanden** (understood)

All verbs that end in **-ieren**, most of which are derived from French and are regular, omit the **ge-** prefix as the stress is on the last syllable of the past participle; this is intended to avoid a cluster of unstressed syllables preceding the final stressed syllable, e.g.

studieren > **studiert** (studied), **organisieren** > **organisiert** (organized)

10.1.5.2 Use of **haben** or **sein** as the auxiliary verb in the perfect tense

One of the hardest aspects of German to master is when to use **haben** versus **sein** in the perfect tense. The following is the basic rule (but in practice there are numerous cases that do not seem to fit the rule): all transitive verbs take **haben** and all verbs of motion and verbs that indicate a change of state take **sein** as their auxiliary in the perfect tense, e.g.

lesen (to read, a transitive verb)

ich habe gelesen	I have read (but also 'I read' and 'I was reading')
du hast gelesen	
er hat gelesen	
wir haben gelesen	
ihr habt gelesen	
sie haben gelesen	

kommen (to come, a verb of motion)

ich bin gekommen	I have come (but also 'I came' and 'I was coming')
du bist gekommen	
er ist gekommen	
wir sind gekommen	
ihr seid gekommen	
sie sind gekommen	

sterben (to die, a verb of change of state)

ich bin gestorben	I have died (but also 'I died' and 'I was dying')
du bist gestorben	
er ist gestorben	
wir sind gestorben	
ihr seid gestorben	
sie sind gestorben	

All verbs which take **sein** in the perfect tense are intransitive (see 10.11), which is not to say that all intransitive verbs take **sein**, but only those indicating motion or a change of state. **Lachen**, for example, is an intransitive verb (you can't laugh something) but it takes **haben**, e.g. **Ich habe gelacht** (I have laughed).

Whether a verb requires **haben** or **sein** in the perfect tense has to do with whether the verb concerned is a verb of motion or change of state. It is a fact that the most common verbs that take **sein** are irregular, as the two previous examples illustrate. For this reason most German grammars refer you to their list of irregular verbs (see 10.12.1) where the fourth column, that containing the past participles, indicates by means of **ist** (other books use a variety of symbols) whether **sein** is the required auxiliary. As regular verbs are never listed in a grammar, simply because their number is infinite and you can derive their past tenses for yourself, you will seldom ever get to see a list of regular verbs that require **sein** in the perfect tense because they indicate motion or a change of state. The following is such a list although quite a number of the verbs in it are not particularly common.

10.1.5.2.1 **Regular verbs that take** sein

See 10.1.5.2.4 for an explanation of the asterisks.

abflauen	to die down, abate
abmagern	to thin off, become skinny
abstürzen	to crash
aufflammen	to flare up
aufrücken	to approach, close ranks
auftauchen	to turn up, surface
aufwachen	to wake up

ausbluten	to bleed to death
ausrasten	to blow one's top
begegnen	to bump into, meet
driften	to drift
einrosten	to rust up
einrücken	to move in
entwischen	to escape
eskalieren	to escalate
explodieren	to explode
folgen	to follow
glücken	to be a success
heimkehren	to return home
irren	to roam, wander
kentern	to capsize
kippen	to tip over
klettern	to climb
kollabieren	to collapse
kollidieren	to collide
landen	to land
paddeln*	to paddle
passieren	to happen
platzen	to burst
radeln *	to cycle
rattern*	to rattle along
reisen	to travel
rodeln*	to toboggan
rudern*	to row

scheitern	to fail
schlüpfen (aus-)	to hatch
schrumpfen	to shrink
segeln*	to sail
starten	to take off (planes), start (a race)
stolpern	to stumble
stürzen	to plunge
tanzen*	to dance
unterschlupfen	to take cover
untertauchen	to go into hiding
verbluten	to bleed to death
verdorren	to wither
verduften	to lose its smell
verheilen	to heal up
vermodern	to decay
versanden	to silt up
versickern	to seep away
verunglücken	to have an accident
verwelken	to wilt
zerschellen	to be smashed to pieces

10.1.5.2.2 **Use of** sein **or** haben **with derived verbs**

Whether a verb takes **sein** or **haben** is determined by the meaning of the verb (i.e. whether it indicates motion or a change of state or not), not by its form. Thus, not only is the fact that a verb is regular or not irrelevant to what auxiliary is required, but many new German verbs are derived from a basic infinitive by means of a whole series of separable (see 10.9.1) and inseparable prefixes (see 10.9.2). Adding such a prefix to a verb, whether it be regular or irregular, can so change the meaning of the verb that where the root verb requires **sein**, the derived verb does not, or vice versa. For example, **kommen** (to come) is a verb of motion that requires **sein**, but **bekommen** (to get) is a transitive verb that no longer bears any semantic relationship to **kommen** and thus it requires **haben**, e.g.

Er ist spät nach Hause gekommen.
He got home late.

Ich habe Geld von meiner Tante bekommen.
I got money from my aunt.

Equally, **brennen** (to burn) is an intransitive verb that does not indicate motion or a change of state and thus requires **haben**, but **niederbrennen** (to burn down) can be used as an intransitive verb that does indicate a change of state and thus requires **sein**, or it can be used transitively, in which case it requires **haben**, e.g.

Das Haus hat stundenlang gebrannt. (state unchanged)
The house burnt for hours.

Das Haus ist leider niedergebrannt. (change of state)
The house unfortunately burnt down.

Rechtsradikale haben das Asylantenheim niedergebrannt. (used transitively)
Neo-Nazis burnt down the home for asylum seekers.

Stehen (to stand) is another example of an intransitive verb that neither indicates motion nor a change of state and thus requires **haben**, but **aufstehen** (to get up/stand up) indicates a change of state (or is it motion?) and requires **sein**, e.g.

Er hat sehr lange vor dem Geschäft gestanden.
He stood in front of the shop for ages.

Er ist jeden Morgen um sieben Uhr aufgestanden.
He got up at seven o'clock every morning.

In southern Germany and Austria the three verbs of position **liegen** (to lie), **sitzen** (to sit) and **stehen** (to stand) take **sein** in the perfect but in northern and standard German they take **haben**.

10.1.5.2.3 Verbs of motion that take haben when used transitively

A number of verbs in the list in 10.12.1 have **hat/ist** before their past participle. This means there is a choice of auxiliary depending on the meaning of the verb, i.e. when it is used as a verb of motion it requires **sein**, but if used transitively it requires **haben**. **Fahren**, for example, normally means 'to drive' or 'to go (by vehicle)' to a place, in which case it acts as a verb of motion and takes **sein**, but if you drive a car, the verb has an object, is thus transitive and takes **haben**, e.g.

Er ist sofort nach Hause gefahren.
He drove home straight away.

Ich habe noch nie einen Mercedes gefahren.
I've never ever driven a Mercedes.

10.1.5.2.4 Verbs of motion that take haben or sein when used intransitively

The presence of **hat/ist** before a past participle in the list of verbs in 10.12.1 indicates a different distinction in the case of a few verbs. Take **schwimmen**, for example. **Schwimmen** can never be used as a transitive verb but it can indicate either motion from x to z or merely where the action took place; in the former case it requires **sein** and in the latter **haben**, e.g.

Er ist von hier bis zur Insel da drüben geschwommen.
He swam from here to that island over there.

Wir haben noch nie in der Ostsee geschwommen.
We have never ever swum in the Baltic Sea.

There are also regular verbs where the same distinction is made (see those marked * in the list in 10.1.5.2.1). **Segeln** is one such verb as the following examples illustrate:

Wir sind in den Ferien nach Schweden gesegelt.
We sailed to Sweden in the holidays.

Wir haben jeden Sommer vor der schwedischen Küste gesegelt.
We sailed off the coast of Sweden every summer.

10.1.5.3 Use of the perfect tense

This tense is used much more in German than in English. The rules of English grammar demand that you use the imperfect when the time of an action performed in the past is mentioned, but German knows no such restriction and prefers to use the perfect, particularly in speech (this issue is dealt with in detail under 10.1.4.3). All that needs to be said about the difference in use between the perfect in English and German that is not dealt with under 10.1.4.3 is the following.

The rule that an English perfect is always rendered by a perfect in German has one exception: when an action that began in the past continues into the present, German uses the present tense as the action of the verb is seen to be still ongoing, e.g.

Ich lerne seit zwei Jahren Deutsch.
I have been learning German for two years (and am still learning it).

Keeping in mind that the perfect is the most usual way of expressing a past event in spoken German, the following two sentences are synonymous, despite the fact that the first sentence might look as if it means 'I have learnt German for two years', but this is synonymous with 'I have been learning German for two years' and is thus expressed as above.

Ich habe zwei Jahre lang Deutsch gelernt. (It's common to insert **lang**.)
Ich lernte zwei Jahre lang Deutsch.
I learnt German for two years (but am no longer learning it).

See 10.1.6 for a parallel construction in rendering the English pluperfect.

10.1.6 The pluperfect tense

The pluperfect tense is sometimes referred to as the past perfect. If the (present) perfect is 'I have done/seen' then the past perfect is 'I had done/seen', i.e. it is the past in the past. It refers to an action having been performed prior to another action that occurred in the past, e.g.

Als sie aufstand, hatte ihr Mann schon gefrühstückt.
When she got up her husband had already had breakfast.

As in English, the pluperfect is formed by 'had + past participle' with the added complexity that 'had' is not necessarily **hatte**, but may be **war** in the case of a verb of motion or change of state, e.g.

Er war schon um fünf Uhr aufgestanden.
He had already got up at five o'clock.

Use of the pluperfect is identical in both languages with the following two exceptions. When an action had already commenced in the past, prior to another action occurring in the past, and the first action was still being performed, that ongoing action is expressed in German by the imperfect, not the pluperfect; this is the past tense of the construction discussed in 10.1.5.3, e.g.

Er lernte seit sechs Jahren Deutsch, als er endlich seine Großeltern in Deutschland besuchte.
He had been learning German for six years (and was still learning it), when he finally visited his grandparents in Germany.

The only other difference from English with regard to the pluperfect you need to be aware of is when a pluperfect subjunctive (10.3.2.1) is required in German as this is identical to the pluperfect indicative in English, e.g.

Wenn ich das gewusst hätte, wäre ich nicht in Urlaub gegangen. (i.e. **hätte** not **hatte**)
If I had known that I would not have gone on holiday.

Wenn er im Unfall umgekommen wäre, wäre seine Frau in einer sehr schwierigen Lage gewesen. (i.e. **wäre** not **war**)
If he had died in the accident his wife would have been in a very difficult situation.

10.1.7 The future perfect tense

The future perfect is formed by combining **werden** (will) with the so-called perfective infinitive (i.e. past participle plus **haben** or **sein**, see 10.2.2) which renders English 'will have done', where 'done' stands for any verb, e.g.

Sie wird bestimmt schon fürs Wochenende eingekauft haben.
She will definitely have already shopped for the weekend.

Er wird schon in Urlaub gegangen sein.
He will already have gone off on holiday.

10.1.8 The conditional tense

The conditional is rendered in English by 'would' + infinitive and thus in German by **würde** + infinitive (i.e. the subjunctive of **werden**); it is called the conditional as it is used in combination with an if-clause (thus in German a **wenn**-clause) which states the condition under which the action *would* be performed, e.g.

Ich würde mitgehen, wenn ich Zeit hätte.
I would go along if I had the time.

When the infinitive that follows **würde** is **haben** or **sein**, it is preferable in German to use **hätte** and **wäre** instead of **würde haben** and **würde sein** respectively, although the latter do exist, e.g.

Wärest du damit zufrieden? (< Würdest du damit zufrieden sein?)
Would you be satisfied with that?

Ich hätte Zeit, wenn ich keine Kinder hätte. (< Ich würde Zeit haben, …)
I would have time if I didn't have kids.

The subjunctive form of **mögen** is **möchte**, which renders 'would like', e.g.

Ich möchte heute Abend Kalbfleisch essen.
I would like to have veal tonight.

In shops the form **hätte gern** is commonly used when requesting something from a shop assistant, e.g.

Ich hätte gern 750 Gramm Kalbfleisch.
I would like 750 grams of veal, please. (**bitte** is not necessary with **hätte gern**)

10.1.9 The conditional perfect tense

The conditional perfect in English is formed by combining 'would' with the so-called perfective infinitive thereby rendering 'would have done', where 'done' stands for any verb. This would normally give you in German **würde gemacht haben**, or **würde gegangen sein** in the case of a verb that takes **sein** in the perfect tenses, but instead of doing that German has a preference here for the following: **würde haben** is contracted to **hätte** and **würde sein** to **wäre**, which reduces the number of verbs you have to cope with in these otherwise quite complicated constructions, e.g.

Sie hätte bestimmt schon fürs Wochenende eingekauft, wenn …
(= Sie würde bestimmt schon fürs Wochenende eingekauft haben, wenn …)
She would definitely already have shopped for the weekend if …

Er wäre schon in Urlaub gegangen, wenn ...
(= Er würde schon in Urlaub gegangen sein, wenn ...)
He would already have gone off on holiday if ...

10.1.9.1 Sequence of tenses with the conditional

When dealing with complex sentences in the conditional you must make sure you use the right sequence of tense, something which English speakers consistently get wrong in English but which you must get right in German. Look at the following examples:

If he went to Italy in February he would still find it a bit cold.
If he had gone to Italy in February he would still have found it a bit cold.

The correct sequence of tense refers to the fact that in the first example 'went' in the first clause must be followed by 'would find' in the second clause; in the second example 'had gone' must be followed by 'would have found' in the second clause. The problem lies in the fact that English speakers are quite capable of using a hybrid of these two, e.g. 'If he had gone to Italy in February he would still find it a bit cold' or 'If he went to Italy in February he would still have found it a bit cold'. You cannot do this in German; only the following are possible as German translations of the above:

Wenn er im Februar nach Italien ginge/gehen würde, würde er es noch ein bisschen kalt finden.
Wenn er im Februar nach Italien gegangen wäre, hätte er es noch ein bisschen kalt gefunden.

Here's another example of the problem:

Ich würde ihm helfen, wenn ich könnte.
I would help him if I could.

Ich hätte ihm geholfen, wenn ich ihm hätte helfen können.
I would have helped him if I could have/had been able to.

Both the following variants in English do not observe the correct sequence of tenses:

I would help him if I could have.
I would have helped him if I could.

10.2 Modal auxiliary verbs

The six modal auxiliary verbs of German, generally referred to simply as modal verbs, differ from all other verbs in a number of ways:

1 They are conjugated in the present tense like no other verbs: there is a difference in vowel between the singular and the plural, the usual endings of the present tense do not apply in the sing. and the first and third persons sing. are the same.
2 Despite their highly irregular present tense forms, modal verbs have more or less regular imperfect forms and past participles.
3 Their past participles are not commonly used because of the frequency of the so-called double infinitive construction.
4 When a modal is the finite verb in a clause and has an infinitive dependent on it, that infinitive is never preceded by **zu** (see 10.5.2).
5 They translate idiosyncratically.

Modal verbs are regarded as auxiliary verbs as they are always used in combination with the infinitive of another verb which is either present or implied, e.g.

A: Musst du gehen? B: Ja, ich muss (gehen).
A: Must you go? B: Yes, I must (go).

These verbs are best dealt with one by one as there are features that are unique to each verb.

a) dürfen (to be allowed to)

present		*imperfect*	
ich darf	I am allowed to, I may	**ich durfte**	I was allowed to
du darfst		**du durftest**	
er darf		**er durfte**	
wir dürfen		**wir durften**	
ihr dürft		**ihr durftet**	
sie dürfen		**sie durften**	

past participle: **gedurft**

conditional/subjunctive: **dürfte** (see 10.3.2.1)

This verb in English has the peculiarity that the past tense of 'may' is 'was allowed to', e.g.

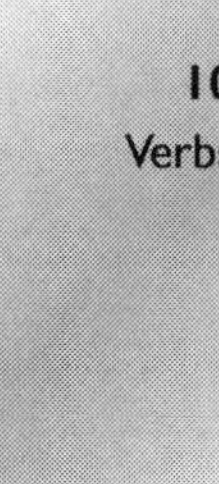

Er darf heute Abend mit uns ins Kino gehen.
He may/is allowed to go to the movies with us tonight.

Er durfte gestern Abend mit uns ins Kino gehen.
He was allowed to go to the movies with us last night.

See **nicht dürfen** under **müssen** below.

b) können **(to be able to)**

present		*imperfect*	
ich kann	I am able to, can	**ich konnte**	I was able to, could
du kannst		**du konntest**	
er kann		**er konnte**	
wir können		**wir konnten**	
ihr könnt		**ihr konntet**	
sie können		**sie konnten**	

past participle: **gekonnt**

conditional/subjunctive: **könnte** (see 10.3.2.1)

When translating 'could' into German, ask yourself whether 'could' means 'was/were able to', in which case you are dealing with the imperfect and the word required is **konnte**, or whether it means 'would be able to', in which case you are dealing with the conditional and the word required is **könnte** (see 10.3.2.1), e.g.

Der Arzt konnte seiner Patientin nicht helfen.
The doctor could not help his patient. (= was not able to)

Der Arzt könnte seiner Patientin nicht helfen.
The doctor could not help his patient. (= would not be able to)

See **mögen** below for cases where **können** renders 'may'.

c) mögen **(to like)**

present		*imperfect*	
ich mag	I like	**ich mochte**	I liked
du magst		**du mochtest**	
er mag		**er mochte**	
wir mögen		**wir mochten**	
ihr mögt		**ihr mochtet**	
sie mögen		**sie mochten**	

past participle: **gemocht**

conditional/subjunctive: **möchte** (see 10.3.2.1)

This verb can be used simply as a transitive verb, where it is usually used to refer to liking people but can be used for food too, e.g.

Ich mag dich (sehr gern).
I like you (a great deal).

Ich habe ihn/Ananas immer gemocht.
I have always liked him/pineapple.

Mögen occurs occasionally in set idioms where it renders 'may' expressing possibility, as opposed to **dürfen** which renders 'may' in the sense of permission, e.g.

Das mag wohl sein.
That may be so./That may well be.

Otherwise 'may', expressing possibility, is normally rendered by **können**, e.g.

Es kann mein Bruder gewesen sein, den Sie auf dem Markt gesehen haben.
It may have been my brother you saw at the market.

Das kann sein.
That may be.

d) müssen **(to have to)**

present		*imperfect*	
ich muss	I have to, must	**ich musste**	I had to
du musst		**du musstest**	
er muss		**er musste**	
wir müssen		**wir mussten**	
ihr müsst		**ihr musstet**	
sie müssen		**sie mussten**	

past participle: **gemusst**

conditional/subjunctive: **müsste** (see 10.3.2.1)

This verb in English has the peculiarity that the past tense of 'must' is 'had to', e.g.

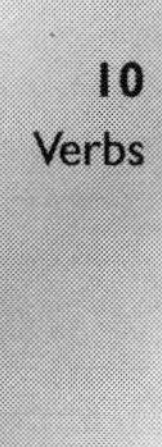

Die Kinder müssen draußen spielen.
The children have to/must play outside.

Die Kinder mussten draußen spielen.
The children had to play outside.

There are complications with this verb when it is used in the negative, both in English and in German. Look at the following English sentences:

You have to/must read this book >	You mustn't read this book.
	You don't have to read this book.

Although 'must' and 'have to' are synonymous, i.e. **Du musst dieses Buch lesen**, 'must not' and 'don't have to' are not. 'Must not' is a prohibition and is expressed by **nicht dürfen**, whereas 'don't have to' implies a lack of obligation and is synonymous with 'don't need to' and is thus expressed by **nicht brauchen**, e.g.

Du darfst dieses Buch nicht lesen.
You mustn't read this book.

Du brauchst dieses Buch nicht (zu) lesen.
You don't have/need to read this book. (= You needn't read this book.)

It is true, however, that **müssen** *is* used with **nicht** in spoken German but, despite appearances, it means 'don't have/need to' not 'mustn't', e.g.

Du musst dieses Buch nicht lesen. = **Du brauchst dieses Buch nicht (zu) lesen.**
You don't have to/don't need to read this book.

Use of **zu** with **brauchen**, which is not a true modal verb, is optional although purists would maintain it is required (see double infinitives under 10.2.1).

e) sollen **(ought to)**

present		*imperfect*	
ich soll	I ought to, shall	**ich sollte**	I should
du sollst		**du solltest**	
er soll		**er sollte**	
wir sollen		**wir sollten**	

ihr sollt		**ihr solltet**	
sie sollen		**sie sollten**	

past participle: **gesollt**

conditional/subjunctive: **sollte** (see 10.3.2.1)

f) wollen **(to want [to])**

present		*imperfect*	
ich will	I want (to)	**ich wollte**	I wanted (to)
du willst		**du wolltest**	
er will		**er wollte**	
wir wollen		**wir wollten**	
ihr wollt		**ihr wolltet**	
sie wollen		**sie wollten**	

past participle: **gewollt**

conditional/subjunctive: **wollte** (see 10.3.2.1)

10.2.1 Double infinitive constructions

Look at the following English sentence which contains a modal verb in the perfect tense:

He hasn't been able to earn much this year.

There are three verbs in this sentence: the finite verb 'has', the past participle 'been able' and the infinitive 'to earn'. Literally in German this would be

Er hat dieses Jahr nicht viel verdienen gekonnt.

But this construction is not possible in German because of the double infinitive rule which states that the past participle of a modal verb cannot be used when the infinitive for which it is acting as an auxiliary is present, but it *is* used when that infinitive is not present, but implied, e.g.

Er hat dieses Jahr nicht viel verdienen können.

A: Hat er viel verdienen können? B: Nein, er hat es nicht gekonnt.
A: Has he been able to earn much? B: No, he hasn't been able to.

When the infinitive is omitted and the past participle of a modal is used in German, it is always used in combination with the object **es**.

When two (or more) infinitives stand at the end of a German clause, they are in the reverse order to English.

Nicht brauchen is one way of rendering the negative of **müssen** (see **müssen** under 10.2 above). **Brauchen** is a verb that cannot make up its mind whether it is a modal or not; originally it was not, but it is being regarded more and more as one. If you treat it as a non-modal verb, you always use **zu** with it and in the perfect tense it behaves as follows:

Du hast den Brief nicht zu schreiben gebraucht.
You didn't have/need to write the letter.

If you treat it as a modal, which is more usually the case in spoken German, you use a double infinitive construction in the perfect tense, e.g.

Du hast den Brief nicht (zu) schreiben brauchen.

When the perfect tense of a modal complete with dependent infinitive occurs in a subordinate clause, the finite verb precedes the two infinitives, i.e.

Hast du gewusst, dass er dieses Jahr nicht viel hat verdienen können?
Did you know that he hasn't been able to earn much this year?

Modals are used most commonly in the imperfect tense (rather than in the perfect tense with a double infinitive construction), even where all other verbs are used in the perfect in speech (see 10.1.4.3).

See 10.3.2.5 for more modals in double infinitive constructions expressing 'could/should have done'.

10.2.1.1 Double infinitives of non-modal verbs

This double infinitive construction is also used with a few other verbs that are not modal verbs, but which behave like modals in contexts where they have an infinitive dependent on them. This construction usually alternates with one utilizing the past participle of the verb concerned, e.g.

fühlen (to feel) **Er hat sein Herz klopfen fühlen.** or (less commonly)

	Er hat sein Herz klopfen gefühlt. He felt his heart beat(ing).
helfen (to help)	**Du hast mir geholfen, Vokabeln zu lernen.** (most usual) or **Du hast mir Vokabeln lernen helfen.** or (but least common) **Du hast mir Vokabeln lernen geholfen.** You helped me (to) learn vocabulary.
hören (to hear)	**Die Mutter hat ihr Baby weinen hören.** or (colloquially) **Die Mutter hat ihr Baby weinen gehört.** The mother heard her baby cry(ing).
sehen (to see)	**Ich habe Alexa tanzen sehen.** or (colloquially) **Ich habe Alexa tanzen gesehen.** I saw Alexa dance/dancing.

Lassen, which translates both 'to let (s.o. do s.t.)' and 'to have (s.o. do s.t.)', is a very common auxiliary verb that always employs a double infinitive construction in the perfect, e.g.

Ich habe meine Kinder alleine ins Kino gehen lassen.
I let my children go to the movies alone.

Ich habe mir die Haare schneiden lassen.
I (have) had my hair cut.

Wir haben ein Ferienhaus in diesem österreichischen Dorf bauen lassen.
We (have) had a holiday home built in this Austrian village.

There are a few pairs of infinitives which render one concept in English that do *not* employ a double infinitive construction in the perfect tense where you might otherwise expect this to be the case (see 10.9.1.1), e.g.

kennen lernen (to meet for the first time)	**Ich lernte ihn in Berlin kennen.** (imperfect) I met him in Berlin. **Ich habe ihn in Berlin kennen gelernt.** (perfect) I met him in Berlin.
spazieren gehen (to go for a stroll)	**Ich gehe jeden Tag spazieren.** (present) I go for a walk/stroll every day.

	Ich bin jeden Tag spazieren gegangen. (perfect) I went for a walk/stroll every day.
sitzen bleiben (to stay down [at school])	**Er blieb auch letztes Jahr sitzen.** (imperfect) He stayed down last year too. **Er ist auch letztes Jahr sitzen geblieben.** (perfect) He stayed down last year too.
stehen bleiben (to stop still/walking)	**Bleib stehen!** (imperative) Stop! (i.e. Don't go any further.) **Warum bist du nicht stehen geblieben?** (perfect) Why didn't you stop?

10.2.2 Modals used with perfective infinitives

A perfective infinitive (see 10.1.7) is a verbal construction consisting of the auxiliary 'to have' used in combination with a past participle, e.g. 'to have read', which in German is **gelesen haben**, whereas 'to have gone' is **gegangen sein** as this is a verb of motion requiring **sein** as its auxiliary. This construction is commonly used in combination with modal verbs, e.g.

Die Feuerwehr muss zu spät gekommen sein.
The fire brigade must have arrived too late.

Er mag den Schlüssel verloren haben.
He may have lost the key.

Wer kann den Brief geschrieben haben?
Who can have written the letter?

Wer soll den Brief geschrieben haben?
Who is supposed/meant to have written the letter?

10.3 The subjunctive

The subjunctive is referred to as a mood, contrasting with the indicative mood, i.e. all the tenses we have looked at so far are officially called the present indicative, the imperfect indicative etc., to give those tenses their full name. In addition to these there are present and past subjunctive forms, called Konjunktiv I and II respectively in German. For this reason we will call them subjunctive I and II here.

10.3.1 The subjunctive I

There are remnants of the present subjunctive in English, e.g. 'The powers that be', 'The new law advocates that one keep to the left' (not 'keeps'). Where it is still used, most native speakers of English are unaware of its continued existence as its forms seldom differ from those of the present indicative (see 'keep' above). But where it is still used in English, it is not used in German, with one exception where it connotes 'let something be the case', i.e.

Lang lebe der König!
Long live the king. (The lack of '-s' on 'live' tells you this is a subjunctive form.)

Gott segne dich!
God bless you.

Gott sei dank!
Thank God. (lit. Thanks be to God)

The forms of the subjunctive I are as follows for every verb in the language, both regular and irregular, except **sein**, which has a separate conjugation:

leben (to live)	**tragen** (to carry)	**geben** (to give)	**sein** (to be)
ich lebe	**ich trage**	**ich gebe**	**ich sei**
du lebest	**du tragest**	**du gebest**	**du seiest**
er/sie/es lebe	**er/sie/es trage**	**er/sie/es gebe**	**er/sie/es sei**
wir leben	**wir tragen**	**wir geben**	**wir seien**
ihr lebet	**ihr traget**	**ihr gebet**	**ihr seiet**
sie leben	**sie tragen**	**sie geben**	**sie seien**

By far the most common use of subjunctive I relates to reporting indirect speech. Compare the following two sentences, where the former quotes directly what was said and the latter expresses it indirectly:

Sie hat ihn gefragt: „Warum kommst du nicht auch mit?“
She asked him, 'Why don't you come along too?'

Sie hat ihn gefragt, warum er nicht auch mitkomme.
She asked him why he isn't coming along too.

When the verb in the subordinate clause is in the past, this is always expressed in German by the past participle plus the subjunctive I of **haben** or **sein**, depending on the auxiliary required for the verb concerned, e.g.

Sie hat ihn gefragt: „Warum hast du mir nicht geholfen?"
She asked him, 'Why didn't you help me?'

Sie hat ihn gefragt, warum er ihr nicht geholfen habe.
She asked him why he didn't help her/hadn't helped her.

Sie hat ihn gefragt, warum er nicht mitgegangen sei.
She asked him why he didn't go along too/hadn't gone along too.

Subjunctive I belongs to the realm of higher style and is found very commonly in journalese, but it is virtually always interchangeable with the present indicative. In fact because three of the six persons of the verb are identical to the present indicative, subjunctive II forms (see 10.3.2) are frequently used instead of subjunctive I forms, for all six persons, when reporting indirect speech. The following are all alternative versions of the previously mentioned examples:

Sie hat ihn gefragt, warum er nicht mitkommt. (present indicative)
Sie hat ihn gefragt, warum er nicht mitkäme. (subjunctive II)
Sie hat ihn gefragt, warum er ihr nicht geholfen hat. (present indicative)
Sie hat ihn gefragt, warum er ihr nicht geholfen hätte. (subjunctive II)

Sie hat ihn gefragt, warum er nicht mitgegangen ist. (present indicative)
Sie hat ihn gefragt, warum er nicht mitgegangen wäre. (subjunctive II)

10.3.1.1 Omission of **dass**

It is not uncommon when reporting indirect speech in a subordinate clause that would otherwise be introduced by **dass**, to omit the conjunction, but then it is necessary to use either form of the subjunctive, not the indicative, and the finite verb in the subjunctive is left in second place, not sent to the end of the clause, e.g.

Er hat gesagt, dass er zwei Wochen in Russland gewesen ist/sei/wäre.
Er hat gesagt, er sei/wäre zwei Wochen in Russland gewesen.
He said he was/had been in Russia for two weeks.

10.3.2 The subjunctive II

You will use subjunctive II much more often than subjunctive I, as it is indispensable. The past subjunctive is complicated, but what you need to know actively is much less than you need to know passively – most forms you can recognize and understand but will rarely need to use yourself.

10.3.2.1 The subjunctive II of strong verbs

There is only one living example of subjunctive II in English (called the past subjunctive in English), which is a good place to start as it corresponds exactly with German, i.e. 'If I were healthy, I would go along too.' 'If I were healthy' states a hypothesis, as opposed to 'I was healthy', which states a fact. German makes the same distinction, e.g. **Wenn ich gesund wäre, würde ich auch mitgehen** versus **Ich war gesund**. But German always makes this distinction between the past subjunctive (i.e. subjunctive II) and the past indicative (i.e. the imperfect), whereas in English it is only obvious with certain persons of the verb 'to be' where 'was' and 'were' alternate, not with any other verb, e.g.

Wenn ich ein Auto hätte, würde ich dich nach Hause bringen.
If I had a car I would take you home.

Here German can continue to show the difference between the fact (**Ich hatte ein Auto**) and the hypothesis (**Wenn ich ein Auto hätte**), whereas English does not bother to. **Wäre** and **hätte** already give you some idea of what you do to form the subjunctive II of strong verbs – here is the full conjugation of those two verbs plus two others to illustrate the regularity:

sein	*haben*	*kommen*	*gehen*
ich wäre	**hätte**	**käme**	**ginge**
du wärest	**hättest**	**kämest**	**gingest**

er wäre	**hätte**	**käme**	**ginge**
wir wären	**hätten**	**kämen**	**gingen**
ihr wäret	**hättet**	**kämet**	**ginget**
sie wären	**hätten**	**kämen**	**gingen**

Although you can apply this pattern to almost any strong verb (e.g. **finden** > **fände, fliegen** > **flöge**), in practice you will find the subjunctive II forms of only a handful of very common verbs being used: **wäre** and **hätte** are of course indispensable, **käme** is not uncommon but **ginge** is less frequently used. Generally speaking, in addition to **wäre** and **hätte**, you will only need actively to use the subjunctive II of modal verbs as well as that of **werden** and **wissen**, i.e. **dürfte, könnte, möchte, müsste, würde** and **wüsste; sollte** and **wollte** do not have separate subjunctive II forms. All of these verbs, with the exception of **wissen**, are commonly used as auxiliary verbs and **wissen** is only here because of the frequency of the expression **Wenn ich nur wüsste!** (If only I knew). Quite a number of strong verbs have irregular subjunctive II forms which are virtually never used any more, e.g. **sterben** > **stürbe** (imperfect **starb**), **helfen** > **hülfe** (imperfect **half**), **empfehlen** > **empföhle** (imperfect **empfahl**).

So how do you avoid using the subjunctive II of strong verbs? Take a sentence like 'It would not surprise me if he died before his wife'. Whenever an if-clause is used in combination with a would-clause, the verb in the if-clause requires a subjunctive II form, thus you would expect here: **Es würde mich nicht erstaunen, wenn er vor seiner Frau stürbe**. Although this is correct German, it sounds very stilted and would seldom be heard (but possibly written); forms like **stürbe** are consistently replaced by **sterben würde** in natural sounding German, i.e. **... wenn er vor seiner Frau sterben würde** (compare the English '... if he were to die before his wife'). With some of the more common verbs, like **kommen** and **gehen** above, you might hear either **käme/ginge** or **kommen würde/gehen würde**, but with less common verbs only the latter will be regularly heard, e.g. not **fände** but **finden würde**, not **flöge** but **fliegen würde**, e.g.

Wenn du über Wien fliegen würdest, würdest du schneller in Athen ankommen.
If you flew via Vienna, you would get to Athens sooner.

Wherever you can use the subjunctive II of **sein, haben, wissen** and the modals, do not avoid doing so by using the **würde**-construction, e.g.

Wenn ich dir helfen müsste ...
If I had to help you ...

Wenn er teilnehmen könnte ...
If he could take part ...

Wenn ich nur wüsste, wo er wohnt!
If only I knew where he's living.

10.3.2.2 Alternative subjunctive II constructions found only in higher style

In higher style in English it is possible to omit the 'if' in an if-clause and to invert the subject and verb instead. This has a direct parallel in German and is regarded as equally high style, e.g.

Wenn Krieg ausbräche, würden alle Ausländer das Land verlassen.
If war broke out/were to break out, all foreigners would leave the country.

Bräche Krieg aus, so würden ...
Were war to break out, ...

It is usual to start the would-clause with **so** when this inversion is applied in the if-clause.

There are three additional ways in which the above could be expressed, the first being the most everyday way and the last two sounding as formal as their English equivalents, i.e.

Wenn Krieg ausbrechen würde, ...
If war broke out, ...

Wenn Krieg ausbrechen sollte, ...
If war should break out, ...

Sollte Krieg ausbrechen, so ...
Should war break out, ...

10.3.2.3 The subjunctive II of regular verbs

In English, with the exception of 'was/were', no attempt is made to distinguish between the past indicative (i.e. the imperfect) and the past subjunctive, usually called subjunctive II in German (see 10.3.2.1), i.e. between fact and hypothesis. Although it is vital to make the distinction in German with strong verbs, the same necessity does not exist with regular verbs, with the result that they can behave exactly as all verbs do in English, e.g.

Wenn du es machtest, würde ich dich dafür bezahlen.
If you did it, I would pay you for it.

Although this is possible, generally speaking German likes to emphasize the hypothetical nature of the action in the if-clause and does so in this case by using the **würde**-construction dealt with under 10.3.2.1 – the addition of an Umlaut is not possible with regular verbs, i.e.

Wenn du es machen würdest, würde ich dich dafür bezahlen.

10.3.2.4 Use of the subjunctive II in would-clauses

Use of the subjunctive II forms described in 10.3.2.1 is not limited to if-clauses, as illustrated there; they are also commonly used in would-clauses, e.g.

Wenn er reicher wäre, hätte er ein besseres Auto. (= **würde er ein besseres Auto haben)**
If he were richer, he would have a better car.

Although would-clauses can be rendered by **würde**-clauses, with the verbs whose subjunctive II is commonly used in if-clauses, it is more usual to use those subjunctive II forms in the would-clauses too, e.g.

Wenn es nicht so kalt wäre, wäre es schon angenehmer. (= **würde es schon angenehmer sein)**
If it weren't so cold, it would indeed be more pleasant.

Wenn du mitkommen würdest, könntest du mir helfen. (= **würdest du mir helfen können)**
If you came along, you could help me.

Du könntest mitkommen (= **du würdest mitkommen können), wenn du möchtest.**
You could come along if you would like to.

10.3.2.5 'Could/should have done'

The most complex subjunctive constructions you will encounter are those German double infinitive constructions that render 'could have done' and 'should have done', where 'done' stands for any verb, i.e. 'could have seen/made/gone' etc., e.g.

Er hätte es machen können.
He could have done it

Er hätte auch mitkommen können.
He could have come along too.

Sie hätte dir helfen sollen.
She should have helped you.

The formula is the same in all cases, i.e. always use **hätte**, regardless of whether the infinitive that follows takes **haben** or **sein** in the perfect because in fact this is a perfect subjunctive form of the modal verbs, not of **machen**, **mitkommen** or **helfen**.

The construction with **können** allows itself to be logically dissected – see the second translation of the following German sentence which is synonymous with the first; it merely expresses 'could' in terms of 'to be able' and illustrates that **würde** and **haben** have been contracted, as is nearly always the case in German, to be expressed by **hätte**:

Der Lehrer hätte die Schüler früher nach Hause schicken können.
The teacher could have sent the pupils home earlier.
The teacher would have been able to send the pupils home earlier.
(would have = **hätte**, been able = **können**, to send = **schicken**)

The construction with **sollen** does not permit logical breakdown like this, so both constructions are simply best learnt parrot-fashion, i.e. 'could have done' is **hätte machen können** and 'should have done' is **hätte machen sollen**.

10.4 The passive

The passive is a so-called voice, not a tense. All tenses of the active extend to the passive too. A passive construction is one where the object of the active sentence becomes the subject of the finite verb:

active:	**Die Polizei untersucht den Mord.** The police are investigating the murder.
passive:	**Der Mord wird (von der Polizei) untersucht.** The murder is being investigated (by the police).

In the passive the agent or doer of the action may be left unmentioned (hence the brackets in the above example) if so desired. The passive is used in German more or less exactly as it is in English (see 10.4.6 for the few exceptions). You use the passive in preference to the active for stylistic reasons, often because who has performed the action is either unknown or irrelevant to the information you wish to relay, e.g. 'The money has been found', where the agent is not mentioned and thus this is the passive equivalent of something like 'Someone has found the money'. If in English you would say the former, do so in German too; and if the latter is the appropriate construction in English, so it is in German too, i.e.

Das Geld ist gefunden worden.
Jemand hat das Geld gefunden.

As the passive is a construction in which the object of the active becomes the subject of the passive, generally speaking only transitive verbs – those that can take an object (see 10.11) – can be used in the passive. Thus verbs like **gehen**, **kommen** and **sterben** cannot be used in the passive in either English or German.

10.4.1 How to construct the passive

The passive is constructed in English by a tense form of the verb 'to be' plus a past participle plus an optional agent introduced by the preposition 'by':

subject	*to be*	*past participle*	*(by + noun/pronoun)*
The murder	is being	investigated	(by the police/them).

The German passive differs in that the verb **werden** is used, not **sein**, to translate the verb 'to be' and 'by' is rendered by **von**:

subject	***werden***	*(**von** + noun/pronoun)*	*past participle*
Der Mord	**wird**	**(von der Polizei/ihnen)**	**untersucht.**

What follows is this sample sentence in all tenses of the passive:

Der Mord wird (von der Polizei) untersucht. (present tense)
The murder is being investigated (by the police).

Der Mord wurde (von der Polizei) untersucht. (imperfect tense)
The murder was [being] investigated (by the police).

Der Mord ist (von der Polizei) untersucht worden. (perfect tense)
The murder has been investigated (by the police).

Der Mord war (von der Polizei) untersucht worden. (pluperfect tense)
The murder had been investigated (by the police).

Der Mord wird (von der Polizei) untersucht werden. (future tense)
The murder will be investigated (by the police).

Der Mord wird (von der Polizei) untersucht worden sein. (future perfect tense)
The murder will have been investigated (by the police).

Der Mord würde (von der Polizei) untersucht werden. (conditional tense)
Der Mord würde (von der Polizei) untersucht. (würde = contracted **würde** + **werden)**
The murder would be investigated (by the police).

Der Mord wäre (von der Polizei) untersucht worden. (conditional perfect tense)
The murder would have been investigated (by the police). (see note below)

Remember the following with regard to how the tenses of the passive are used. Just as in the active (see 10.1.2), the present tense is commonly used in German to express the future as well, especially when an adverb of future time is mentioned, e.g.

Der Mord wird bald von der Polizei untersucht.
The murder will soon be investigated by the police.

And once again, just as in the active (see 10.1.4.3), the English imperfect is commonly expressed by the perfect in German, especially in speech, e.g.

Der Mord ist von der Polizei untersucht worden.
The murder was (being) investigated by the police.

The use of **war** in the example in the pluperfect tense above looks suspiciously like it is rendering 'The murder was investigated ...', but this is precisely what this does *not* mean as **war** here translates 'had'; both **wurde untersucht** and **ist untersucht worden** render 'was investigated'.

The example in the conditional perfect tense above is a contraction of the following, but would nearly always be expressed in that contracted way:

Der Mord würde von der Polizei untersucht worden sein.
The murder would by the police investigated been have.

Sein is used to render the infinitive 'have' here, because **werden** requires **sein** as its auxiliary in all perfect tenses.

10.4.2 The passive with a modal verb

Modal verbs often act as auxiliaries in the passive, as in English, and should simply be translated literally, and the infinitive 'to be' is of course rendered by **werden**, not **sein**:

Der Mord muss (von der Polizei) untersucht werden.
The murder must be investigated (by the police).

Der Mord musste (von der Polizei) untersucht werden.
The murder had to be investigated (by the police).

Der Mord hat (von der Polizei) untersucht werden müssen.
The murder has had to be investigated (by the police).
The murder had to be investigated (by the police).

The following modal constructions differ considerably from English (see 10.3.2.5):

Das hätte gemacht werden können.
That could have been done.

Das hätte gemacht werden sollen.
That should have been done.

10.4.3 Action versus state with the passive

German grammars talk of 'das Vorgangs- versus das Zustandspassiv' which we'll call the action versus the state, sometimes called the false passive. What is dealt with under 10.4 to 10.4.2 is the true passive (or Vorgangspassiv) where an action being performed by someone is described, even though that someone may not be mentioned. But take a sentence like 'The table is laid.' If you are describing an action, i.e. if the sentence is 'The table is (being) laid (by her)', then the present tense of **werden** must be used: **Der Tisch wird (von ihr) gedeckt.** Similarly, in the past 'The table was laid'; if it means 'The table was (being) laid (by her)', it will be in German **Der Tisch wurde (von ihr) gedeckt.**

But perhaps only a state, not an action, is implied, i.e. 'The table is/was laid.' Here the past participle can be regarded simply as a normal adjective like 'large' in the sentence 'The table is/was large', where no agent is implied. If this is the case then the sentence is translated as **Der Tisch ist/war gedeckt.**

10.4.4 *Passives with indirect objects*

A special difficulty arises in passive sentences such as the following: 'I/he was given a book (by them).' If you look firstly at the active of this sentence 'They gave a book to me/him', you see that the English 'I' and 'he' are indirect objects in meaning: I/he was not given, but a book was given to me/him; thus this 'I' and 'he' are translated by **mir** and **ihm** in German, e.g.

Mir/ihm wurde ein Buch gegeben.
I/he was given a book.

This must also be observed when a verb that takes a dative object is used in the passive in German:

Ihm konnte nicht geholfen werden.
He could not be helped.

This is the passive of the active sentence:

Niemand konnte ihm helfen.
Nobody could help him.

10.4.5 *Passives with a dummy subject* es

A dummy subject **es** is commonly used in combination with the passive in German, especially when the agent is not mentioned.

Es sind viele Computer installiert worden.
Many computers have been installed.
There have been a lot of computers installed.

Es muss etwas getan werden.
Something must be done.

As these two English examples illustrate, the equivalent construction in English uses 'there', but this is often not possible in English where an es construction *is* possible in German. There are more examples of this concept under 10.4.6.

10.4.6 *Passive use of intransitive verbs*

No intransitive verb in English can be used in the passive because the passive is by definition a construction in which the object of the active becomes the subject of the passive and a verb that has no object therefore cannot occur in the passive. Broadly speaking the same applies in German too with the following exception. Intransitive verbs that are not verbs of motion or change of state can be used in the passive in impersonal constructions, and are especially found where the sentence is introduced by a dummy subject **es** or an adverb of place (note that none of the following English translations contain a passive), e.g.

Es wird zu viel geredet.
There is too much talking going on.

Hier wird weder getanzt noch gelacht.
There is neither dancing nor laughter here.

In dieser Kirche wird nicht gesungen. (a trans. verb being used intransitively)
There's no singing in this church./People don't sing in this church.

These **es**-constructions are very common in German. If such sentences begin with an adverbial expression, **es** is dropped, e.g.

Hier wird nicht geraucht. (= Es wird hier nicht geraucht.)
People don't smoke here.

Auch am Wochenende wird gearbeitet. (= Es wird auch am Wochenende gearbeitet.)
Work is also done on weekends.

10.4.7 *Alternatives to the passive*

a) The passive is frequently avoided in German by using alternative constructions, the most common of which is **man** ('one', see 7.1.1.2 and 7.7.2). This is sometimes possible in English too, where it usually sounds stilted, which is certainly not the case in German, e.g.

Hier wird Deutsch gesprochen. (passive)
Hier spricht man Deutsch.
German is spoken here.

In dieser Fabrik werden Staubsauger hergestellt. (passive)
In dieser Fabrik stellt man Staubsauger her.
Vacuum cleaners are manufactured in this factory.

b) **Sich lassen** is used in combination with an infinitive to express what might otherwise be expressed by a passive with **können** or **man** + **können**, e.g.

Das lässt sich bestimmt reparieren.
Das kann bestimmt repariert werden.
Das kann man bestimmt reparieren.
That can certainly be repaired.

c) And finally a construction consisting of **sein** + **zu** + infinitive is yet another stylistic alternative to the passive that you will encounter, e.g.

Es war niemand zu sehen.
There was nobody to be seen.

So was ist in Deutschland nicht zu finden.
Something like that is not to be found in Germany.

10.4.8 Passive alternatives to the use of participles in extended adjectival phrases

See 7.6.4 for the use of participles in extended adjectival phrases in lieu of relative clauses containing a passive.

10.5 The infinitive

10.5.1 Characteristics of the infinitive

The infinitive or basic undeclined form of the verb nearly always ends in **-en** in German: **laufen** 'to run', **sehen** 'to see' etc. There are only two monosyllabic verbs whose infinitives end in **-n**, i.e. **tun** (to do) and **sein** (to be) (see 10.1.1.1).

English always puts 'to' before the infinitive in isolation; one should learn each new verb as follows: **laufen** = to run. In context, however, there are occasions when this 'to' may or may not be used. Similarly in German, although the infinitive in isolation is never preceded by **zu**; in a sentence there are rules for when **zu** is and is not used before an infinitive.

10.5.2 *Rules for the use of* zu *with infinitives*

As a general rule one can say that an infinitive at the end of a clause is always preceded by **zu**, e.g.

Dieser Ausdruck ist nicht leicht zu übersetzen.
This expression is not easy to translate.

Er versucht dir zu helfen.
He's trying to help you.

Wir hoffen in den Sommerferien nach Norwegen fahren zu können.
We're hoping to be able to go to Norway in the summer holidays.

But in the following extremely numerous cases **zu** before the infinitive is omitted:

a) When the infinitive is used as a general impersonal imperative (see 10.1.3), e.g.

Nicht rauchen!
Don't smoke.

Nicht so viel Krach machen!
Don't make so much noise.

Nicht so schnell fahren!
Don't drive so fast.

b) It is never used after modal verbs, i.e. when a modal is the finite verb in the clause (see 10.2); German shares this feature with English:

Er kann es nicht machen.
He can't do it./He isn't able to do it.

Wir müssen drei Romane auf Französisch lesen.
We must (= have to) read three novels in French.

Wir haben drei Romane auf Französisch lesen müssen.
We had to read thee novels in French.

Note the English modal 'to want to', where the second 'to' is part of the verb (compare 'to be able to' and 'to have to' above), unlike German.

Er will auch mitgehen.
He wants to go along too.

Er muss auch mitgehen.
He has to go along too.

10.5.3 *Use of* um ... zu *before infinitives*

a) When 'to' before an infinitive means 'in order to', you need to use **um ... zu**, which construction is called an infinitive clause. Compare the archaic English form 'She went to town for to buy a bonnet', which comes close to the literal meaning and feeling of German **um ... zu**:

Ich gehe in die Stadt, um einen Schirm zu kaufen.
I am going to town to buy an umbrella.

Es ist nicht notwendig, die Straße zu überqueren, um zur Post zu kommen.
It is not necessary to cross the road to get to the post office.

The first 'to' in the previous example does not mean 'in order to', whereas the second 'to' does and thus **zu** and **um ... zu** alternate here.

b) When a sentence begins with an infinitive clause, where 'to' also means 'in order to', **um ... zu** is required, e.g.

Um eine Fremdsprache gut zu lernen, muss man das Land besuchen.
To learn a foreign language well, you must visit the country. (= in order to)

c) There is one specific use of **um ... zu** which renders English 'only to ...', e.g.

Er überlebte die Operation, um kurz danach an einem Herzinfarkt zu sterben.
He survived the operation only to die of a heart attack soon thereafter.

Despite appearances, common sense prevents this being interpreted as 'He survived the operation in order to die of a heart attack soon thereafter.'

10.5.3.1 Other infinitive clauses (see 11.3)

10.5.4 *Double infinitive constructions* (see *10.2.1*)

10.5.5 *The infinitive used as a noun*

The infinitive of any verb can be used as a noun in the same way that the gerund (i.e. the '-ing' form of a verb) can be in English. Such nouns are always neuter (see 6.1.3.b), e.g.

bellen (to bark), thus **das Bellen** (the barking)
kochen (to cook), thus **das Kochen** (cooking)

Ich bin gegen (das) Rauchen.
I am against smoking.

Das Lernen von neuen Vokabeln macht Spaß.
Learning new vocabulary is fun.

Vermeide das Trinken von Wodka, wenn du in Russland bist.
Avoid drinking vodka when you're in Russia.

10.6 Participles

10.6.1 *Present participles*

The present participle in German is formed by adding **-d** to the infinitive, e.g. **laufend** (walking), **klingelnd** (ringing). The present participle is not as commonly used in German, as most English '-ing' constructions are expressed in other ways. It is used in the following instances:

a) Many attributive adjectives are formed from the present participle, in which case the usual adjectival endings are added to the form in **-d** wherever the adjective needs to be inflected:

eine lachende Frau a laughing woman

kochendes Wasser	boiling water
kommende Woche	the coming week/next week
die folgende Geschichte	the following story
wachsende Begeisterung	growing enthusiasm

b) It is commonly used as an adverb of manner, in which case it often has a direct parallel in English:

Das Kind kam weinend zurück.
The child returned crying.

Er reagierte wütend.
He reacted angrily. (lit. seethingly)

c) It can also be used to form adjectival nouns, e.g.

die Überlebenden	the survivors
alle Wartenden	all those waiting

10.6.2 *Past participles*

In addition to its verbal functions in forming the perfect tenses of verbs (see 10.1.5.1), the past participle of a verb can be used as an adjective, in much the same way as it is in English, e.g.

eine gehasste Frau	a hated woman
ein mit der Hand geschriebener Brief	a handwritten letter
der übersetzte Film	the translated film
Der Tisch ist gedeckt.	The table is laid. (see passive, 10.4.3)
der gedeckte Tisch	the laid table

10.6.3 *Use of present and past participles in extended adjectival phrases* (see relative pronouns, 7.6.4)

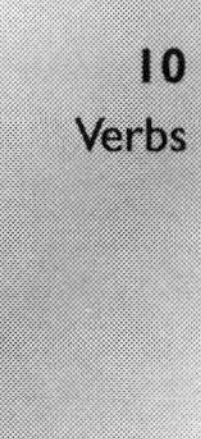

10.7 Progressive tenses

The subtle distinction made in English between 'I am reading a German novel at the moment' (occurring now) and 'I read one German novel a year at most' (a repetitive action) is not usually made in German, e.g.

Ich lese im Augenblick einen deutschen Roman.
Ich lese höchstens einen deutschen Roman pro Jahr.

The same applies to such progressive tenses in the past, e.g.

Ich habe den neuesten Roman von Grass gelesen.
I have been reading Grass's latest novel.
I have read Grass's latest novel.

What is being expressed by progressive forms of the tenses in English can also be expressed in German, if need be; however, it is not done verbally but rather by means of adverbs or other constructions, e.g.

Sie duscht sich gerade.
She is having a shower. (lit. She is just showering.)

Ich komme schon.
I'm coming.

The construction **gerade dabei sein, etwas zu tun** is very commonly used where there is a need to emphasize that an action is ongoing, e.g.

Er war gerade dabei, das Auto aus dem Schlamm zu ziehen, als das Tau auf einmal riss.
He was (in the process of) pulling the car out of the mud when the rope suddenly snapped.

Beim + an infinitival noun (see 10.5.5) is another common option, context and syntax permitting, e.g.

Wir waren beim Essen, als das Telefon klingelte.
We were eating when the phone rang.

A: Was machst du? B: Ich bin beim Kochen./Ich koche.
A: What are you doing? B: I'm cooking.

10.8 Reflexive verbs

Reflexive verbs are dealt with under reflexive pronouns (see 7.3).

10.9 Verbal prefixes

German has a very elaborate system of verbal prefixes. These prefixes can be separable or inseparable, this distinction being explained below. There are subtle distinctions between **antworten** and **beantworten** (to answer), and **folgen, befolgen, erfolgen** and **verfolgen** (to follow), for example. Many prefixes, when applied to a root verb, produce an entirely new verb that has semantically little or nothing to do with the original verb (e.g. **suchen** 'to seek' and **besuchen** 'to visit'), whereas the semantic connection between others is more obvious (e.g. **fahren** 'to travel' and **abfahren** 'to depart').

10.9.1 Verbs with separable prefixes (separable verbs)

Many German verbs take a prefix which separates from the verb in certain circumstances. Let's take a look at a typical separable verb, **aufmachen** (to open):

present tense:	**Er macht die Tür auf.** He opens the door.
imperfect tense:	**Er machte die Tür auf.** He opened the door.
imperative:	**Mach die Tür bitte auf!** Please open the door.
perfect tense:	**Er hat die Tür aufgemacht.** He has opened the door.
in an infinitive clause:	**Er hat versucht, die Tür aufzumachen.** He tried to open the door.
in a subordinate clause:	**Als er die Tür aufmachte, sah er sie.** When he opened the door, he saw her.

Verbs like this with a separable prefix always stress the prefix, which is how you can tell that a verb with such a prefix is a so-called separable verb. In addition a large number of prefixes are always stressed, but not all.

Verbs with these prefixes are called separable verbs because, as illustrated above,

1 in the present and imperfect tenses, as well as in the imperative, the prefix stands separate from the verb at the end of the clause. However, in a subordinate clause the prefix and the verb, by both having to stand at the end of the clause, recognize each other and join up again as in the infinitive.
2 in the past participle **ge-** is inserted between the prefix and the root of the verb
3 in infinitive clauses (see 11.3) **zu** is inserted between the prefix and the root of the verb.

These prefixes are applied to both regular and irregular verbs.

The prefixes that separate are of two kinds:

a) The most common prefixes are prepositions.

   These are always separable:

   ab-, an-, auf-, aus-, bei-, mit-, nach-, vor-, zu-

   Examples: **abfahren** (to depart), **ankommen** (to arrive), **aufgehen** (to rise [of sun]), **ausgehen** (to go out), **beitragen** (to contribute), **mitgehen** (to go along), **nachschicken** (to forward [mail]), **vorstellen** (to introduce), **zugeben** (to admit)

   For **hin** and **her** in combination with such prepositional verbal prefixes, see 9.7.3.

b) Quite a number of somewhat less common prefixes are adverbs (this list is not complete), e.g.

   dar-, fort-, her-, hin-, los-, nieder-, statt-, teil-, voran-, voraus-, vorbei-, vorüber-, weg-, zurück-, zusammen-

   Examples: **vorbeifahren** (to drive past), **weggehen** (to go away), **zurückkommen** (to come back). The literal meaning of these adverbs is usually evident in the new compound verb. Some occur in only a couple of verbs, e.g. **statt-** and **teil-**.

10.9.1.1

There is a small group of very common verbs consisting of two infinitives that together form a new concept, e.g. **kennen lernen** (to meet [for the first time]), **sitzen bleiben** (to stay down [at school]), **spazieren gehen** (to go for a walk) and **stehen bleiben** (to stop/stand still). Under the old spelling these were written as one word and thus the first verb in each couplet acted as a de facto separable prefix. They are now written as two words but otherwise nothing has changed, e.g.

Ich habe ihn in Wien kennen gelernt.
I (first) met him in Vienna.

Ich habe keine Zeit spazieren zu gehen.
I have no time to go for a walk.

Compare double infinitive constructions like **fallen lassen**, which differ markedly (see 10.2.1.1).

10.9.2 Verbs with inseparable prefixes (inseparable verbs)

Many German verbs take a prefix which is never stressed and never separates from the verb. The most common inseparable prefixes are the following, which are to be compared with prefixes such as those in 'to believe', 'to discover', 'to release' and 'to forget', which are not stressed in English either:

be-, emp-, ent-, er-, ge-, miss-, ver-, zer-

Examples: **beschreiben** (to describe), **empfehlen** (to recommend), **entwickeln** (to develop), **erzählen** (to relate, tell), **geschehen** (to happen), **misslingen** (to fail), **vergessen** (to forget), **zerbrechen** (to smash)

Let's take a look at a typical inseparable verb, **besuchen** (to visit):

present tense:	**Er besucht seine Großeltern.** He is visiting his grandparents.
imperfect tense:	**Er besuchte seine Großeltern.** He visited his grandparents.
imperative:	**Besuch deine Großeltern!** Visit your grandparents.
perfect tense:	**Er hat seine Großeltern besucht.** He has visited his grandparents.
in an infinitive clause:	**Er hat versucht, seine Großeltern zu besuchen.** He tried to visit his grandparents.

in a subordinate clause: **Als er seine Großeltern besuchte, waren sie krank.**
When he visited his grandparents, they were sick.

10.9.3 Verbs with variable prefixes (separable or inseparable verbs)

There is a small group of chiefly prepositional prefixes that can be either separable or inseparable, e.g.

durch-, hinter-, um-, über-, unter-, voll-, wider-, wieder-

Examples of separable verbs: **durchgehen** (to go through), **umbringen** (to kill), **volltanken** (to fill up [car with fuel]), **wiedersehen** (to see again)

Examples of inseparable verbs: **durchsuchen** (to search), **überholen** (to overtake), **umgeben** (to surround), **unterschreiben** (to sign), **wiederholen** (to repeat)

When faced with a new verb with one of these prefixes that you have never seen before, you will not automatically know if it is separable or not, e.g. **umsteigen** (to change [trains, buses etc.]) or **umarmen** (to embrace). A good dictionary should have some means of indicating which category a given verb belongs to, e.g. **'umsteigen, um'armen** where the marker stands in front of the stressed syllable. Once you know a prefix is stressed, you also know it is separable and thus the past participles of these two verbs are **umgestiegen** and **umarmt** respectively and when used together with **zu** act as follows: **umzusteigen, zu umarmen.**

Very occasionally the same verb is found with both a separable and an inseparable prefix but with totally different meanings; separable verbs tend to be more literal and inseparable more figurative in meaning, e.g. **'umgehen** (to associate with), **um'gehen** (to get round, evade), **'überfahren** (to pass over), **über'fahren** (to run over), **'unterhalten** (to hold under), **unter'halten** (to entertain, maintain).

Let's take a look at a typical inseparable verb that has one of these prefixes, **widersprechen** (to contradict + dat.); compare these forms with **aufmachen** in 10.9.1.

present tense: **Er widerspricht seiner Mutter.**
He contradicts his mother.

imperfect tense: **Er widersprach seiner Mutter.**
He contradicted his mother.

imperative: **Widersprich deiner Mutter nicht!**
Don't contradict your mother.

perfect tense: **Er hat seiner Mutter widersprochen.**
He has contradicted his mother.

in an infinitive clause: **Er hat versucht, seiner Mutter zu widersprechen.**
He tried to contradict his mother.

in a subordinate clause: **Wenn er seiner Mutter widerspricht, wird sie böse.**
When he contradicts his mother, she gets angry.

10.10 Verbs followed by prepositional objects

Both English and German have verbs that are connected to their objects by means of a preposition, but the problem here lies in the fact that the preposition required is often different in German from that used in English, e.g.

Er hat mich um Geld gebeten.
He asked me for money. (**um** translates 'for' here, not **für**)

For this reason it is best to learn such verbs not, for example, as **bitten** = to ask, but as **bitten um** + acc. = to ask for.

The verbs below are grouped under the German prepositions they are followed by in order to give the learner a feeling for the use of prepositions in German. This approach thereby fulfils a function the dictionary does not. The following list does not attempt to be complete, but merely to give an indication of the concept. This is the sort of additional information about verbs that you need to be on the lookout for when consulting a good bilingual dictionary.

There are also verbs that require a prepositional object in English, but govern the dative in German instead of employing a preposition, e.g.

geben + dat. (to give to)
Er hat seinem Sohn sein altes Auto gegeben.
He gave his son his old car.

sich unterwerfen + dat. (to subject to)
Alle Einwohner haben sich dem neuen Regime unterwerfen müssen.
All inhabitants had to subject themselves to the new regime.

There are verbs that do not take a prepositional object in English, but do in German, e.g.

zweifeln an + dat. (to doubt)
Ich zweifle an der Wahrheit von dem, was er sagt.
I doubt the truth of what he says.

Sometimes what is expressed by a verb followed by a prepositional object in English is expressed by a transitive verb with a separable prefix in German, e.g.

anbellen (to bark at)
Der Hund hat die Kinder angebellt.
The dog barked at the children.

auslachen (to laugh at, ridicule)
Seine Kollegen haben ihn ausgelacht.
His colleagues laughed at him.

an + acc.

binden	to tie to
denken	to think of
erinnern	to remind s.o. of s.t.
sich erinnern	to remember s.o. or s.t.
glauben	to believe in (God)
grenzen	to border on
schicken	to send to
sich gewöhnen	to get used/accustomed to
sich wenden	to turn to (s.o. for help)

an + dat.

arbeiten	to work at
erkennen	to recognize by
sich freuen	to take pleasure in/rejoice at
hindern	to prevent from
leiden	to suffer from (a disease)

sterben	to die of
teilnehmen	to take part in
vorbeigehen	to pass (by)
zweifeln	to doubt s.t.

auf + acc. (many verbs take **auf** + acc.; very few take **auf** + dat.)

antworten	to answer to (a question)
aufmerksam machen	to call (s.o.'s) attention to
aufpassen	to keep an eye on
sich beziehen	to refer to
sich freuen	to look forward to
gucken	to look at (a watch)
hoffen	to hope for
kommen	to hit upon/think of
sich konzentrieren	to concentrate on
reagieren	to react to
rechnen	to count on
schätzen	to assess/value at
schauen	to look at (a watch)
schießen	to shoot at
sich spezialisieren	to specialize in
trinken	to drink to
sich verlassen	to rely, depend on
verzichten	to do without
warten	to wait for
weisen	to point to/at
wetten	to bet on
zielen	to aim at

zukommen	to come up to (s.o.)
zurückkommen	to return to (a topic)

auf + dat.

beruhen	to be founded/based on
bestehen	to insist on

aus + dat.

ableiten	to infer/deduce from
bestehen	to consist of
datieren	to date from
entkommen	to escape from
entstehen	to arise/spring from
kommen	to come from (a country, town)
stammen	to hail from
trinken	to drink from (a glass, bottle)
übersetzen	to translate from
werden	to become of

bei + dat.

sich entschuldigen	to apologize to s.o.
helfen	to help with (work)
nehmen	to take by (the hand)
wohnen	to live with (i.e. at s.o.'s place)

für + acc.

sich begeistern	to be enthusiastic about
danken	to thank for
sich entscheiden	to decide on
gelten	to apply/be applicable to

halten	to consider to be
sich interessieren	to be interested in
sich schämen	to be ashamed of s.t.
sorgen	to take care of/look after

in + acc. (most verbs followed by **in** take the acc.)

einsteigen	to get into (i.e. a bus, train etc.)
eintreten	to enter (into)
geraten	to get into (problems)
sich mischen	to meddle in
übersetzen	to translate into
sich verlieben	to fall in love with
sich vertiefen	to become engrossed in
(sich) verwandeln	to change into

in + dat.

ankommen	to arrive in/at
sich irren	to be mistaken in (your judgement) about s.o./s.t.
sich täuschen	to be wrong about s.t.

mit + dat.

sich abfinden	to be satisfied with, accept
sich beschäftigen	to occupy/busy o.s. with
handeln	to trade/deal in
nicken	to nod (one's head)
rechnen	to count on s.t.
reden	to speak/talk to
sprechen	to speak to
sich unterhalten	to converse with

vergleichen	to compare to/with
sich verheiraten	to marry/get married to
versehen	to provide with

nach + dat.

aussehen	to look like (rain)
fischen	to fish for
fragen	to ask after, enquire about
graben	to dig for
greifen	to clutch at/grab for
hungern	to hunger after/for
riechen	to smell of
rufen	to call for s.o.
schicken	to send for (a doctor)
schmecken	to taste of
schreien	to yell/scream for s.o.
sich sehnen	to long for
stinken	to stink/smell of
streben	to strive for
suchen	to look for
telefonieren	to call for (a doctor)
verlangen	to long for/crave

über + acc. (**über** always governs the accusative after verbs)

sich ärgern	to be annoyed/irritated at
sich freuen	to be glad/pleased about
klagen	to complain about
lachen	to laugh about/at s.t.
nachdenken	to think about/ponder on

reden	to talk about
schreiben	to write about
spotten	to mock
sprechen	to talk about
sich unterhalten	to talk/converse about
urteilen	to judge s.t./pass judgement on
verfügen	to have at one's disposal
weinen	to cry/weep about

um + acc.

bangen	to worry about, fear for (one's life)
beneiden	to envy s.o. s.t.
betteln	to beg for
sich bewerben	to apply for (a job)
bitten	to ask for
fürchten	to fear for (s.o.'s life)
sich handeln	to be a question/matter of
sich kümmern	to take care of/worry about

von + dat.

abhängen	to depend on
befreien	to liberate/free from
sich erholen	to recover from
halten	to think (well) of s.o.
leben	to live on
überzeugen	to convince of
wimmeln	to swarm/teem with
wissen	to know of/about

vor + dat. (**vor** always governs the dative after verbs)

sich in Acht nehmen	to be on one's guard against, to mind

Angst haben	to be afraid of
beschützen	to protect from s.o./s.t.
fliehen	to flee from
sich fürchten	to be afraid of
sich hüten	to beware of
retten	to save s.o. from s.t.
sich schämen	to be ashamed in front of s.o.
(sich) verbergen	to hide/conceal (oneself) from
warnen	to warn against
weichen	to give way to/yield to
weinen	to weep/cry for (joy)

wegen + gen.

loben	to praise for
sich schämen	to be ashamed of
tadeln	to reprimand for

zu + dat.

beitragen	to contribute to
bewegen	to induce/move to
dienen	to serve as s.t.
einladen	to treat/invite to
führen	to lead to
gehören	to belong to (a group, club)/be part of
gratulieren	to congratulate on
neigen	to tend to/towards
provozieren	to provoke to
raten	to advise to
sagen	to say to s.o. (also just dat.)

treiben	to drive to (despair)
verführen	to seduce to
wählen	to elect as
sich wenden	to turn round to s.o.
zwingen	to force s.o. into s.t.

10.10.1 *Use of prepositional adverbs before subordinate clauses*

It is sometimes the case that the object following many of the verbs given under 10.10 is a whole clause rather than a noun or pronoun. In such cases it is common practice with some verbs, and compulsory with others, to combine that verb's preposition with **da(r)-** (see 7.1.4), thereby creating a prepositional adverb, before proceeding with the dependent clause, which might be either a subordinate clause (mostly introduced by **dass**) or an infinitive clause introduced by **zu**, e.g.

Er hat mich an ihren Geburtstag erinnert. (with a prepositional object)
He reminded me of her birthday.

Er hat mich daran erinnert, dass sie heute Geburtstag hat. (followed by a clause)
He reminded me (of the fact that) it's her birthday today.

Er hat mich daran erinnert, ein Geburtstagsgeschenk für sie zu kaufen.
He reminded me to buy her a birthday present.

Where such constructions are required is not easy to give rules for, all the more so as not all verbs that take a prepositional object necessarily require it; it is often optional. The best advice that can be given is to do it when in doubt, e.g.

Sie hat mich (davon) überzeugt, dass es nicht der Mühe wert wäre.
She convinced me it would not be worth the effort.

Wir freuen uns (darauf), dass wir dieses Jahr wieder nach Australien reisen.
We're looking forward to going to Australia again this year.

The meaning of the prepositional adverb in all these examples is something like 'the fact that', e.g. 'We're looking forward to the fact that we are going to Australia again this year.'

10.11 Transitive and intransitive verbs

Transitive verbs are those that can take a direct object and intransitive verbs are those that can't. For example, 'to lay' (**legen**) and 'to raise' (**erhöhen**) can both take an object and are thus transitive, whereas 'to lie' (**liegen**) and 'to rise' (**steigen**) cannot take an object and are thus intransitive. As illustrated, German too uses separate verbs here. But verbs that can be used both transitively and intransitively in English may not necessarily be so in German, where you will need to use a different verb in each case. For example, if you want to say 'He answered the question' you will find in the dictionary under 'to answer' the words **antworten** and **beantworten**. A good dictionary will indicate that the former is intransitive and the latter transitive. The above example can thus be translated as either **Er hat die Frage beantwortet** or **Er hat auf die Frage geantwortet** (intransitive verbs often take prepositional objects, i.e. they are only capable of taking an object if connected to that object by a preposition; see 10.10).

It is not possible to give rules for such difficulties, but the following common examples will serve to illustrate what you have to be wary of:

to burn	=	**brennen** (intr.):	**Das Haus brannte.** The house was burning.
		verbrennen (trans.):	**Er verbrannte die Zeitschrift.** He burnt the magazine.
to leave	=	**abfahren** (intr.):	**Der Zug fuhr um zehn Uhr ab.** The train left at ten o'clock.
		verlassen (trans.):	**Der Zug verließ Berlin um zehn Uhr.** The train left Berlin at ten o'clock.
to taste	=	**schmecken** (intr.):	**Dieser Apfel schmeckt gut.** This apple tastes good.
		probieren (trans.):	**Probier mal diesen Apfel!** Just taste this apple.

10.11.1 *Use of* sein *and* lassen *with intransitive verbs*

All verbs that take **sein** in the perfect (see 10.1.5.2) are intransitive, which is not to say that all intransitive verbs take **sein**, e.g.

Er hat gelacht.
He laughed.

This also explains why a verb like **fahren**, which normally takes **sein**, takes **haben** if it is ever used transitively, e.g.

Er hat das neue Auto gefahren.
He drove the new car.

It is not generally speaking usual for an intransitive verb to be used transitively like this in German. Another similar, although not identical, example is **zerbrechen**. When used with an object there is no problem, e.g.

Ich habe die Tasse zerbrochen.
I broke the cup.

But if this verb is used intransitively, it is seen as belonging to the category of verbs that render a change of state and thus **sein** is used, e.g.

Die Tasse ist zerbrochen.
The cup has broken.

A verb like **explodieren**, for example, can only be used intransitively, e.g.

Die Bombe ist explodiert.
The bomb exploded.

But 'to explode' can take an object in English and this is a typical instance where German resorts to **lassen** to be able to use such a verb with an object, e.g.

Die Wissenschaftler haben eine Bombe explodieren lassen.
The scientists exploded a bomb. (= made a bomb explode)

Here's another example incorporating **laufen** (to run), a typical intransitive verb of motion that by definition cannot take a direct object, e.g.

Ich habe das Pferd am Strand laufen lassen.
I ran the horse along the beach.

To the German mind of course there is no difference in meaning between a sentence like the previous one and **Ich habe ein Haus bauen lassen** (where **bauen** is per chance a transitive verb), but which renders quite a different

English structure, i.e.'I had a house built' (see 10.2.1.1). The above example could also be translated as 'I had/let the horse run along the beach.'

10.11.2 Intransitive verbs and the passive

Intransitive verbs cannot generally be used in the passive as the passive is by definition a construction where the object of the active sentence becomes the subject (see 10.4), but see 10.4.6 for a few notable exceptions.

10.12 List of irregular verbs

The following list of all the most common irregular verbs groups the verbs according to their irregularities. What are called groups 1 to 7 here constitute the seven historical Ablaut series common to all Germanic languages, and thus those that are strictly speaking strong not just irregular verbs, and which you will need to be acquainted with if you go on to study the history of German. If, as will usually be the case, you merely want to learn the irregular verbs of German, it is useful to have them grouped according to their irregularities in order to get a feeling for the relatively consistent patterns that occur among irregular verbs.

For easy reference when wanting to check whether a given verb is irregular or not and, if so, how it is irregular, this list of verbs is repeated in 10.12.1, but in alphabetical order regardless of group. Remember that when checking on the irregularity of a verb, this list only contains root forms on the whole, not derived verbs, i.e. **einladen** (to invite), a verb with a separable prefix, is not in the list but **laden** (to load) is and of course **einladen** is conjugated in the same way. The same applies to verbs with unstressed prefixes, i.e. **erfinden** (to invent) is not in the list, but **finden** (to find) is.

Column 1 contains the infinitive, column 2 the third person sing. of the present tense where an irregularity may occur, column 3 the third person sing. of the imperfect, from which all other persons can be derived (see **schreiben, finden, halten** and **lesen** in 10.1.4.2), and column 4 contains the past participle together with the third person of the auxiliary verb when the auxiliary is either **sein** or both **haben** and **sein** (see perfect tense 10.1.5 for more on this).

Group I

This group contains verbs with **ei** in the infinitive but they follow one of two patterns, i.e. sub-groups a) and b):

a)

bleiben	**bleibt**	**blieb**	**ist geblieben**	to remain
leihen	**leiht**	**lieh**	**geliehen**	to lend
meiden	**meidet**	**mied**	**gemieden**	to avoid
preisen	**preist**	**pries**	**gepriesen**	to praise
reiben	**reibt**	**rieb**	**gerieben**	to rub
scheiden	**scheidet**	**schied**	**hat/ist geschieden**	to separate
scheinen	**scheint**	**schien**	**geschienen**	to shine
schreiben	**schreibt**	**schrieb**	**geschrieben**	to write
schweigen	**schweigt**	**schwieg**	**geschwiegen**	to be silent
steigen	**steigt**	**stieg**	**ist gestiegen**	to climb
treiben	**treibt**	**trieb**	**getrieben**	to drive
verzeihen	**verzeiht**	**verzieh**	**verziehen**	to forgive
weisen	**weist**	**wies**	**gewiesen**	to point

b)

beißen	**beißt**	**biss**	**gebissen**	to bite
gleichen	**gleicht**	**glich**	**geglichen**	to resemble
gleiten	**gleitet**	**glitt**	**ist geglitten**	to glide
greifen	**greift**	**griff**	**gegriffen**	to grab
kneifen	**kneift**	**kniff**	**gekniffen**	to pinch
leiden	**leidet**	**litt**	**gelitten**	to suffer
pfeifen	**pfeift**	**pfiff**	**gepfiffen**	to whistle
reißen	**reißt**	**riss**	**hat/ist gerissen**	to tear
reiten	**reitet**	**ritt**	**hat/ist geritten**	to ride
scheißen	**scheißt**	**schiss**	**geschissen**	to shit
schleichen	**schleicht**	**schlich**	**ist geschlichen**	to sneak
schmeißen	**schmeißt**	**schmiss**	**geschmissen**	to chuck
schneiden	**schneidet**	**schnitt**	**geschnitten**	to cut
schreiten	**schreitet**	**schritt**	**ist geschritten**	to stride
streichen	**streicht**	**strich**	**hat/ist gestrichen**	to delete
streiten	**streitet**	**stritt**	**gestritten**	to argue
verbleichen	**verbleicht**	**verblich**	**ist verblichen**	to fade

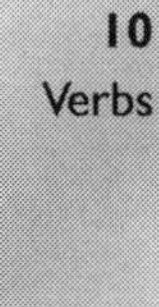

Group 2

This group contains verbs with a variety of vowels in the infinitive, but most contain **ie**.

befehlen	**befiehlt**	**befahl**	**befohlen**	to order
biegen	**biegt**	**bog**	**gebogen**	to bend
bieten	**bietet**	**bot**	**geboten**	to offer
fliegen	**fliegt**	**flog**	**hat/ist geflogen**	to fly
fliehen	**flieht**	**floh**	**ist geflohen**	to flee
fließen	**fließt**	**floss**	**ist geflossen**	to flow
frieren	**friert**	**fror**	**hat/ist gefroren**	to freeze
genießen	**genießt**	**genoss**	**genossen**	to enjoy
gießen	**gießt**	**goss**	**gegossen**	to pour
heben	**hebt**	**hob**	**gehoben**	to lift
kriechen	**kriecht**	**kroch**	**ist gekrochen**	to crawl
lügen	**lügt**	**log**	**gelogen**	to lie
riechen	**riecht**	**roch**	**gerochen**	to smell
saufen	**säuft**	**soff**	**gesoffen**	to booze
schelten	**schilt**	**scholt**	**gescholten**	to scold
schieben	**schiebt**	**schob**	**geschoben**	to push
schießen	**schießt**	**schoss**	**geschossen**	to shoot
schließen	**schließt**	**schloss**	**geschlossen**	to shut
schmelzen	**schmilzt**	**schmolz**	**hat/ ist geschmolzen**	to melt
schwellen	**schwillt**	**schwoll**	**ist geschwollen**	to swell
schwören	**schwört**	**schwor**	**geschworen**	to swear
trügen	**trügt**	**trog**	**getrogen**	to deceive
verlieren	**verliert**	**verlor**	**verloren**	to lose
wiegen	**wiegt**	**wog**	**gewogen**	to weigh
ziehen	**zieht**	**zog**	**gezogen**	to pull

Group 3

The verbs in this group all have a stem that ends in **n** + another consonant.

binden	**bindet**	**band**	**gebunden**	to tie
finden	**findet**	**fand**	**gefunden**	to find
gelingen	**gelingt**	**gelang**	**ist gelungen**	to succeed
klingen	**klingt**	**klang**	**geklungen**	to sound

schlingen	**schlingt**	**schlang**	**geschlungen**	to wind
schwinden	**schwindet**	**schwand**	**ist geschwunden**	to dwindle
schwingen	**schwingt**	**schwang**	**hat/ ist geschwungen**	to swing
singen	**singt**	**sang**	**gesungen**	to sing
sinken	**sinkt**	**sank**	**ist gesunken**	to sink
springen	**springt**	**sprang**	**ist gesprungen**	to jump
stinken	**stinkt**	**stank**	**gestunken**	to stink
trinken	**trinkt**	**trank**	**getrunken**	to drink
zwingen	**zwingt**	**zwang**	**gezwungen**	to force

Group 4

beginnen	**beginnt**	**begann**	**begonnen**	to begin
bergen	**birgt**	**barg**	**geborgen**	to rescue
brechen	**bricht**	**brach**	**gebrochen**	to break
erschrecken	**erschrickt**	**erschrak**	**ist erschrocken**	to be startled
gebären	**gebärt**	**gebar**	**geboren**	to give birth
gelten	**gilt**	**galt**	**gegolten**	to be valid
gewinnen	**gewinnt**	**gewann**	**gewonnen**	to win
helfen	**hilft**	**half**	**geholfen**	to help
kommen	**kommt**	**kam**	**ist gekommen**	to come
nehmen	**nimmt**	**nahm**	**genommen**	to take
schwimmen	**schwimmt**	**schwamm**	**hat/ist geschwommen**	to swim
spinnen	**spinnt**	**spann**	**gesponnen**	to spin
sprechen	**spricht**	**sprach**	**gesprochen**	to speak
stechen	**sticht**	**stach**	**gestochen**	to sting
stehlen	**stiehlt**	**stahl**	**gestohlen**	to steal
sterben	**stirbt**	**starb**	**ist gestorben**	to die
treffen	**trifft**	**traf**	**getroffen**	to meet
verderben	**verdirbt**	**verdarb**	**hat/ist verdorben**	to spoil
werben	**wirbt**	**warb**	**geworben**	to recruit
werfen	**wirft**	**warf**	**geworfen**	to throw

Group 5

The verbs in this group, generally speaking, differ from those in group 4 in that the vowel of the infinitive usually recurs in the past participle.

bitten	**bittet**	**bat**	**gebeten**	to ask
essen	**isst**	**aß**	**gegessen**	to eat
fressen	**frisst**	**fraß**	**gefressen**	to eat, scoff
geben	**gibt**	**gab**	**gegeben**	to give
genesen	**genest**	**genas**	**ist genesen**	to recover
geschehen	**geschieht**	**geschah**	**ist geschehen**	to happen
lesen	**liest**	**las**	**gelesen**	to read
liegen	**liegt**	**lag**	**gelegen**	to lie
messen	**misst**	**maß**	**gemessen**	to measure
sehen	**sieht**	**sah**	**gesehen**	to see
sitzen	**sitzt**	**saß**	**gesessen**	to sit
treten	**tritt**	**trat**	**hat/ist getreten**	to tread
vergessen	**vergisst**	**vergaß**	**vergessen**	to forget

Group 6

The verbs in this group all have in common that the vowel of the infinitive recurs in the past participle and this vowel is always an **a**, which is not the case in group 5.

fahren	**fährt**	**fuhr**	**hat/ist gefahren**	to drive
graben	**gräbt**	**grub**	**gegraben**	to dig
laden	**lädt**	**lud**	**geladen**	to load
schaffen	**schafft**	**schuf**	**geschaffen**	to create
schlagen	**schlägt**	**schlug**	**geschlagen**	to hit
tragen	**trägt**	**trug**	**getragen**	to carry
wachsen	**wächst**	**wuchs**	**ist gewachsen**	to grow
waschen	**wäscht**	**wusch**	**gewaschen**	to wash

Group 7

This group contains verbs that follow one of two patterns in the imperfect. What they all have in common is that the vowel of the infinitive recurs in the past participle.

a)

blasen	**bläst**	**blies**	**geblasen**	to blow
braten	**brät**	**briet**	**gebraten**	to roast
fallen	**fällt**	**fiel**	**ist gefallen**	to fall

halten	**hält**	**hielt**	**gehalten**	to hold
heißen	**heißt**	**hieß**	**geheißen**	to be called
lassen	**lässt**	**ließ**	**gelassen**	to let, leave
laufen	**läuft**	**lief**	**ist gelaufen**	to run
raten	**rät**	**riet**	**geraten**	to advise
rufen	**ruft**	**rief**	**gerufen**	to call
schlafen	**schläft**	**schlief**	**geschlafen**	to sleep
stoßen	**stößt**	**stieß**	**gestoßen**	to push

b)

fangen	**fängt**	**fing**	**gefangen**	to catch
gehen	**geht**	**ging**	**ist gegangen**	to go
hängen	**hängt**	**hing**	**gehangen**	to hang

Totally irregular verbs that don't follow any of the above seven patterns

haben	**hat**	**hatte**	**gehabt**	to have
sein	**ist**	**war**	**ist gewesen**	to be
stehen	**steht**	**stand**	**gestanden**	to stand
tun	**tut**	**tat**	**getan**	to do
werden	**wird**	**wurde**	**ist geworden**	to become
wissen	**weiß**	**wusste**	**gewusst**	to know

Mixed verbs a)

Verbs in this group are mixed in the sense that the imperfect is regular but the past participle is irregular.

backen	**backt**	**backte**	**gebacken**	to bake
mahlen	**mahlt**	**mahlte**	**gemahlen**	to grind
salzen	**salzt**	**salzte**	**gesalzen**	to salt
spalten	**spaltet**	**spaltete**	**gespalten**	to split

Mixed verbs b)

Verbs in this group are mixed in the sense that they have a vowel change in the past tenses like a strong verb, but the imperfect ends in **-te** etc. and the past participle ends in -t like a weak verb. **Senden** and **wenden** both have alternative weak forms, i.e. **sendete/wendete** and **gesendet/gewendet**.

brennen	**brennt**	**brannte**	**gebrannt**	to burn
bringen	**bringt**	**brachte**	**gebracht**	to bring
denken	**denkt**	**dachte**	**gedacht**	to think
kennen	**kennt**	**kannte**	**gekannt**	to know
nennen	**nennt**	**nannte**	**genannt**	to name
rennen	**rennt**	**rannte**	**ist gerannt**	to run
senden	**sendet**	**sandte**	**gesandt**	to send
wenden	**wendet**	**wandte**	**gewandt**	to turn

Modal verbs (see 10.2)

dürfen	**darf**	**durfte**	**gedurft**	to be allowed to/may
können	**kann**	**konnte**	**gekonnt**	to be able to/can
mögen	**mag**	**mochte**	**gemocht**	to like; may
müssen	**muss**	**musste**	**gemusst**	to have to/must
sollen	**soll**	**sollte**	**gesollt**	shall/to be supposed to
wollen	**will**	**wollte**	**gewollt**	to want (to)

10.12.1 Alphabetical list of irregular verbs

backen	**backt**	**backte**	**gebacken**	to bake
befehlen	**befiehlt**	**befahl**	**befohlen**	to command
beginnen	**beginnt**	**begann**	**begonnen**	to begin
beißen	**beißt**	**biss**	**gebissen**	to bite
bergen	**birgt**	**barg**	**geborgen**	to rescue
biegen	**biegt**	**bog**	**gebogen**	to bend
bieten	**bietet**	**bot**	**geboten**	to offer
binden	**bindet**	**band**	**gebunden**	to tie
bitten	**bittet**	**bat**	**gebeten**	to ask
blasen	**bläst**	**blies**	**geblasen**	to blow
bleiben	**bleibt**	**blieb**	**ist geblieben**	to remain
braten	**brät**	**briet**	**gebraten**	to roast
brechen	**bricht**	**brach**	**gebrochen**	to break
brennen	**brennt**	**brannte**	**gebrannt**	to burn

bringen	**bringt**	**brachte**	**gebracht**	to bring
denken	**denkt**	**dachte**	**gedacht**	to think
dürfen	**darf**	**durfte**	**gedurft**	may
erschrecken	**erschrickt**	**erschrak**	**ist erschrocken**	to be startled
essen	**isst**	**aß**	**gegessen**	to eat
fahren	**fährt**	**fuhr**	**hat/ist gefahren**	to drive
fallen	**fällt**	**fiel**	**ist gefallen**	to fall
fangen	**fängt**	**fing**	**gefangen**	to catch
finden	**findet**	**fand**	**gefunden**	to find
fliegen	**fliegt**	**flog**	**hat/ist geflogen**	to fly
fliehen	**flieht**	**floh**	**ist geflohen**	to flee
fließen	**fließt**	**floss**	**ist geflossen**	to flow
fressen	**frisst**	**fraß**	**gefressen**	to eat, scoff
frieren	**friert**	**fror**	**hat/ist gefroren**	to freeze
gebären	**gebärt**	**gebar**	**geboren**	to give birth
geben	**gibt**	**gab**	**gegeben**	to give
gehen	**geht**	**ging**	**ist gegangen**	to go
gelingen	**gelingt**	**gelang**	**ist gelungen**	to succeed
gelten	**gilt**	**galt**	**gegolten**	to be valid
genesen	**genest**	**genas**	**ist genesen**	to recover
genießen	**genießt**	**genoss**	**genossen**	to enjoy
geschehen	**geschieht**	**geschah**	**ist geschehen**	to happen
gewinnen	**gewinnt**	**gewann**	**gewonnen**	to win
gießen	**gießt**	**goss**	**gegossen**	to pour
gleichen	**gleicht**	**glich**	**geglichen**	to resemble
gleiten	**gleitet**	**glitt**	**ist geglitten**	to glide
graben	**gräbt**	**grub**	**gegraben**	to dig
greifen	**greift**	**griff**	**gegriffen**	to grab
haben	**hat**	**hatte**	**gehabt**	to have
halten	**hält**	**hielt**	**gehalten**	to hold
hängen	**hängt**	**hing**	**gehangen**	to hang
heben	**hebt**	**hob**	**gehoben**	to lift
heißen	**heißt**	**hieß**	**geheißen**	to be called
helfen	**hilft**	**half**	**geholfen**	to help
kennen	**kennt**	**kannte**	**gekannt**	to know
klingen	**klingt**	**klang**	**geklungen**	to sound
kneifen	**kneift**	**kniff**	**gekniffen**	to pinch
kommen	**kommt**	**kam**	**ist gekommen**	to come
können	**kann**	**konnte**	**gekonnt**	can
kriechen	**kriecht**	**kroch**	**ist gekrochen**	to crawl
laden	**lädt**	**lud**	**geladen**	to load

lassen	**lässt**	**ließ**	**gelassen**	to let, leave
laufen	**läuft**	**lief**	**ist gelaufen**	to run
leiden	**leidet**	**litt**	**gelitten**	to suffer
leihen	**leiht**	**lieh**	**geliehen**	to lend
lesen	**liest**	**las**	**gelesen**	to read
liegen	**liegt**	**lag**	**gelegen**	to lie
lügen	**lügt**	**log**	**gelogen**	to lie
mahlen	**mahlt**	**mahlte**	**gemahlen**	to grind
meiden	**meidet**	**mied**	**gemieden**	to avoid
messen	**misst**	**maß**	**gemessen**	to measure
mögen	**mag**	**mochte**	**gemocht**	may, to like
müssen	**muss**	**musste**	**gemusst**	must
nehmen	**nimmt**	**nahm**	**genommen**	to take
nennen	**nennt**	**nannte**	**genannt**	to name
pfeifen	**pfeift**	**pfiff**	**gepfiffen**	to whistle
preisen	**preist**	**pries**	**gepriesen**	to praise
raten	**rät**	**riet**	**geraten**	to advise
reiben	**reibt**	**rieb**	**gerieben**	to rub
reißen	**reißt**	**riss**	**hat/ist gerissen**	to tear
reiten	**reitet**	**ritt**	**hat/ist geritten**	to ride
rennen	**rennt**	**rannte**	**ist gerannt**	to run
riechen	**riecht**	**roch**	**gerochen**	to smell
rufen	**ruft**	**rief**	**gerufen**	to call
salzen	**salzt**	**salzte**	**gesalzen**	to salt
saufen	**säuft**	**soff**	**gesoffen**	to booze
schaffen	**schafft**	**schuf**	**geschaffen**	to create
scheiden	**scheidet**	**schied**	**hat/ ist geschieden**	to separate
scheinen	**scheint**	**schien**	**geschienen**	to shine
scheißen	**scheißt**	**schiss**	**geschissen**	to shit
schelten	**schilt**	**scholt**	**gescholten**	to scold
schieben	**schiebt**	**schob**	**geschoben**	to push
schießen	**schießt**	**schoss**	**geschossen**	to shoot
schlafen	**schläft**	**schlief**	**geschlafen**	to sleep
schlagen	**schlägt**	**schlug**	**geschlagen**	to hit
schleichen	**schleicht**	**schlich**	**ist geschlichen**	to sneak
schließen	**schließt**	**schloss**	**geschlossen**	to shut
schlingen	**schlingt**	**schlang**	**geschlungen**	to wind
schmeißen	**schmeißt**	**schmiss**	**geschmissen**	to chuck
schmelzen	**schmilzt**	**schmolz**	**hat/ ist geschmolzen**	to melt

schneiden	**schneidet**	**schnitt**	**geschnitten**	to cut
schreiben	**schreibt**	**schrieb**	**geschrieben**	to write
schreiten	**schreitet**	**schritt**	**ist geschritten**	to stride
schweigen	**schweigt**	**schwieg**	**geschwiegen**	to be silent
schwellen	**schwillt**	**schwoll**	**ist geschwollen**	to swell
schwimmen	**schwimmt**	**schwamm**	**hat/ ist geschwommen**	to swim
schwinden	**schwindet**	**schwand**	**ist geschwunden**	to disappear
schwingen	**schwingt**	**schwang**	**hat/ ist geschwungen**	to swing
schwören	**schwört**	**schwor**	**geschworen**	to swear
sehen	**sieht**	**sah**	**gesehen**	to see
sein	**ist**	**war**	**ist gewesen**	to be
senden	**sendet**	**sandte sendete**	**gesandt gesendet**	to send
singen	**singt**	**sang**	**gesungen**	to sing
sinken	**sinkt**	**sank**	**ist gesunken**	to sink
sitzen	**sitzt**	**saß**	**gesessen**	to sit
sollen	**soll**	**sollte**	**gesollt**	shall
spalten	**spaltet**	**spaltete**	**gespalten**	to split
spinnen	**spinnt**	**spann**	**gesponnen**	to spin
sprechen	**spricht**	**sprach**	**gesprochen**	to speak
springen	**springt**	**sprang**	**ist gesprungen**	to jump
stechen	**sticht**	**stach**	**gestochen**	to sting
stehen	**steht**	**stand**	**gestanden**	to stand
stehlen	**stiehlt**	**stahl**	**gestohlen**	to steal
steigen	**steigt**	**stieg**	**ist gestiegen**	to climb
sterben	**stirbt**	**starb**	**ist gestorben**	to die
stinken	**stinkt**	**stank**	**gestunken**	to stink
stoßen	**stößt**	**stieß**	**gestoßen**	to push
streichen	**streicht**	**strich**	**hat/ ist gestrichen**	to stroke, rub
streiten	**streitet**	**stritt**	**gestritten**	to argue
tragen	**trägt**	**trug**	**getragen**	to carry
treffen	**trifft**	**traf**	**getroffen**	to meet
treiben	**treibt**	**trieb**	**getrieben**	to drive
treten	**tritt**	**trat**	**hat/ist getreten**	to tread
trinken	**trinkt**	**trank**	**getrunken**	to drink
trügen	**trügt**	**trog**	**getrogen**	to deceive
tun	**tut**	**tat**	**getan**	to do
verbleichen	**verbleicht**	**verblich**	**ist verblichen**	to fade

verderben	**verdirbt**	**verdarb**	**hat/ ist verdorben**	to spoil
vergessen	**vergisst**	**vergaß**	**vergessen**	to forget
verlieren	**verliert**	**verlor**	**verloren**	to lose
verzeihen	**verzeiht**	**verzieh**	**verziehen**	to forgive
wachsen	**wächst**	**wuchs**	**ist gewachsen**	to grow
waschen	**wäscht**	**wusch**	**gewaschen**	to wash
weisen	**weist**	**wies**	**gewiesen**	to point
wenden	**wendet**	**wandte wendete**	**gewandt gewendet**	to turn
werben	**wirbt**	**warb**	**geworben**	to recruit
werden	**wird**	**wurde**	**ist geworden**	to become
werfen	**wirft**	**warf**	**geworfen**	to throw
wiegen	**wiegt**	**wog**	**gewogen**	to weigh
wissen	**weiß**	**wusste**	**gewusst**	to know
wollen	**will**	**wollte**	**gewollt**	will
ziehen	**zieht**	**zog**	**gezogen**	to pull
zwingen	**zwingt**	**zwang**	**gezwungen**	to force

Chapter 11

Conjunctions

A sentence that consists of just one clause, i.e. one that has just one finite verb, contains simply a main clause. A sentence that has more than one clause, i.e. one that has more than one finite verb, is a compound or complex sentence as it consists of more than simply a main clause; the additional clause or clauses must by necessity be either coordinate or subordinate clauses, which means they are joined to the main clause by means of either a coordinating or a subordinating conjunction. These conjunctions or joining words have important ramifications for word order in German and they are the topic of this chapter.

German employs a handy syntactical tool that is unknown in English when stringing clauses together to make compound and complex sentences.

A compound sentence is one that consists of a main clause plus one or more coordinate clauses, i.e. a clause joined to the main clause by means of a coordinating conjunction which has no effect on word order, thereby indicating that both clauses are of equal value (see 11.1).

A complex sentence is one that consists of a main clause plus one or more subordinate clauses, i.e. a clause joined to the main clause by means of a subordinating conjunction which has does have an effect on the word order of the subordinate clause – it sends the finite verb of the subordinate clause to the end of that clause, thereby indicating that this clause is dependent on the main clause (see 11.2).

In English, where this distinction in word order does not exist, the difference between a coordinating and a subordinating conjunction lies in the fact that you cannot put the coordinate clause before the main clause, whereas this is always possible with subordinate clauses in both languages, e.g.

Er hat selbst keine Kinder, aber er hat Kinder sehr gern. (only possibility)
He has no children himself but he likes children a lot.

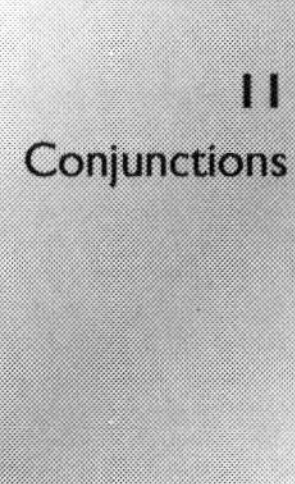

Er hat ihr gekündigt, weil sie immer zu spät ins Büro gekommen ist.
He fired her because she always arrived late at the office.

Weil sie immer zu spät ins Büro gekommen ist, hat er ihr gekündigt.
Because she always arrived late at the office, he fired her.

Note: The footnote numbers next to the conjunctions in the lists below do not indicate true footnotes but refer to the notes that follow these lists.

11.1 Coordinating conjunctions

The main distinguishing feature of a coordinating conjunction in German is that it does not have any effect on the word order of the following clause.

aber	but
denn[1]	for, because
oder	or
sondern[2]	but
und	and

Er hat selbst keine Kinder, aber er hat Kinder sehr gern.
He has no children himself but he likes children a lot.

Die Bäckerei hatte heute Morgen zu, denn der Bäcker war krank.
The bakery was shut this morning for (= because) the baker was sick.

Kommst du heute(,) oder komst du morgen?
Are you coming today or tomorrow?

Die Schmidts haben ein Ferienhaus an der Küste(,) und sie verbringen jeden Sommer dort.
The Schmidts have a holiday home on the coast and they spend every summer there.

Previously a comma was always placed between such clauses but the new spelling (since 1998) has made a comma before **oder** and **und** optional. Note, however, that if the subject of the coordinate clause is in the main clause, i.e. it is not repeated in the second clause, you must not separate the finite verb in that clause from its subject in the first clause as the second clause is seen to be not totally independent, e.g.

Die Schmidts haben ein Ferienhaus an der Küste und verbringen jeden Sommer dort. (**sie** has been omitted before **verbringen**).

Notes:

1 The conjunction 'for' is rather formal in English and is usually replaced by 'because', but in German the reverse is the case. A sentence such as 'He dropped the cup because it was too hot' would usually be rendered **Er hat die Tasse fallen lassen, denn sie war zu heiß**, although **weil** plus subordinate word order would be quite correct too: **Er hat die Tasse fallen lassen, weil sie zu heiß war**. Just as English 'because' cannot always be replaced by 'for', so **weil** cannot always be replaced by **denn**, i.e. when a complex sentence begins with the dependent clause, then 'because' and **weil** must be used:

Weil die Tasse zu heiß war, hat er sie fallen lassen.
Because the cup was too hot, he dropped it.

2 **Sondern** is used instead of **aber** to translate 'but' when the main clause contains a negative and the but-clause contradicts the main clause, e.g.

Wir gehen zu Weihnachten nicht zu meinen Eltern, sondern (wir gehen) zu meinen Schwiegereltern.
We are not going to my parents' place for Christmas but (we're going) to my parents-in-laws'.

Er kommt nicht am Montag zurück, sondern am Dienstag.
He's not returning on Monday but on Tuesday

For word order with adverbs of time in coordinate clauses see 9.4.5.

11.2 Subordinating conjunctions

There is a large number of such conjunctions, most of which are listed below. The distinguishing feature of these is that the verb of the dependent clause is sent to the end of that clause. The following pitfalls with subordinating conjunctions should be noted.

Be careful with word order when a subordinating conjunction governs two subordinate clauses which are joined by a coordinating conjunction, e.g.

Ich bin zu Hause geblieben, weil ich etwas erkältet war und (weil) im Büro sowieso nicht viel los war.
I stayed home because I had a bit of a cold and (because) there wasn't much to do at the office anyway.

Was war sie froh, als sie seine Stimme hörte und (als sie) sein Gesicht wieder sah.
How glad she was when she heard his voice and (when she) saw his face again.

Unsere Freunde hatten uns gesagt, dass es eine sehr interessante Ortschaft sei und (dass) wir da unbedingt ein paar Tage verbringen sollten.
Our friends had told us that it was a very interesting place and (that) we should definitely spend a few days there.

It is nearly always possible for stylistic reasons in both English and German to place a subordinate clause in front of the main clause in a complex sentence. In English this has no effect on word order but in German the subordinate clause assumes the role of first idea in the main clause (i.e. in the sentence as a whole) and thus inversion of subject and verb is required in the main clause. It is compulsory to insert a comma between the two clauses to keep the finite verbs of each clause apart, e.g.

Ich machte die Betten, während meine Frau abwusch.
I made the beds while my wife washed up.

Während meine Frau abwusch, machte ich die Betten.
While my wife washed up I made the beds.

When a coordinating conjunction is followed by a subordinating conjunction, the subordinating one governs the word order of the following clause, but not that of the coordinate clause in which it is embedded; the subject and verb of the following coordinate clause invert as above because the subordinate clause takes on the role of first idea in the overall sentence:

Ich bleibe zu Hause, und weil ich nicht gut geschlafen habe, gehe ich wieder ins Bett.
I'm staying home and because I didn't sleep well, I'm going back to bed.

A subordinate clause can be embedded in another subordinate clause, in which case you must remember to put the verb of the interrupted clause to the end when you return to it. In the following example, which is stylistically not ideal but nevertheless possible, **wenn man eine Fremdsprache lernt** has been embedded in the clause **dass man gewöhnlich seine eigene Sprache besser verstehen kann**, e.g.

Ich meine, dass, wenn man eine Fremdsprache lernt, man gewöhnlich seine eigene Sprache besser verstehen kann.
I think that if you learn a foreign language you can usually understand your own language better.

This is stylistically better expressed as follows and the above problem is avoided:

Ich meine, dass man gewöhnlich seine eigene Sprache besser verstehen kann, wenn man eine Fremdsprache lernt.

Get into the habit of completing your clauses before launching off into a new one and problems of word order as illustrated here will not occur.

als[1, 2]	when; than
als ob	as if
auch wenn	even if, even though
bevor[3]	before
bis[4]	until
da[5]	since, as
damit[6]	so that (purpose)
dass[7]	that
indem[8]	by
nachdem[9]	after
ob[10]	whether, if
obwohl	although
seit(dem)[11]	since (temporal)
so dass[6]	so that (result)
sobald	as soon as
solange	as long as
soweit, sofern	as far as
während[12]	while, whilst
weil[13]	because, as, since
wenn[1]	when, if
wie[14]	as
anstatt dass[15]	instead of
ohne dass[15]	without

Interrogatives (question words)

wann[1, 16]	when
warum[16]	why
was[16]	what
wer/wen/wem[16]	who/whom
wie[14, 16]	how
wie viel(e)[16]	how much (many)
wo[16]	where
woher[16]	where (from)
wohin[16]	where (to)

Notes:

1 The translation of English 'when' into German is a complex issue. There are three words: **als, wann** and **wenn**.

Wann, as an interrogative (question word, see 9.7) rather than a subordinating conjunction, must always be used in both direct and indirect questions, e.g.

Wann kommt er nach Hause? (direct question)
When is he coming home?

Ich weiß nicht, wann er nach Hause kommt. (indirect question)
I don't know when he is coming home.

Wenn is used to translate 'when' in subordinate clauses when the verb is in the present or future tense, e.g.

Wenn das Wetter im Juli schön ist, fahren wir nicht in Urlaub sondern bleiben lieber zu Hause
When/if the weather is fine in July, we don't go on holiday but prefer to stay at home.

As this example illustrates, the subtle distinction between 'when' and 'if' is not made in German. See 10.3.2.2 for cases where **wenn** meaning 'if' is omitted.

Wenn can only be used with a verb in the past when it means 'whenever' (see 7.7.e), i.e. 'when on repeated occasions', otherwise **als** is used (see below), e.g.

Wenn er in Großbritannien war, hat er immer seine Tante in Chester besucht.
Whenever he was in the UK, he would always visit his aunt in Chester.

Als is used, not **wenn**, when the verb is in the past, i.e. when the meaning is 'when on one occasion', e.g.

Als er in Großbritannien war, hat er seine Tante in Chester besucht.
When he was in the UK, he visited his aunt in Chester.

2 'Than' as used after comparatives (see 8.2.1) is **als**; it is often followed simply by a noun or pronoun rather than a whole clause.

Er ist größer als ich
He is taller than I.

Er hat's besser gemacht, als ich es hätte machen können.
He did it better than I could have done it.

3 Take care when translating 'before' as this can be either an adverb (e.g. **nie zuvor** 'never before'), a preposition (**vor dem Abendessen** 'before dinner', see 5.1.1.d and 12.3.h) or a conjunction, e.g.

Ich vesuchte mit ihm zu reden, bevor der Film begann.
I tried to talk to him before the film began.

4 **Bis**, like 'until/till', is also a preposition (see 12.1), which function must not be confused with its function as a conjunction, e.g.

Er hat die ganze Nacht hindurch bis zum Sonnenaufgang gearbeitet. (prep.)
He worked right through the night till sunrise.

Er hat die ganze Nacht hindurch gearbeitet, bis die Sonne aufging. (conj.)
He worked right through the night till the sun came up.

5 **Da** only translates 'since' where 'since' has the meaning of 'because/as', e.g.

Da das Konzert eine Viertelstunde zu spät angefangen hat, haben wir glücklicherweise nichts verpasst.
Since/as the concert started 15 minutes late we fortunately didn't miss anything.

6 **Damit** means 'so that' in the sense of 'with the purpose of' whereas **so dass** means 'so that' in the sense of 'with the result that', e.g.

Nimm einen Schirm mit, damit du nicht nass wirst.
Take an umbrella with you so you don't get wet.

Ich habe vergessen einen Schirm mitzunehmen, so dass ich durch und durch nass geworden bin.
I forgot to take an umbrella with me so that I got wet through.

7 The subordinating conjunction 'that' is often omitted in English but **dass** is never omitted in German (see 10.3.1.1 for the one possible exception), e.g.

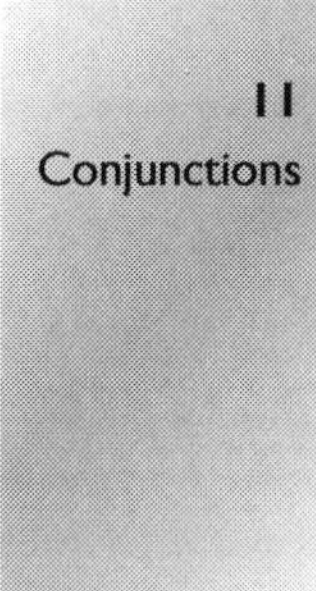

Ich weiß, dass er so was nie versprochen hätte.
I know (that) he would never have promised anything like that.

Das erste Mal, dass sie es erwähnt hat, war ich erstaunt.
The first time (that) she mentioned it, I was amazed.

Not only the subordinating conjunction 'that' is dropped in English but also the relative pronoun 'that'; nor may this pronoun ever be omitted in German (see 7.6).

8 **Indem** means 'by' and introduces a clause that expresses 'by doing something', e.g.

Ich trage der Luftverschmutzung weniger bei, indem ich jeden Tag mit dem Rad zur Arbeit fahre.
I contribute less to air pollution by cycling to work every day.

9 **Nachdem** renders the conjunction 'after', whereas **nach** renders the preposition (see 12.2), e.g.

Nachdem die Verkäuferin mich bedient hat, hat sie den schönen, jungen Mann hinter mir bedient, statt der alten Dame, die an der Reihe war. (conjunction)
After the shop assistant served me, she served the handsome young man behind me instead of the old lady whose turn it was.

Gleich nach mir hat sie den schönen, jungen Mann bedient. (preposition)
She served the handsome young man immediately after me.

10 **Ob** means 'whether', but must also be used to translate any 'if' that is interchangeable with 'whether'; otherwise 'if' must be rendered by **wenn** (see note 1 above), e.g.

Ich weiß nicht, ob er morgen oder übermorgen abfährt.
I do not know if/whether he is leaving tomorrow or the next day.

11 Take care when translating 'since' as this can be either an adverb, a preposition or a conjunction, e.g.

Ich habe ihn seitdem/seither nie wiedergesehen. (adverb)
I haven't seen him (again) since.

Ich habe ihn seit letzter Woche nicht gesehen. (preposition)
I haven't seen him since last week.

Seit(dem) er in Bremen wohnt, habe ich ihn nicht wiedergesehen. (conjunction)
Since he's been living in Bremen I haven't seen him again.

12 **Während** is both a preposition meaning 'during' (see 12.4) and a conjunction meaning 'while/whilst', but context always makes its function clear, e.g.

Er wollte ständig während des Films mit mir reden.
(preposition)
He continually wanted to talk to me during the film.

Der Sturm hat angefangen, während wir im Kino saßen.
(conjunction)
The storm began while we were sitting in the cinema.

13 **Weil** translates 'because' but you will frequently hear **denn** (lit. 'for' in the sense of 'because') being used (see 11.1). As **weil** and **denn** are synonymous, coordinate word order is commonly heard after **weil** in colloquial German, but do not copy it; you will never see it in writing and Germans are generally unaware that they do it in speech, e.g.

Er hat ihr nicht helfen wollen, weil sie ihm früher auch nicht geholfen hatte.
Er hat ihr nicht helfen wollen, denn (weil?) sie hatte ihm früher auch nicht geholfen.
He didn't want to help her because she hadn't helped him previously.

14 The conjunction 'as' is rendered by **wie**, as is 'how' (see reference to 9.7 in note 16 below), e.g.

Wie du hören kannst, kann er immer noch gut Deutsch.
As you can hear, he still speaks German well.

Er kann Deutsch genau so gut wie du.
He speaks German just as well as you (do).

Wie is commonly used with **hören** and **sehen** when you 'see/hear' s.o. doing s.t., but this can also be expressed by the infinitive without the need for a subordinate clause (see 10.2.1.1), e.g.

Ich hörte/sah, wie er die Treppe heraufkam.
Ich habe ihn die Treppe heraufkommen hören/sehen.
I heard/saw him come/coming up the stairs.

15 See conjunctions introducing infinitive clauses under 11.3.

16 In clauses introduced by these interrogatives (see 9.7) the verb is always in second position in a direct question, but in an indirect question the finite verb is sent to the end of the clause, in which case these words all behave like subordinating conjunctions, e.g.

Wann kommt sie aus Japan zurück? (direct question)
When is she returning from Japan?

Ich habe keine Ahnung, wann sie aus Japan zurückkehrt.
(indirect question)
I haven't any idea when she's coming back from Japan.

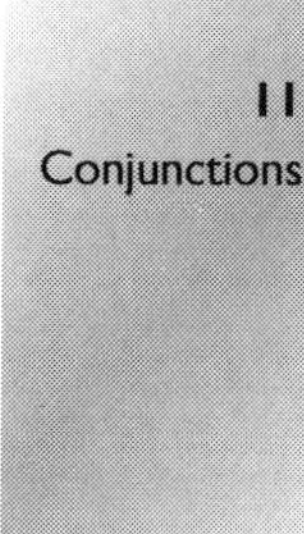

For how to say 'whenever', 'wherever' etc. see 7.7.e.

11.3 Conjunctions introducing infinitive clauses

Infinitive clauses contain no finite verb but rather an infinitive preceded by **zu**. The subject of an infinitive clause is the same as that of the main clause and thus repetition of the subject and a finite verb is unnecessary. **Um** is by far the most common of these three conjunctions.

um[1]	in order to, only to (a much less common meaning)
(an)statt[2]	instead of
ohne[2]	without

Notes:

1 Where 'to' before an infinitive can be replaced by 'in order to' you require **um … zu** (see 10.5.3), e.g.

Er hat ein Taxi nach Hause genommen, um seine Schlüssel zu holen.
He took a taxi home (in order) to fetch his keys.

Compare the following example where 'in order to' cannot be substituted, thereby indicating that **zu** alone is sufficient (see 10.5.2):

Er hat versucht, ihr zu helfen.
He tried to help her.

Occasionally **um … zu** occurs in German where in English we say 'only to …'; the German looks ambiguous but context makes it clear whether **um … zu** means 'in order to' or 'only … to', e.g.

Das Flugzeug startete ohne Problem, um plötzlich einige Kilometer vom Flughafen entfernt abzustürzen.
The plane took off without a problem only to suddenly crash a few kilometres from the airport. (obviously it did not take off in order to crash)

2 **(An)statt** and **ohne** are also both prepositions (see 12.4 and 12.1 respectively), but as conjunctions there is a complication associated with them that is unique to them. When they introduce a clause that has the same subject as that of the main clause, they introduce an infinitive clause and are thus used in combination with **zu**, e.g.

Er hat bei mir zu Hause gegessen, (an)statt allein in der Stadt zu essen.
He ate at my place instead of eating alone in town.

(i.e. he ate at my place and he would otherwise have eaten alone in town)

Er kam herein, ohne ein Wort zu sagen.
He came in without saying a word.
(i.e. he came in and he said nothing)

But when the performer of the action in the two clauses is different, an infinitive clause is no longer possible and must be replaced by a subordinate clause, which requires the use of **dass**, e.g.

Er hat ihr das Geld geliehen, (an)statt dass ich es machen musste.
He lent her the money instead of me/my having to.
(i.e. he her lent her the money and I didn't have to)

Er kam herein, ohne dass ich ihn sah.
He came in without me/my seeing him.
(i.e. he came in and I didn't see him)

11.4 Correlative conjunctions

Correlative conjunctions are couplets of coordinating conjunctions that correlate two clauses of a sentence, i.e. each clause begins with a conjunction that forms a sense pair with the other. More often than not the second clause is not completed but is implied, but if it is included, it too employs coordinate word order, i.e. the finite verb is not sent to the end of the clause.

entweder … oder	either … or
weder … noch	neither … nor
sowie … als/wie auch	both … and/as well as
nicht nur … sondern auch	not only … but also

Entweder du bringst deinen Mann mit, oder du kommst überhaupt nicht.
Either you bring your husband along or you don't come at all.

Ich habe sie leider weder nach Hause noch zum Bus bringen können.
Unfortunately I was able neither to take her home nor to take her to the bus.

Sowohl der Lehrer wie auch alle in der Klasse hatten den Roman gelesen.
Both the teacher and/as well as everyone in the class had read the novel.

Nicht nur die Jungen, sondern auch die Mädchen haben Fußball gespielt.
Not only the boys played football but also the girls.

Chapter 12

Prepositions

Because prepositions are the most idiomatic part of speech, each with a vast number of meanings in many cases, the following can only serve as a guide to the usage of German prepositions. To have listed English prepositions with their various translations into German would have been unwieldy and the student would have been prevented from getting a feeling for the nuances of meaning associated with each individual German preposition. By doing the reverse you can get some idea of the various meanings of each German preposition. It should be noted that some prepositions can be used as adverbs too, e.g.

Das Geschäft ist zu.
The shop is shut.

Das Licht war aus.
The light was off.

Only the most usual meanings of each preposition in English are given next to the German form at the beginning of each entry (e.g. **an** [on, at]), although in reality they may be rendered in myriad ways in English.

Specific to German prepositions is that they govern a given case, i.e. any noun or pronoun following a preposition must be in the accusative, dative or genitive case, depending on the preposition, but sometimes also depending on the connotation of the preposition concerned as there is a group of very common prepositions that are called two-way prepositions since they can take either the accusative or the dative case. Prepositions are dealt with in the following order: those that take the accusative (12.1), those that take the dative (12.2), those that take either the accusative or the dative (12.3) and those that take the genitive (12.4). 12.5 deals with prepositions that must or can be contracted with a following definite article and 12.6 deals with translating English 'to' into German.

There are many verbs in both German and English that take a prepositional object, but the preposition required in German is often different from that used in English, e.g. **sterben an** + dat. (to die of), **warten auf** + acc. (to wait for) (see 10.10).

There are also quite a lot of adjectives in both German and English that take a prepositional object, but the preposition required in German is often different from that used in English, e.g. **reich an** + dat. (rich in), **stolz auf** + acc. (proud of) (see 8.4).

12.1 Prepositions that take the accusative case

The following eight prepositions require any noun or pronoun that follows them to be in the accusative case: **für, um, durch, gegen, entlang, bis, ohne, wider**. A mnemonic for remembering them, if you take the first letter of each, is FUDGEBOW.

a) **bis** (until, by, as far as)
The underlying meaning of this preposition is 'up to a certain point in time or place'.

i) The most common meaning of this preposition is 'until/till' with reference to time, e.g.

Er bleibt bis nächste Woche.
He's staying till next week.

Bis morgen.
See you tomorrow. (lit. till tomorrow)

ii) To Germans 'by' with reference to time is also rendered by **bis**, as they see this as synonymous with the above, e.g.

Ich will das Buch bitte bis nächste Woche zurück haben.
I want to have the book back by next week, please.

Bis wann muss ich wieder hier sein?
By when must I be back here?

iii) Closely related in meaning for Germans, and thus **bis** is used here too, is 'as far as' with reference to place, e.g.

Ich fahre nur bis Hannover.
I'm only going as far as Hanover.

iv) Idioms like the following incorporating **bis**, where it translates as 'to', illustrate its underlying meaning of 'from A right up to B', e.g.

von Kopf bis Fuß
from head to toe

von oben bis unten
from top to bottom

v) It is a peculiarity of **bis**, and only of this preposition, that when a determiner stands between it and the following noun, it must be used together with another preposition and that second preposition determines the case of the noun (note that there are no determiners in the above examples). A variety of prepositions are used with **bis** and it is extremely difficult to formulate rules for which one is appropriate for a given context, e.g.

Es muss bis zum Jahr 2015 eine Lösung gefunden werden.
By 2015 a solution has to be found.

Wir werden bis in das nächste Jahrhundert eine Lösung suchen.
We'll be searching for a solution till next century.

Das Wasser kam bis an seinen Mund.
The water came (up) as far as his mouth.

Er ging bis an den Zaun und nicht weiter.
He walked as far as the fence and no further.

vi) **Bis** is also a subordinating conjunction (see 11.2).

b) **durch** (through, by)
i) The primary meaning of **durch** is 'through', e.g.

Wir sind quer durch die Mitte der Stadt gefahren.
We drove straight through the centre of town.

ii) There is a minority of cases where **durch** is better rendered by 'by' in English, e.g.

Ich habe es durch Zufall gehört.
I heard it through/by chance.

iii) **Durch** can also render 'by' in the passive when the agent of the action is not a person (see **von** for personal agents), e.g.

Die Gaststätte ist durch Feuer zerstört worden.
The restaurant was destroyed by fire.

c) **entlang** (along)

i) **Entlang** differs from nearly all other prepositions (but see **gegenüber**) in that it follows its noun, e.g.

Sie gingen den Fluss entlang.
They walked along the river.

ii) It is possibly somewhat more common, however, to use **entlang** in combination with **an** + dat. with exactly the same meaning, e.g.

Sie gingen am Fluss entlang.
They walked along the river.

d) **für** (for)

i) **Für** nearly always equates to 'for', e.g.

Ich habe ein Geschenk für dich.
I have a gift for you.

Wie viel hast du dafür bezahlt?
How much did you pay for it?

ii) In idioms of the following sort it renders English 'by', e.g.

Schritt für Schritt
step by step/little by little

Das ist Wort für Wort, was er gesagt hat.
That is verbatim (lit. word for/by word) what he said.

e) **gegen** (against)

i) The primary meaning of **gegen** is 'against', e.g.

Stell die Leiter gegen die Wand!
Put the ladder (up) against the wall.

Ich habe nichts gegen ihn.
I have nothing against him.

ii) A common secondary meaning of **gegen** is 'approximately/around' with numerical quantities, e.g.

Er kam so gegen acht Uhr an.
He arrived at about eight o'clock. (lit. getting on towards eight, but no later)

Es tauchten plötzlich gegen fünfzig Kinder auf.
All of a sudden about fifty children turned up.

f) **ohne** (without)
i) **Ohne** is never followed by an indefinite article (see 5.3.1), e.g.

Nur er war ohne Schlips.
Only he was without a tie.

Er geht nie ohne seinen Hund spazieren.
He never goes for a walk without his dog.

ii) **Ohne** is also used as a conjunction (see 11.3).

g) **um** (around)
i) The primary meaning of **um** is 'around', e.g.

Ich bin zweimal um die Welt geflogen.
I have flown around the world twice.

ii) **Um** also renders 'at' with the time of day, e.g.

Der Film fängt um halb acht an.
The film starts at half past seven.

iii) **Um** is also used as a conjunction (see 11.3).

h) **wider** (against)
Wider is not commonly used in everyday German. It is a formal synonym of **gegen** and is usually found with the meaning 'against' in compounds, e.g. **Widerstand** (opposition, i.e. stand against s.t.) and **widersprechen** (to contradict, i.e. to say against), but also occurs as a preposition in some standard expressions, e.g.

Wider (alles) Erwarten ist das Wetter auf einmal umgeschlagen.
Contrary to/Against (all) expectations the weather suddenly changed.

12.2 Prepositions that take the dative case

There is a traditional mnemonic to help remember these prepositions, which is 'out from midnight, tight by two', an indirect way of listing **aus**, **von**, **mit**, **nach**, **seit**, **bei** and **zu**. If you find it useful, well and good, but although it covers all the common dative prepositions, there are two more, **außer** and **gegenüber**. **Gegenüber** is a bit of an odd man out anyway as the description of it below reveals. Even where prepositions like **aus**, **nach**, **von** and **zu** indicate a motion from or towards a place, they are always followed by the dative, unlike the two-way prepositions (see 12.3).

a) **aus** (out of, from)
   i) The primary meaning of **aus** is 'out of', e.g.

Er rannte aus dem Haus.
He ran out of the house.

ii) It also renders 'from' towns and countries when expressing s.o.'s or s.t.'s origins, the answer to **Wo kommen Sie her?** (Where do you come from?), e.g.

Ich komme aus Frankreich/Paris.
I come from France/Paris.

Der Brief kam aus Polen.
The letter was from Poland.

iii) To drink 'from' s.t. is also rendered by **aus**, e.g.

Er hat sein Bier aus der Flasche getrunken.
He drank his beer from the bottle.

iv) Less commonly **aus** renders 'made of' with reference to materials, e.g.

ein Gürtel aus Leder
a belt made of leather

Meine Socken sind aus Nylon.
My socks are made of nylon.

v) There is another very idiomatic use of **aus** where it renders the motivation for doing s.t., e.g.

Aus welchem Grund hat er ihr €20 gegeben?
For what reason did he give her €20?

Er hat es ihr aus Mitleid gegeben.
Her gave it to her out of pity.

b) **außer** (apart from, except for, besides, other than, out of)

i) Depending on context **außer** can be translated in a variety of ways, e.g.

Er kennt niemand in dieser Stadt außer mir.
He doesn't know anyone in this city apart from/besides/other than me.

ii) There are a few idiomatic contexts where 'out of' must be rendered by **außer**, not **aus**, e.g.

Das Telefon an der Ecke ist außer Betrieb.
The phone on the corner is out of order.

Sie war außer sich (vor Angst).
She was beside herself (with fear).

Ich musste rennen und war deswegen völlig außer Atem.
I had to run and was thus completely out of breath.

c) **bei** (at, with)

i) **Bei** has many idiomatic uses and very seldom means 'by'. First and foremost it renders 'at' s.o.'s place (compare French **chez**), which is sometimes expressed by 'with' in English; German uses **bei** not **mit** in such cases, e.g.

Dieses Jahr feiern wir meinen Geburtstag bei meinen Großeltern.
This year we are celebrating my birthday at my grandparents' place.

Meine Freundin wohnt noch bei ihren Eltern.
My girlfriend is still living with her parents.

ii) **Bei** in combination with the definite article is used with professions to render 'at' or 'in' their places of work, e.g.

Meine Frau ist beim Arzt.
My wife is at the doctor's.

Ich bin ihr beim Bäcker begegnet.
I bumped into her at the baker's/in the bakery.

iii) When you state that you bought s.t. 'at' a particular shop or that you work 'at' a particular place, i.e. referring to the names of firms, **bei** is required, e.g.

Ich habe unseren neuen Fernseher bei Hertie gekauft.
I bought our new television set at Hertie. (compare Harrods or Macy's)

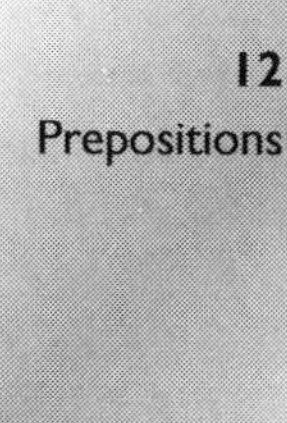

Mein Onkel arbeitet bei VW.
My uncle works for VW.

iv) **Bei** also renders 'near' or 'in the vicinity of', which is also most commonly expressed quite literally by **in der Nähe von**, e.g.

Wir wohnen bei Frankfurt/in der Nähe von Frankfurt.
We live near/close to/in the vicinity of Frankfurt.

v) A little known village might be referred to in German as **Winkelstadt bei Kassel** (i.e. W which is not far from K), which helps the listener to roughly place a village he is not likely otherwise to have heard of.

vi) **Bei** plus a reflexive pronoun (see 7.3.2) renders 'on one's person', e.g.

Er hatte keinen Pfennig bei sich.
He didn't have a penny on him.

vii) **Beim** + an infinitive used as a noun (see 10.7), and thus capitalized, renders 'while doing' whatever the infinitive in question is, e.g.

Ich singe sehr gern beim Duschen.
I like to sing while (I'm) showering.

Beim Fahren hat man Zeit über Gott und die Welt nachzudenken.
You have time to think about everything under the sun when you're driving.

viii) **Beim** is used with the names of meals to render 'during/at breakfast/lunch/dinner' (see **zum** + meals under **zu**, point vii), e.g.

Beim Abendessen hat keiner was gesagt.
During dinner no one said anything.

ix) **Bei** is used very idiomatically with forms of weather, roughly translating 'when', e.g.

Bei schönem Wetter gehen wir aus und bei schlechtem (Wetter) bleiben wir zu Hause.
When it's fine we go out and when the weather is bad we stay at home.

Bei Schnee verbringen die Kinder den ganzen Tag draußen.
When there's snow/when it's snowing the kids spend all day outside.

d) **gegenüber** (opposite, towards)

i) **Gegenüber** is a preposition with a difference; it follows the noun or pronoun when it refers to a person, but usually precedes it when the noun is non-personal, e.g.

Er saß mir gegenüber.
He sat opposite me.

Er wohnt der alten Dame gegenüber.
He lives opposite the old lady.

Die Bäckerei befindet sich gegenüber dem Postamt.
The bakery is (situated) opposite the post office.

ii) **Gegenüber** after a noun or pronoun referring to one or more people can render 'to/toward(s)' in a figurative sense (i.e. not indicating movement towards), e.g.

Mir gegenüber ist er immer sehr höflich/nett gewesen.
He has always been very polite/nice to me.

e) **mit** (with)

i) Generally speaking **mit** corresponds to 'with', e.g.

Er ging mit seinem Hund im Park spazieren.
He went for a walk with his dog in the park.

Mit diesem Messer kann man kein Brot schneiden.
You can't cut bread with this knife.

ii) **Mit** + the definite article is used to express 'by' various modes of transport, e.g.

Sie ist mit der Straßenbahn in die Stadt gefahren.
She went to town by tram.

f) **nach** (to, after)

i) The most usual meaning of **nach** is 'after', e.g.

Unmittelbar nach dem Konzert ist der Dirigent in Ohnmacht gefallen.
Straight after the concert the conductor fainted.

ii) For cases where **nach** translates 'to' see 12.6.

iii) **Nach** also translates 'past' with reference to telling the time, e.g.

Der Zug ist erst um zehn nach sechs angekommen.
The train did not arrive till ten past six.

iv) There is a common idiomatic use of **nach**. In a few standard expressions **nach** means 'according to', in which case it usually follows the noun, e.g.

Meiner Meinung nach hat sie nicht alle Tassen im Schrank.
In my opinion she is not alright in the head.

v) The expression **nach Hause** (home, i.e. indicating motion towards) is very common (see **zu Hause** under **zu**, point iv), e.g.

Wann kommst du nach Hause?
When are you coming home?

g) **seit** (since, for)
i) **Seit** translates 'since' as a preposition, e.g.

Ich habe sie seit letzter Woche nicht gesehen.
I haven't seen them since last week.

ii) **Seit** is also used with expressions of time together with the present tense to render 'for (a particular length of time)', see 9.4.6 and 10.1.5.3), e.g.

Ich lerne seit zwei Jahren Deutsch.
I have been learning German for two years.

iii) 'Since' in English is also a conjunction (see 11.2) and an adverb (see 9.4.7, General expressions of time), in which instances it is rendered by other words in German, i.e. **seit/seitdem** and **seitdem/seither** respectively.

h) **von** (from, off, of)
i) The most usual meaning of **von** is 'from' (see **aus**), e.g.

Wie weit ist es von München nach Nürnberg?
How far is it from Munich to Nuremberg?

ii) The distinction we make in English between 'from' and 'off' is not made in German; both meanings are rendered by **von**, e.g.

Er ist vom Dach gefallen.
He fell off/from the roof.

iii) When 'of' is not possessive **von** is required, e.g.

Das ist sehr lieb von dir.
That is very sweet of you.

iv) Where the genitive is not used to render possessive 'of', **von** is used, often being an alternative in colloquial German to the genitive (see 4.4), e.g.

die Hauptstadt von Deutschland (= die Hauptstadt Deutschlands)
the capital city of Germany

der Schwager von meinem Bruder (= der Schwager meines Bruders)
my brother's brother-in-law

v) **Von** also renders 'by' in the passive (see 10.4.1), e.g.

Dieser Brief ist deutlich von einem Deutschen geschrieben worden.
This letter was clearly written by a German.

i) **zu** (to)

i) The primary meaning of **zu** is 'to' (a place); see 12.6.
Compare **Gib mir deine Hand!** (Give me your hand.), which is a typical case of the dative expressing 'to', with **Komm zu mir!** (Come to me.) which involves physical movement.

ii) Good/nice 'to' s.o. is rendered by **zu**, e.g.

Er war sehr gut/nett zu mir.
He was very good/nice to me.

iii) **Zu** is usually not an option where a dative renders 'to' a person except after the verb **sagen**, where it used when **sagen** means 'to say s.t. to s.o.' as opposed to 'to tell s.o. s.t.', e.g.

Was hat er zu dir gesagt?
What did he say to you?

Was hat er dir gesagt?
What did he tell you?

iv) The very common expression **zu Hause** means 'at home'. Compare **nach Hause** (home) under **nach**, point v.

v) **Zu** renders 'at' with reference to religious festivities, e.g.

zu Ostern/Pfingsten/Weihnachten
at Easter/Whitsuntide/Christmas

vi) **Zu** occurs in many idiomatic phrases where it is rendered by various English prepositions, e.g.

zu Fuß	on foot
zu zweit/dritt/viert	in twos/threes/fours
zum Schluss	at the end (= finally)
zum ersten/zweiten/letzten Mal	for the first/second/last time
zum Beispiel	for example

Ich habe eine digitale Kamera zum Geburtstag bekommen.
I got a digital camera for my birthday.

vii) **Zu** + the definite article is used with meals to render 'for' breakfast/lunch/dinner (compare **bei** with meals, point viii), e.g.

Was esst ihr normalerweise zum Frühstück?
What do you (guys) normally have for breakfast?

Compare **zu** without the definite article with reference to meals, which has quite a different meaning, e.g.

Wo habt ihr zu Mittag/Abend gegessen?
Where did you have lunch/dinner?

viii) **Zu** is also used as an adverb meaning 'closed' of doors, windows and shops, e.g.

Die Tür/Aldi war zu.
The door/Aldi was shut. (Aldi is a German supermarket chain.)

j) **ab** (from)
The most usual function of **ab** is as a prepositional verbal prefix (see 10.9.1.a), but it also has a limited function as an independent preposition meaning 'from' in expressions of time, where it is synonymous with **von ... an**, e.g.

Ab zehn Uhr bin ich wieder im Büro. (= von zehn Uhr an)
From ten o'clock (on) I'll be back in my office.

12.3 Prepositions that take both the accusative and the dative case, i.e. two-way prepositions

These prepositions take either the accusative or the dative case depending on whether motion towards (acc.) or place (dat.) is being indicated: **hinter, an, auf, unter, über, zwischen, vor, in, neben.** Try HAAUUZVIN (think of 'housewine') as a mnemonic; it's not perfect but better than nothing.

With these prepositions you will often be faced with the dilemma of not being able to decide whether a given context indicates motion or place, as it would not seem to be either; in such cases you simply have to learn which case is appropriate to the context, e.g.

Sie ist über neunzig Jahre alt.
She is over ninety years old.

This example is in the acc., as indicated by the lack of a dat. plural **-n** on **Jahre**.

a) **an** (on, at)
i) This preposition is often confused by English speakers with **auf**. First and foremost vertical 'on' is rendered by **an** (but a horizontal 'on' is rendered by **auf**), e.g.

Der Lehrer hat die Weltkarte an die Wand gehängt. (accusative)
The teacher hung the map of the world on the wall.

Er klopfte ans Fenster. (accusative)
He knocked on the window.

Die Karte hängt an der Wand. (dative)
The map is hanging on the wall.

ii) 'On' or 'at' the edge of things is also **an**, e.g.

an der Grenze	on the border (dative)
an der Küste	on the coast (dative)
am Rand des Waldes	on the edge of the forest

iii) 'On' in expressions of time is rendered by **an** + dative, e.g.

an meinem Geburtstag	on my birthday
am Montag	on Monday
am nächsten Tag	the next day

b) **auf** (on)
When s.t. is (placed) 'on' a horizontal surface, 'on' is rendered by **auf**, e.g.

Ich habe die Zeitung auf den Tisch gelegt. (accusative)
I put the newspaper on the table.

Die Zeitung liegt auf dem Tisch. (dative)
The newspaper is lying on the table.

c) **hinter** (behind)
Hinter corresponds almost exactly to 'behind', e.g.

Der Dackel lief hinter einen Baum. (accusative)
The sausage dog ran behind a tree.

Er hat den Dackel hinter einem Baum gefunden. (dative)
He found the sausage dog behind a tree.

d) **in** (in, into)
In this case we make a distinction between motion and place in English too, but where German does this with case, we do it with 'into' and 'in' respectively, e.g.

Sie ging ins Badezimmer. (accusative)
She went into the bathroom.

Sie ist im Badezimmer. (dative)
She is in the bathroom.

e) **neben** (next to, beside, alongside)
Neben corresponds almost exactly to 'next to', e.g.

Er setzte sich neben mich. (accusative)
He sat down next to me.

Er saß neben mir. (dative)
He was sitting next to/alongside me.

f) **über** (above, over, across)
i) The primary meaning of **über** is 'over', but more or less the same meaning is expressed in certain contexts in English by 'above' and 'across' – German makes do with the one word here, e.g.

Der Bus ist über die Brücke gefahren. (accusative)
The bus drove over/across the bridge.

Sie haben einen Spiegel über ihrem Bett. (dative)
They have a mirror over/above their bed.

ii) 'Over' meaning 'more than' with reference to quantities is also rendered by **über** (+ acc.), e.g.

Als er verhaftet wurde, hatte er über fünftausend Euro bei sich.
When he was arrested he had over five thousand euros on him.

iii) **Über** (+ acc.) also translates 'via' with reference to places, e.g.

Wir sind über Innsbruck/den Brenner von Italien zurückgefahren.
We drove back from Italy via Innsbruck/the Brenner Pass.

g) **unter** (under)

i) Generally speaking **unter** corresponds quite closely to 'under', e.g.

Die Katze ist unter das Bett gelaufen. (accusative)
The cat ran under the bed.

Ich habe meine Brille endlich unter dem Bett gefunden. (dative)
I finally found my glasses under the bed.

ii) **Unter** (+ dat.) also translates 'beneath', as this is more or less synonymous with 'under' even if 'under' cannot be used in all contexts in English, e.g.

unter der See
beneath/under the sea

Das war bestimmt unter ihrer Würde.
That was definitely beneath her (dignity).

iii) 'Among' is also rendered by **unter** (+ dat.), e.g.

Sie sind hier unter Freunden.
You are among friends here.

h) **vor** (in front of, before)

i) **Vor** can refer to the physical position of s.t., in which case it translates 'in front of', e.g.

Er hat sein Auto vor die Garage gefahren.
He drove his car in front of the garage. (accusative, i.e. where he drove it *to*)

Die Kinder haben anderthalb Stunden vor dem Supermarkt gewartet.
The children waited in front of the supermarket for an hour and a half.

ii) **Vor** can just as commonly refer to time, in which case it translates 'before' and always takes the dative, e.g.

Wir haben vor dem Konzert ein Glas Wein in einer Wirtschaft getrunken.
We had a glass of wine in a pub before the concert.

iii) **Vor** is used to translate 'to' when telling the time (see **nach**, point iii), e.g.

Es ist Viertel vor sechs.
It is a quarter to six.

i) zwischen (between)
Zwischen corresponds more or less exactly to 'between', e.g.

Er setze sich zwischen mich und meine Frau.
He sat down between me and my wife.

Er saß zwischen mir und meiner Frau.
He was sitting between me and my wife.

12.4 Prepositions that take the genitive case

There are only six prepositions that take the genitive case: **anstatt, außerhalb, innerhalb, trotz, während, wegen**. The genitive case has been losing functions over a long period of time in German. This process of erosion is evidenced by the fact that many Germans these days commonly use the dative after **wegen** in speech, and even after **während**, but you are advised to adhere to the genitive. The English equivalents of all but one of these prepositions contain 'of', which is an indicator of their taking the genitive case; even **während** can be seen as meaning 'during the course of'.

a) **(an)statt** (instead of)
i) The **an-** prefix is optional, but inclusion of the prefix is more formal, e.g.

Er hat seine neuen Sandalen getragen statt seiner alten Schuhe.
He wore his new sandals instead of his old shoes.

ii) When a masculine or neuter noun immediately follows **statt**, i.e. with no determiner between them, a genitive **s** is not applied to the noun, as might otherwise be expected, e.g.

Wir haben alle Tee statt Kaffee getrunken.
We all drank tea instead of coffee.

iii) Note the adverb **stattdessen** (instead of that, instead), e.g.

Was hast du denn stattdessen gemacht?
Then what did you do instead (of that)?

iv) **(An)statt** is also a conjunction (see 11.2 and 11.3).

b) **außerhalb** (outside [of])
This preposition differs in meaning from the adverb **draußen** (outside), e.g.

Er wohnt heutzutage außerhalb der Stadt.
These days he lives outside (of) town.

c) **innerhalb** (inside [of], within)
i) This preposition differs in meaning from the adverb **drinnen** (inside). It can be used with reference to place, in which case it is the opposite of **außerhalb**, e.g.

Alle entkommenen Tiger sind zum Glück innerhalb des Tiergartens geblieben.
All escaped tigers fortunately stayed within/inside the zoo.

ii) **Innerhalb** is more usually used to render 'within' in a temporal sense, in which case **von** + dat. commonly replaces the genitive, e.g.

Wenn du nicht innerhalb eines Monats/von einem Monat zahlst, gibt es Krach.
If you don't pay up within a month, there'll be trouble.

d) **trotz** (in spite of, despite)
i) **Trotz** corresponds exactly to 'in spite of' and its synonym 'despite', e.g.

Die Party wurde trotz des schlechten Wetters draußen im Garten gehalten.
The party was held outside in the garden despite the bad weather.

ii) The adverbial expressions **trotz allem** (in spite of everything) and **trotzdem** (nevertheless) betray the historical tendency of this preposition to take the dative.

e) **während** (during)
i) **Während** as a preposition corresponds exactly to 'during', e.g.

Während des Krieges hat die Familie in Bosnien gewohnt.
The family lived in Bosnia during the war.

ii) **Während** is also a subordinating conjunction meaning 'while' (see 11.2).

f) **wegen** (because of, on account of, due to)
i) This preposition is very commonly followed by the dative in spoken German, although when followed by a feminine noun, there is no difference anyway, e.g.

Wegen des Wetters/wegen dem Wetter sind wir zu Hause geblieben.
We stayed at home because of/due to the weather.

Irmgard konnte wegen ihrer Mutter nicht mitkommen.
Irmgard was not able to come along because of/on account of her mother.

If a personal pronoun follows **während**, you have no choice but to use a dative form, e.g.

Irmgard konnte wegen mir nicht mitgehen.
Irmgard was not able to go along because of me/on account of me.

ii) When this preposition is used in combination with a personal pronoun, rather than a noun, special forms are used which can also translate differently into English, e.g.

meinetwegen	because of me, for my sake, on my account
deinetwegen	because of you, for your sake, on your account
seinetwegen	because of him, for his sake, on his account
ihretwegen	because of her, for her sake, on her account
unseretwegen	because of us, for our sake, on our account
euretwegen	because of you, for your sake, on your account

Ihretwegen	because of you, for your sake, on your account
ihretwegen	because of them, for their sake, on their account

iii) The adverbs **weswegen** (why), a synonym of **warum**, and **deswegen** (therefore, i.e. because of that) are derived from **wegen. Weshalb** and **deshalb** are synonymous with **weswegen** and **deswegen**.

12.5 Contraction of prepositions with the definite article

In both spoken and written German it is usual to contract certain prepositions with the following definite article. Some of these contractions are mandatory whereas others are merely possible, but not necessarily applied. The following contractions should always be applied in the dative to masculine and neuter nouns:

an dem > **am, bei dem** > **beim, in dem** > **im, von dem** > **vom, zu dem** > **zum**

e.g.

am Bahnhof (at the station), **beim Abendessen** (during dinner), **im Wasser** (in the water)

There is only one feminine contraction, namely **zu der** > **zur**, e.g.

Ich gehe jetzt zur Post.
I'm going to the post office now.

The accusative neuter forms **an das** > **ans** and **in das** > **ins** are also mandatory, e.g.

Wir gehen heute Abend ins Theater.
We're going to a play tonight.

All the following accusative contractions are optional in the spoken language but are rarely written:

auf das > **aufs, durch das** > **durchs, für das** > **fürs, hinter das** > **hinters, über das** > **übers, unter das** > **unters, vor das** > **vors, um das** > **ums**

e.g.

Er ist aufs Dach geklettert.
He climbed onto the roof.

The dative forms **unter dem** > **unterm** and **vor dem** > **vorm** also occur in speech, but seldom in writing.

Other forms like **auf dem** > **auf'm** and **nach dem** > **nach'm** are considered even more colloquial but are nevertheless extremely commonly used in natural speech.

Whenever forms of **der/die/das** are emphasized, as in cases where they mean 'that/those' (see 5.2), such contractions cannot be used, e.g.

Sie haben früher in d e m Haus gewohnt.
They used to live in that house.

12.6 How to translate 'to' into German

Although it would be an endless task to attempt to explain how every English preposition is rendered in German, there are a few hard and fast rules that apply to 'to' which are worth heeding as this is such a common preposition in English and is translated into German in several different ways.

a) 'To' a town or country is always rendered by **nach**, which always requires the dative despite indicating motion towards a place, e.g.

Wir fahren morgen in Urlaub nach Italien/Rom.
We're going on holiday to Italy/Rome tomorrow.

Only those countries that are preceded by the definite article require **in** + acc., not **nach**, to render 'to' before them, e.g.

Wir fliegen morgen in die Türkei/Vereinigten Staaten.
We're flying to Turkey/the USA tomorrow.

b) As a general rule **in** + acc. is the most common way of rendering 'to' a place if that place is preceded by a definite article, as is the case for example with shops, e.g.

Sie ist in die Konditorei/Apotheke gegangen.
She went to the cake shop/chemist's.

In + acc. is also the most usual form for going 'to' town, church and school, e.g.

Sie geht um acht Uhr in die Stadt/Kirche/Schule.
She's going to town/church/school at eight o'clock.

Such forms contrast nicely with **in** + dat. rendering position at such places, not motion towards them, e.g.

Ich habe sie in der Konditorei/Apotheke/Stadt/Kirche/Schule getroffen.
I met her in the cake shop/chemist's/town/church/school.

c) It is usually also possible to use **zu** + dat. in cases like those immediately above to render 'to', e.g.

Sie ist zur Konditorei/Apotheke/Stadt/Kirche/Schule gegangen.

With public buildings the form with **zu** is preferable (but see d), e.g.

Sie ist zum Bahnhof/Postamt gegangen.
She went to the station/post office.

d) A little less commonly you will find **auf** + acc. being used to translate 'to' public buildings, e.g.

Sie ging auf den Markt/die Post/die Bank.
She went to the market/post office/bank.

This has a parallel in the dative rendering 'at', as was the case with **in** above, e.g.

Ich bin ihr auf dem Markt/der Post/der Bank begegnet.
I bumped into her at the market/post office/bank.

e) **Zu** must be used when going 'to' s.o.'s place, e.g.

Wir gingen nach dem Abendessen zu meinen Großeltern/zu Oma.
We went to my grandparents'/granny's (place) after dinner.

f) The dative case on its own can also render 'to', which is, for example, always the case after **geben** (to give), e.g.

Er hat seiner Mutter sein ganzes Gehalt gegeben.
He gave his whole salary to his mother.

With verbs like 'to write to' and 'to send to' you have the choice of either using the dative alone or **an** + acc., e.g.

Er hat seiner Mutter einen Brief geschrieben/geschickt.
He wrote/sent his mother a letter.

Er hat einen Brief an seine Mutter geschrieben/geschickt.
He wrote/sent a letter to his mother.

Word order changes in both languages depending on which construction you use.

g) For figurative 'to' as in 'polite to someone', see definition two of **gegenüber** and **zu** under 12.2.

Chapter 13

Numerals

13.1 Cardinal numerals

gerade Zahlen	even numbers
ungerade Zahlen	uneven numbers

Compound numerals, if ever written out in full, are written as one word, as illustrated below.

0	**null**	15	**fünfzehn**
1	**eins**[1]	16	**sechzehn**[3]
2	**zwei**[2]	17	**siebzehn**[4]
3	**drei**	18	**achtzehn**
4	**vier**	19	**neunzehn**
5	**fünf**	20	**zwanzig**
6	**sechs**[3]	21	**einundzwanzig**[1]
7	**sieben**	22	**zweiundzwanzig**
8	**acht**	23	**dreiundzwanzig**
9	**neun**	24	**vierundzwanzig**
10	**zehn**	25	**fünfundzwanzig**
11	**elf**	26	**sechsundzwanzig**
12	**zwölf**	27	**siebenundzwanzig**
13	**dreizehn**	28	**achtundzwanzig**
14	**vierzehn**	29	**neunundzwanzig**

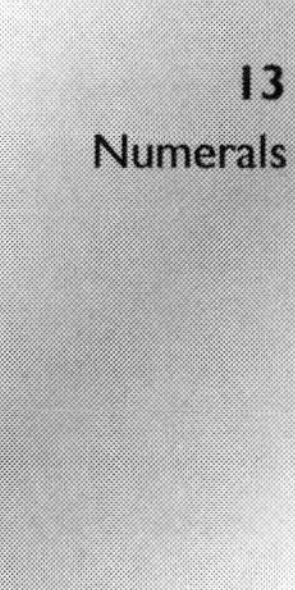

30	**dreißig**[5]	266	**zweihundert-sechsundsechzig**
40	**vierzig**	1,000	**tausend**[6]
50	**fünfzig**	1,008	**tausendacht**
60	**sechzig**[3]	5,010	**fünftausendzehn**
70	**siebzig**[4]	6,788	**sechstausendsieben-hundertachtundachtzig**
80	**achtzig**	200,000	**zweihunderttausend**
90	**neunzig**	1,000,000	**eine Million**
100	**hundert**[6]	2,000,000	**zwei Millionen**
101	**hunderteins**[7]	one billion	**eine Milliarde** (i.e. 1,000 million)
153	**hundertdreiund-**	one trillion	**eine Billion** (a million million)

Notes:

1 The raw numeral is **eins** but when followed by a noun, 'one' is identical in form to the indefinite article 'a/an' (see 5.3). When **ein** means 'one' it is emphasized in speech, e.g.

Er hat nur e i n Kind.
He has only one child.

In compound numerals like **einundzwanzig** etc. the **s** is dropped.

Eins is the only numeral to be inflected for case and gender, in which case its inflections are the same as those for the indefinite article, e.g.

Er hat nur e i n e n Sohn.
He has only one son.

2 Colloquially **zwei** is commonly pronounced **zwo**, particularly when spelling out numbers (e.g. when on the phone), e.g.

Meine Postleitzahl ist vier zwo drei zwo.
My post code is 4232.

This form also applies to the ordinal number, i.e. **der/die/das zwote** (the second) (see 13.2).

3 The **s** of **sechs** is dropped in **sechzehn** and **sechzig**, which also changes the pronunciation of the **ch**, i.e. **sechs** is pronounced 'zeks' but the **ch** in **sech-** in the other two numerals is an **ich**-Laut (see 1.3).

4 Note that although 'seven' is **sieben**, the **-en** is dropped in **siebzehn** and **siebzig** as well as in **siebte** (seventh) (see 13.2).

5 Only **dreißig** ends in **-ßig** rather than **-zig**.

6 **Hundert** and **tausend** on their own render 'a hundred' and 'a thousand', whereas **einhundert** and **eintausend** mean 'one hundred' and 'one thousand'.

'Hundreds/thousands of' is expressed as follows:

hunderte/tausende Mäuse or **hunderte/tausende von Mäusen**
hundreds/thousands of mice

7 With numerals after 101 German omits 'and' between the hundreds and the tens, just as is done in American English, e.g. **zweihundertvierundsechzig** (two hundred [and] sixty-four).

13.1.1 Use of commas and full-stops/periods with numerals

The Germans use a full-stop when writing thousands, not a comma, but a comma may be used where we use a full-stop, i.e. instead of a decimal point: **10.000** and **28.000,00** (English 10,000 and 28,000.00) Thus a price is written like this **€25,95** (pron. **fünfundzwanzig Euro fünfundneunzig**) and a temperature like this **16,8°** (pron. **sechzehn Komma acht Grad**, i.e. sixteen point eight degrees).

13.2 Ordinal numerals

The following are adjectives and are given here in the nom. m. form as found after **ein/eine/ein**.

1st	**erster**	10th	**zehnter**
2nd	**zweiter**	11th	**elfter**
3rd	**dritter**	12th	**zwölfter**
4th	**vierter**	13th	**dreizehnter**
5th	**fünfter**	14th	**vierzehnter**
6th	**sechster**	15th	**fünfzehnter**
7th	**siebter**	16th	**sechzehnter**
8th	**achter**	17th	**siebzehnter**
9th	**neunter**	18th	**achtzehnter**

19th	**neunzehnter**	40th	**vierzigster**
20th	**zwanzigster**	50th	**fünfzigster**
21st	**einundzwanzigster**	60th	**sechzigster**
22nd	**zweiundzwanzigster**	70th	**siebzigster**
23rd	**dreiundzwanzigster**	80th	**achtzigster**
24th	**vierundzwanzigster**	90th	**neunzigster**
25th	**fünfundzwanzigster**	100th	**hundertster**
26th	**sechsundzwanzigster**	101st	**hunderterster**
27th	**siebenundzwanzigster**	121st	**hunderteinund-zwanzigster**
28th	**achtundzwanzigster**	1,000th	**tausendster**
29th	**neunundzwanzigster**	8,452nd	**achttausendvier-hundertzweiund-fünfzigster**
30th	**dreißigster**	1,000,000th	**millionster**

All ordinals from 'twentieth' on end in **-ster/-ste/-stes** etc. in German. Ordinals can be used as both adjectives and adjectival nouns and thus inflect like all other adjectives, e.g.

A: Steht es im fünften Kapitel des Buches? B: Nein, im sechsten.
A: Is it (mentioned) in the fifth chapter of the book? B: No, in the sixth.

ein zweiter Sohn (m.), **eine dritte Tochter** (f.), **ein viertes Kind** (n.)
a second son, a third daughter, a fourth child

der zweite Sohn (m.), **die dritte Tochter** (f.), **das vierte Kind** (n.)
the second son, the third daughter, the fourth child

13.2.1 *The German equivalent of the abbreviations 'st', 'nd', 'rd' and 'th'*

The English abbreviations 'st', 'nd', 'rd' and 'th' are all rendered in German by merely placing a full-stop after the numeral, e.g.

Ich bin am 25. August geboren.
I was born on the 25th of August.

13.3 Fractions

¼	**ein Viertel** (n.)
½	**die Hälfte, ein halber**[1]
1½	**anderthalb, eineinhalb**[1]
2½, 3½ etc.	**zweieinhalb, dreieinhalb** etc.
⅛	**ein Achtel** (n.)
⅔	**zwei Drittel** (n.)
⅜	**drei Achtel** (n.)
1/16	**ein Sechzehntel** (n.)
0,5% (point five per cent)	**null Komma fünf Prozent**
1,8% (one point eight per cent)	**eins Komma acht Prozent**

Notes:

1 The English word 'half' causes difficulties because the noun and the adjective in German are different words, unlike English, i.e. **die Hälfte, halb**. The way the two are used is best illustrated by examples:

die Hälfte der Leute	half the people
die halbe Flasche	half the bottle

Sie hat die Hälfte der Torte aufgegessen.
Sie hat die halbe Torte aufgegessen.
She ate half the cake.

Ich habe die Hälfte des Buches schon gelesen.
Ich habe das halbe Buch schon gelesen.
I have already read half the book.

Ich habe es für die Hälfte des Preises gekauft.
Ich habe es zum halben Preis gekauft.
I bought it for half the price.

'One and a half' is expressed by either **anderthalb** or **eineinhalb**, which do not inflect, e.g.

anderthalb/eineinhalb Stunden	one and a half hours
anderthalb/eineinhalb Meter	one and a half metres

Similarly with **zweieinhalb, dreieinhalb, viereinhalb** etc.

13.4 Arithmetic/calculation

Acht plus acht ist sechzehn.
Eight plus eight is/equals sixteen.

Vier mal vier ist sechzehn.
Four times four is sixteen.

Acht multipliziert mit zwei ist sechzehn.
Four multiplied by four is sixteen.

Sechzehn dividiert/geteilt durch vier ist vier.
Sixteen divided by four is four.

13.5 Age

Wie alt bist du/sind Sie?	How old are you?
Er ist erst zehn (Jahre alt).	He is only ten (years old).
Wann bist du/sind Sie geboren?	When were you born?
Ich bin am dritten (März) geboren.	I was born on the third (of March).
Ich bin am dritten dritten geboren.	I was born on the third of March.
Ich bin (im Jahre) 1978[1] **geboren.**	I was born in 1978.
Ich habe heute Geburtstag.	It is my birthday today.
im Alter von vierzehn Jahren	at the age of fourteen
Mit vierzehn Jahren war er ...	At the age of fourteen he was ...
Er ist in den Sechzigern.	He is in his sixties.
Er ist Anfang/Mitte/Ende sechzig.	He is in his early/mid/late sixties.
Er ist unter/über sechzig.	He is under/over sixty.
der Einunddreißigjährige etc.	the thirty-one-year-old etc.
eine Dame in den mittleren Jahren	a middle-aged lady
eine Dame mittleren Alters	a middle-aged lady

Note:

1 Note that if **im Jahre** is omitted no **in** is used before a year. In addition, years are always read as follows, not omitting the word for hundred as is usually done in English:

neunzehnhundertachtundsiebzig
nineteen (hundred and) seventy-eight

13.6 Money

Currency units, like all forms of measurement (e.g. **Gramm, Millimeter, Meter, Kilometer, Kilo**), are left in the singular after a numeral, e.g. **zehn Mark, zwanzig Euro, sieben (Schweizer) Franken, fünfzehn Dollar, sechs Rubel, fünf Cent**. Only **Krone** (crown), ending in **-e** as it does, takes a plural **-n** after a numeral, e.g. **zehn Kronen**.

Euro is masculine, which is relevant for employing the correct case in contexts such as the following:

Ein Eis kostet einen Euro.
An ice-cream costs a/one euro.

Ich habe einen Euro dafür bezahlt.
I paid a/one euro for it.

For this reason you need to know the gender of all currency units, i.e. **der Cent, der Franken** (Swiss), **die Krone, das Pfund, der Rappen** (Swiss centime), **der Rubel. Der Groschen, die Mark, der Pfennig** and **der Schilling** are now all of course obsolete but are still found in many pre-2003 texts.

Prices in Germany are written and expressed as follows:

€54,60 (pron. **vierundfünfzig Euro sechzig**)
€1,20 (pron. **eins zwanzig** or **ein Euro zwanzig**)

13.7 Telling the time

Wie viel Uhr ist es? **Wie spät ist es?**	What is the time?
Es ist ein[1]/zwei/drei Uhr.	It is one/two/three o'clock.
Es ist fünf nach eins[1].	It is five past one.
Es ist Viertel nach eins.	It is a quarter past one.
Es ist zwanzig nach eins.	It is twenty past one.

Es ist zehn vor halb zwei.	It is twenty past one.
Es ist fünfundzwanzig nach eins.	It is twenty-five past one.
Es ist fünf vor halb zwei.	It is twenty-five past one.
Es ist halb zwei.	It is half past one.
Es ist fünfundzwanzig vor zwei.	It is twenty-five to two.
Es ist fünf nach halb zwei.	It is twenty-five to two.
Es ist zwanzig vor zwei.	It is twenty to two.
Es ist zehn nach halb zwei.	It is twenty to two.
Es ist Viertel vor zwei.	It is a quarter to two.
Es ist zehn vor zwei.	It is ten to two.

Note:

1 Note the alternation of **ein** and **eins**.

The 24-hour clock is popular in Germany. It is always used in official contexts but is not uncommon in informal conversation either, e.g.

Der nächste Zug nach Wien fährt um einundzwanzig Uhr dreißig von Gleis 5 ab.
The next train to Vienna leaves from platform 5 at 9.30 pm.

When not using the 24-hour clock 'am' and 'pm' are expressed as follows if necessary:

um zehn Uhr morgens/vormittags
at ten o'clock in the morning/10.00 am

um vier Uhr nachmittags
at four in the afternoon/4.00 pm

um sechs Uhr abends
at six o'clock in the evening/6.00 pm

um ein Uhr nachts/in der Nacht
at one o'clock in the morning/1.00 am

13.7.1 *Expressions of time with reference to the clock*

um acht (Uhr)	at eight o'clock

um acht Uhr genau	at exactly eight o'clock
pünktlich um acht Uhr	at exactly eight o'clock
Punkt acht Uhr	at eight o'clock on the dot
ungefähr um acht Uhr	at about eight
gegen acht (Uhr)	at about eight (but no later)
kurz nach acht (Uhr)	shortly after eight

Although **Viertel** renders 'a quarter' in telling the time, 'a quarter of an hour' is **eine Viertelstunde** and 'three quarters of an hour' is **eine Dreiviertelstunde**, e.g.

Ich habe eine Dreiviertelstunde auf sie gewartet.
I waited for her for three quarters of an hour.

13.8 Dates

Days of the week (see 9.4.7)

Sonntag (So.)
Montag (Mo.)
Dienstag (Di.)
Mittwoch (Mi.)
Donnerstag (Do.)
Freitag (Fr.)
Samstag/Sonnabend (Sa.)

Sonnabend is typically North German but **Samstag**, although originally southern German, is quite widely used.

Months of the year

Januar (Jan.)
Februar (Feb.)
März (März)
April (Apr.)
Mai (Mai)
Juni (Jun.)
Juli (Jul.)
August (Aug.)
September (Sept.)
Oktober (Okt.)
November (Nov.)
Dezember (Dez.)

Some German speakers feel that **Juni** and **Juli** sound very similar and to avoid ambiguity in deliberate speech they are pronounced **Juno** and **Julei** (stress on second syllable).

When reading out years in dates, German never omits the word 'hundred' as is usually the case in English, e.g.

Er ist im Jahr(e) neunzehnhundertachtundvierzig geboren.
He was born in nineteen (hundred and) forty-eight.

Asking the date in German can be expressed in two ways, i.e.

Der wievielte ist heute? or **Den wievielten haben wir heute?**
What is the date today?

Likewise the answer can be expressed in two ways, i.e.

Heute ist der dritte (Mai). or **Heute haben wir den dritten Mai.**
Today is the third (of May).

Dates are otherwise expressed as in English but omit 'of' before the month, e.g.

Er kommt am neunzehnten (August) zurück.
He's returning on the nineteenth (of August)/on August nineteenth.

Dates at the top of letters are expressed in the accusative and are written as follows:

den 18. September 2006

If abbreviated to pure numerals, dates follow the British, not the American, system of day-month-year, e.g. **12.11.2005** (i.e. 12th of November).

Dates are commonly abbreviated in speech as follows:

Er bleibt bis zum neunten elften auf Rhodos.
He's staying in Rhodes till the ninth of November.

13.9 Weights

Germans express weight in grams (**das Gramm**) and kilos (**das Kilo**), which, like all other such measures, are left in the singular after a numeral, e.g.

Siebenhundertfünfzig Gramm Gehacktes, bitte.
750 grams of mince, please.

Ich wiege fünfundachtzig Kilo.
I weigh 85 kilo(gram)s.

Ich habe in drei Wochen fünf Kilo zugenommen/abgenommen.
I have put on/lost five kilos in three weeks.

Remember that an imperial pound is 454 grams. German does use the word **Pfund** (i.e. 500 grams) as a measure of weight, but not with reference to personal weight, only foodstuffs, e.g.

ein halbes Pfund/250 Gramm Schabefleisch
half a pound/250 grams of minced meat (a speciality eaten raw)

13.10 Measurement

13.10.1 Height, length

die Größe	height (of people), size (of objects, clothing)
Wie groß bist du?	How tall are you?
Ich bin 1,72 groß. (pron. **ein Meter zweiundsiebzig**)	I am one metre seventy-two centimetres tall.

The height of a tree, building etc. is **die Höhe**, e.g.

Wie hoch ist dieser Baum?
How tall is this tree?

Length up to one metre is expressed in millimetres (**Millimeter**) and centimetres (**Zentimeter**).

die Breite	width
die Größe	size (i.e. both largeness and clothing size)
Welche Größe tragen/haben Sie?	What size do you take?
Ich trage/habe Größe 42.	I take a size 42. (in shoes)

13.10.2 Square and cubic measurements

fünf mal fünf (Meter)	five by five (metres)
drei Quadratmeter	three square metres
sechs Kubikmeter	six cubic metres

13.10.3 Distance and petrol/gas consumption

Distances are measured in kilometres in all German-speaking countries and the word **Kilometer**, like **Zentimeter** and **Meter**, is never used in the plural after numerals, although in this case the singular of all three words happens to be the same as the plural in German, e.g.

Wir sind heute 200 Kilometer gefahren.
We drove 200 kilometres today.

Meile (mile) can be used when talking of distances in English-speaking countries, e.g. **zehn Meilen** (ten miles). Being a feminine noun ending in **-e**, **Meile** is pluralized after numerals.

Petrol consumption of a car is rendered as follows:

Wie viel verbraucht Ihr Auto?
How many miles per gallon does your car do? (lit. use)

Mein Auto verbraucht fünf Liter pro/auf 100 Kilometer.
(i.e. five litres for every 100 kilometres driven)
My car does twenty kilometres to the litre.

Speed is expressed as follows:

Er ist mit achtzig um die Ecke gerast.
He drove around the corner at 80 kilometres an hour.

13.11 School marks/grades

A school or university 'mark/grade' is a **Note** (f.). At German schools, marks or grades are given out of six where **eine Eins** (pl. **zwei Einsen**) is the best score and **eine Sechs** the worst, e.g.

Ich habe eine zwei in Mathe bekommen.
I got a 2 for maths.

Eine Fünf and **eine Sechs** are both fails. Synonymous with the six grades are the following:

1 – ausgezeichnet/sehr gut	excellent/very good
2 – gut	good
3 – befriedigend	fair

4 – genügend/ausreichend	satisfactory
5 – mangelhaft	poor
6 – ungenügend	unsatisfactory

Ich habe mangelhaft in Chemie bekommen.
I got a 5 for chemistry./I failed chemistry.

Passing and failing subjects can also be expressed verbally, e.g.

durchfallen (to fail)

Ich bin (in Mathe) durchgefallen.
I failed (maths).

bestehen, durchkommen (to pass)

The former is transitive and the latter intransitive, e.g.

Ich habe Mathe bestanden. (subject must be mentioned)
I passed maths.

Ich bin (in Mathe) durchgekommen. (subject can be omitted)
I passed (maths).

Chapter 14

Negation

14.1 Position of nicht (not) and nie(mals) (never)

One of the trickiest aspects of negating a sentence in German is deciding just where to place the negative particle.

14.1.1 *The negative follows:*

a) adverbs of specific time, e.g.

Ich komme heute nicht mit.
I'm not coming with you today.

Wir wollen es diese Woche nicht machen.
We don't want to do it this week.

However, **nicht** always precedes general adverbs of time like **immer** (always), **oft** (often) and **selten** (seldom), e.g.

Er ist nicht immer so faul gewesen.
He has not always been so lazy.

b) definite direct objects
The negative follows the direct object as long as that object is preceded by a definite determiner, i.e. **der/die/das, dieser,** a possessive adjective or is a personal pronoun, e.g.

Ich habe das/dieses/sein Buch nicht finden können. (definite)
I have not been able to find the/this, that/his book.

Er hat sie nicht getroffen. (definite pronominal object)
He didn't meet her.

Kennst du ihn nicht? (definite pronominal object)
Don't you know him?

Compare the following where the direct objects are indefinite:

Er hat nie ein Buch gelesen.
He has never read a book.

Ich habe nie eine wirklich gute Schere kaufen können.
I have never been able to buy a really good pair of scissors.

14.1.2 *The negative precedes:*

a) indefinite direct objects
The negative precedes a direct object as long as it is indefinite, i.e. a noun preceded by **ein** or **viel(e)** or is an indefinite pronoun like **etwas, jemand, niemand** etc., e.g.

Er hat nie ein Auto gehabt.
He's never had a car.

Wir werden nicht viel/viele Sachen mit dem Geld kaufen können.
We won't be able to buy much/many things with the money.

For **nicht** in combination with **ein** see 14.2.a.

b) adverbial expressions of manner, e.g.

Ich fahre nicht mit dem Zug, (sondern mit dem Auto).
I'm not going by train (but by car).

Sie will nicht alleine zum Arzt gehen.
She does not want to go to the doctor on her own.

c) adverbial expressions of place, e.g.

Ich wohne nicht im achten Stock.
I don't live on the eighth floor.

Sie ist nie in England gewesen.
She has never been to England.

Er hat nicht im Garten gearbeitet.
He hasn't been working in the garden.

d) prepositional objects, e.g.

Hast du nie von ihm gehört?
Have you never heard of him?

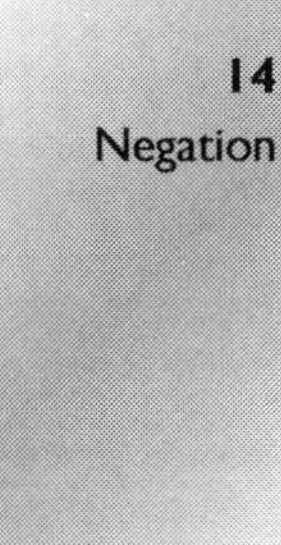

Ich hätte niemals an so was gedacht.
I would never have thought of such a thing.

Ich kann das Brot nicht damit schneiden.
I can't cut the bread with it/that.

Ich habe noch nicht an meine Nichte geschrieben.
I haven't written to my niece yet.

The previous example but one could be expressed with a dative instead of with a preposition, in which case **nicht** follows this definite (indirect) object, e.g.

Ich habe meiner Nichte noch nicht geschrieben.

e) predicative adjectives, e.g.

Die Fensterscheibe ist nicht kaputt.
The window pane isn't broken.

Ich bin nicht blöd.
I'm not stupid.

f) any word or phrase which is specifically negated, even where this conflicts with the rules for the position of **nicht** given in 14.1.1, e.g.

Wir wollen es nicht diese Woche machen (sondern nächste Woche). (emphatic)
We don't want to do it this week (but next week).

Er hat im Garten nicht gearbeitet, sondern gespielt.
He wasn't working in the garden (but playing).

Nicht der Kanzler hat das gesagt.
It wasn't the prime minister who said it.

14.2 Notes on negatives

a) 'Not ... a/any' or 'no + noun' are usually translated by **kein**, e.g.

Ich habe kein Auto. (nicht ein is not possible here)
I don't have a car./I have no car.

Er gibt kein Geld aus.
He doesn't spend any money./He spends no money.

The combination **nicht … ein** *is* possible when **ein** is stressed meaning 'not a/one single', e.g.

Wir sind vier Wochen in Südafrika gewesen und haben nicht e i n e n Löwen gesehen.
We were in South Africa for four weeks and did not see one lion.

But this might also be expressed as follows:

Wir sind vier Wochen in Südafrika gewesen und haben keinen einzigen Löwen gesehen.
We were in South Africa for four weeks and did not see a single lion.

b) 'Not one' is **nicht ein** or **keiner**, e.g.

Nicht einer meiner Freunde hat mich besucht, als ich krank war.
Not one of my friends visited me when I was sick.

Keiner meiner Freunde hat mich besucht, als ich krank war.
None of my friends visited me when I was sick.

Compare **keiner meiner Freunde/keine meiner Freundinnen** 'none of my friends' (definitely takes a singular verb in German).

c) Further uses of **kein**:
The following examples show how **kein** sometimes renders a simple English 'not':

Diese Tiere fressen kein Gras.
These animals don't eat grass.

But this can also be expressed as follows:

Gras fressen diese Tiere nicht.

Es waren keine normalen Katzen.
They were not/no ordinary cats.

Er kann/spricht kein Deutsch.
He doesn't know (any) German./He can't speak German.

The following expressions are all negated by **kein**, not **nicht**: **Dienst haben** (to be on duty), **Durst haben** (to be thirsty), **Eile haben** (to be in a hurry), **Hunger haben** (to be hungry), e.g.

Ich habe keine Eile.
I'm not in a hurry.

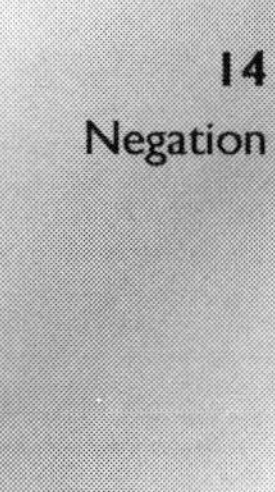

Ich habe keinen Hunger.
I'm not hungry.

d) 'No(t) ... at all' is rendered by either **gar nicht/kein** or **überhaupt nicht/kein**, which are completely synonymous and interchangeable, e.g.

Ich hatte gar nicht daran gedacht./Ich hatte überhaupt nicht daran gedacht.
I hadn't thought of it at all.

Ich habe gar kein Auto./Ich habe überhaupt kein Auto.
I haven't got a car at all.

Er hat gar kein Geld./Er hat überhaupt kein Geld.
He has no money at all.

e) 'Not ... until' is translated by **erst** (never **nicht ... bis**), which can also be rendered by 'only' in English (see use of **erst** with age in 13.5), e.g.

Er kommt erst morgen.
He's not coming until tomorrow./He's only coming tomorrow.

Sie kommen erst nächsten Montag.
They are not coming till next Monday.

Erst dann wird's passieren.
Only then/Not till then will it happen.

f) 'Not ... either' is translated simply by **auch nicht/kein**.

Ich gehe auch nicht.
I'm not going either.

Sie hat auch keins.
She hasn't got one either. (i.e. a car, neuter acc.)

g) 'Not yet' is translated by **noch nicht**, e.g.

Das neue Krankenhaus ist noch nicht eröffnet worden.
The new hospital hasn't been opened yet.

Nie, but never **niemals**, is also very frequently used in combination with **noch**, without the meaning changing much; it possibly adds a slight connotation of 'never ever' e.g.

Er hat (noch) nie ein Versprechen eingehalten.
He's never (yet) kept a promise.

Noch nie can never be used with reference to a future activity, e.g.

Die Regierung wird dieses Gesetz nie verabschieden.
The government will never pass this law.

h) Note the following affirmative/negative couplets:

etwas	something	**jemand**	someone, somebody
nichts	nothing	**niemand**	no-one, nobody
irgendwo	somewhere	**je(mals)**	ever
nirgendwo	nowhere	**nie(mals)**	never

Note: **nie zuvor** (never before) (see 9.4.8).

i) When contradicting a negative question, 'yes' is rendered by **doch**, not **ja** (compare French **si**), e.g.

A: Du bist nicht verheiratet, oder? B: Doch.
A: You're not married, are you? B: Yes, (I am).

English question tags such as 'Is he/Isn't he?', 'Will they/Won't they?', 'Are there/Aren't there?' etc., which vary according to the subject and verb previously mentioned, are all rendered in German simply by **nicht wahr?**, e.g.

Aber er hat's nicht alleine geschafft, nicht wahr?
But he didn't manage it on his own, did he?

Er fliegt morgen nach Japan, nicht wahr?
He's flying to Japan tomorrow, isn't he?

Southern Germany and Austria mostly use **gell?** instead of **nicht wahr?** and the latter is very commonly abbreviated in speech to **nicht?** or even **ne?**, e.g.

Du bist um sechs wieder da, gell/nicht/ne?
You'll be back here at six, won't you?

Also commonly heard in spoken German is **oder?** See the first example above in section i).

j) 'Even' is usually rendered by **sogar**, while 'not even' is normally rendered by **nicht einmal**, e.g.

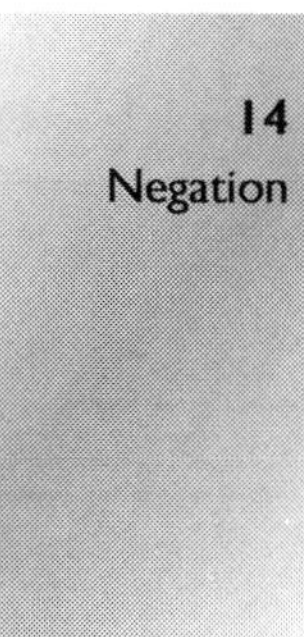

Sogar er ist mitgekommen.
Even he came along.

but

Sein Name wurde nicht einmal erwähnt.
His name wasn't even mentioned.

Chapter 15

Common German abbreviations

d.h.	**das heißt**	i.e.	that is
u.	**und**	&	and
u.a.	**unter anderen/-em**	i.a.	inter alia
u. dgl.	**und dergleichen**		and such like
u.s.f.	**und so fort**	etc.	et cetera, and so on
u.s.w.	**und so weiter**	etc.	et cetera
z.B.	**zum Beispiel**	e.g.	for example

Appendix I

List of countries, inhabitants and adjectives/languages

Male inhabitants ending in **-er** do not change in the plural and the females add **-in** with a plural in **-innen**. Male inhabitants ending in **-e** are weak nouns (see 6.1.1.h), as are **Ungar** and **Zypriot**; the female equivalent ends in **-in** and is of course not weak. Only **Deutscher** is an adjectival noun, the female equivalent consequently being **Deutsche** (see 6.5.1).

	Country	*Inhabitant*	*Female inhabitant*	*Adjective/language*
Afghanistan	**Afghanistan**	**Afghane**	**Afghanin**	**afghanisch**
Africa	**Afrika**	**Afrikaner**	**Afrikanerin**	**afrikanisch**
Albania	**Albanien**	**Albaner**	**Albanerin**	**albanisch**
Algeria	**Algerien**	**Algerier**	**Algerierin**	**algerisch**
America	**Amerika**	**Amerikaner**	**Amerikanerin**	**amerikanisch**
Angola	**Angola**	**Angolaner**	**Angolanerin**	**angolanisch**
Arabia	**Saudi-Arabien**	**Araber**	**Araberin**	**arabisch**
Argentina	**Argentinien**	**Argentinier**	**Argentinierin**	**argentinisch**
Armenia	**Armenien**	**Armenier**	**Armenierin**	**armenisch**
Asia	**Asien**	**Asiat**	**Asiatin**	**asiatisch**
Australia	**Australien**	**Australier**	**Australierin**	**australisch**
Austria	**Österreich**	**Österreicher**	**Österreicherin**	**österreichisch**
Azerbaidjan	**Aserbaidschan**	**Aserbaidschaner**	**Aserbaidschanerin**	**aserbaidschanisch**
Belarus	**Weißrussland**	**Weißrusse**	**Weißrussin**	**weißrussisch**
Belgium	**Belgien**	**Belgier**	**Belgierin**	**belgisch**

	Country	*Inhabitant*	*Female inhabitant*	*Adjective/language*
Flanders	**Flandern**	**Flame**	**Flamin, Flämin**	**flämisch**
Wallonia	**Wallonien**	**Wallone**	**Wallonin**	**wallonisch**
Bolivia	**Bolivien**	**Bolivianer**	**Bolivianerin**	**bolivianisch**
Bosnia	**Bosnien**	**Bosnier**	**Bosnierin**	**bosnisch**
Botswana	**Botswana**	**Botswaner**	**Botswanerin**	**botswanisch**
Brazil	**Brasilien**	**Brasilianer**	**Brasilianerin**	**brasilianisch**
Bulgaria	**Bulgarien**	**Bulgare**	**Bulgarin**	**bulgarisch**
Burkina Fasso	**Burkina Faso**			
Burma	**Burma**	**Burmese**	**Burmesin**	**burmesisch**
	Birma	**Birmane**	**Birmanin**	**birmanisch**
Burundi	**Burundi**	**Burundier**	**Burundierin**	**burundisch**
Cambodia	**Kambodscha**	**Kambodschaner**	**Kambodschanerin**	**kambodschanisch**
Cameroon	**Kamerun**	**Kameruner**	**Kamerunerin**	**kamerunisch**
Canada	**Kanada**	**Kanadier**	**Kanadierin**	**kanadisch**

	Country	*Inhabitant*	*Female inhabitant*	*Adjective/language*
Central African Republic	**die Zentralafrikanische Republik**	**Zentralafrikaner**	**Zentralafrikanerin**	**zentralafrikanisch**
Chad	**(der) Tschad**	**Tschader**	**Tschaderin**	**tschadisch**
Chile	**Chile**	**Chilene**	**Chilenin**	**chilenisch**
China	**China**	**Chinese**	**Chinesin**	**chinesisch**
Columbia	**Kolumbien**	**Kolumbianer**	**Kolumbianerin**	**kolumbianisch**
Comores	**die Komoren**	**Komorer**	**Komorerin**	**komorerisch**
Congo	**Kongo**	**Kongolese**	**Kongolesin**	**kongolesisch**
Costa Rica	**Costarika**	**Costarikaner**	**Costarikanerin**	**costarikanisch**
Croatia	**Kroatien**	**Kroate**	**Kroatin**	**kroatisch**
Cuba	**Kuba**	**Kubaner**	**Kubanerin**	**kubanisch**
Cyprus	**Zypern**	**Zypriot**	**Zypriotin**	**zypriotisch**
Czech Republic	**Tschechien**	**Tscheche**	**Tschechin**	**tschechisch**
Denmark	**Dänemark**	**Däne**	**Dänin**	**dänisch**
Dominican Republic	**die Dominikanische Republik**			

	Country	*Inhabitant*	*Female inhabitant*	*Adjective/language*
Ecuador	**Ecuador**	**Ecuadorianer**	**Ecuadorianerin**	**ecuadorianisch**
Egypt	**Ägypten**	**Ägypter**	**Ägypterin**	**ägyptisch**
El Salvador	**El Salvador**	**Salvadorianer**	**Salvadorianerin**	**salvadorianisch**
England	**England**	**Engländer**	**Engländerin**	**englisch**
Estonia	**Estland**	**Este**	**Estin**	**estnisch**
Ethiopia	**Ethiopien**	**Ethiopier**	**Ethiopier**	**ethiopisch**
Europe	**Europa**	**Europäer**	**Europäerin**	**europäisch**
Fiji	**Fidschi**	**Fidschianer**	**Fidschianerin**	**fidschianisch**
Finland	**Finnland**	**Finne**	**Finnin**	**finnisch**
		Finnländer	**Finnländerin**	**finnländisch**
France	**Frankreich**	**Franzose**	**Französin**	**französisch**
Gabon	**Gabun**	**Gabuner**	**Gabunerin**	**gabunisch**
Gambia	**Gambia**	**Gambier**	**Gambierin**	**gambisch**
Georgia	**Georgien**	**Georgier**	**Georgierin**	**georgisch**
Germany	**Deutschland**	**Deutscher**	**Deutsche**	**deutsch**

	Country	*Inhabitant*	*Female inhabitant*	*Adjective/language*
Federal Republic of Germany	**die Bundesrepublik Deutschland (die BRD)**			
Ghana	**Ghana**	**Ghanaer**	**Ghanaerin**	**ghanaisch**
Great Britain	**Großbritannien**	**Brite**	**Britin**	**britisch**
Greece	**Griechenland**	**Grieche**	**Griechin**	**griechisch**
Greenland	**Grönland**	**Grönländer**	**Grönlanderin**	**grönländisch**
Guatemala	**Guatemala**	**Guatemalteke**	**Guatemaltekin**	**guatemaltekisch**
Guinea	**Guinea**	**Guineer**	**Guineerin**	**guineisch**
Guyana	**Guyana**	**Guyaner**	**Guyanerin**	**guyanisch**
Haiti	**Haiti**	**Haitianer**	**Haitianerin**	**haitianisch**
		Haitier	**Haitierin**	**haitisch**
Holland	**Holland**	**Holländer**	**Holländerin**	**holländisch**
Honduras	**Honduras**	**Honduraner**	**Honduranerin**	**honduranisch**
Hungary	**Ungarn**	**Ungar**	**Ungarin**	**ungarisch**
Iceland	**Island**	**Isländer**	**Isländerin**	**isländisch**

	Country	*Inhabitant*	*Female inhabitant*	*Adjective/language*
India	**Indien**	**Inder**	**Inderin**	**indisch**
Indonesia	**Indonesien**	**Indonesier**	**Indonesierin**	**indonesisch**
Iran	**(der) Iran**	**Iraner**	**Iranerin**	**iranisch**
Iraq	**(der) Irak**	**Iraker**	**Irakerin**	**irakisch**
Ireland	**Irland**	**Ire**	**Irin**	**irisch**
Israel	**Israel**	**Israeli**	**Israelin**	**israelisch**
Italy	**Italien**	**Italiener**	**Italienerin**	**italienisch**
Ivory Coast	**die Elfenbeinküste**			
Jamaica	**Jamaika**	**Jamaikaner**	**Jamaikanerin**	**jamaikanisch**
Japan	**Japan**	**Japaner**	**Japanerin**	**japanisch**
Jordan	**Jordanien**	**Jordanier**	**Jordanierin**	**jordanisch**
Kazakhstan	**Kasachstan**	**Kasache**	**Kasachin**	**kasachisch**
Kenya	**Kenia**	**Kenianer**	**Kenianerin**	**kenianisch**
Korea	**Korea**	**Koreaner**	**Koreanerin**	**koreanisch**
Kuwait	**Kuwait**	**Kuwaiter**	**Kuwaiterin**	**kuwaitisch**

	Country	*Inhabitant*	*Female inhabitant*	*Adjective/language*
Kyrgyzstan	**Kirgisien/Kirgisistan**	**Kirgisier**	**Kirgisierin**	**kirgisisch**
Laos	**Laos**	**Laote**	**Laotin**	**laotisch**
Lappland	**Lappland**	**Lappe**	**Lappin**	**lappisch**
		Lappländer	**Lappländerin**	**lappländisch**
Latvia	**Lettland**	**Lette**	**Lettin**	**lettisch**
Lebanon	**(der) Libanon**	**Libanese**	**Libanesin**	**libanesisch**
Liberia	**Liberien**	**Liberier**	**Liberierin**	**liberisch**
Libya	**Libyen**	**Libyer**	**Libyerin**	**libysch**
Liechtenstein	**Liechtenstein**	**Liechtensteiner**	**Liechtensteinerin**	**liechtensteinisch**
Lithuania	**Litauen**	**Litauer**	**Litauerin**	**litauisch**
Luxembourg	**Luxemburg**	**Luxemburger**	**Luxemburgerin**	**luxemburgisch**
Macedonia	**Mazedonien**	**Mazedonier**	**Mazedonierin**	**mazedonisch**
Malawi	**Malawi**	**Malawier**	**Malawierin**	**malawisch**
Malaysia	**Malaysia**	**Malaysier**	**Malaysierin**	**malaysisch**
Maldives	**die Malediven**	**Malediver**	**Malediverin**	**maledivisch**

	Country	*Inhabitant*	*Female inhabitant*	*Adjective/language*
Mali	**Mali**	**Malier**	**Malierin**	**malisch**
Malta	**Malta**	**Malteser**	**Malteserin**	**maltesisch**
Mauritania	**Mauretanien**	**Mauretanier**	**Mauretanierin**	**mauretanisch**
Mexico	**Mexiko**	**Mexikaner**	**Mexikanerin**	**mexikanisch**
Moldova	**Moldawien**	**Moldawier**	**Moldawierin**	**Moldawisch**
Monaco	**Monaco**	**Monegasse**	**Monegassin**	**monegassisch**
Mongolia	**die Mongolei**	**Mongole**	**Mongolin**	**mongolisch**
Morocco	**Marokko**	**Marokkaner**	**Marokkanerin**	**marokkanisch**
Mozambique	**Mosambik**	**Mosambikaner**	**Mosambikanerin**	**mosambikanisch**
Namibia	**Namibia**	**Namibier**	**Namibierin**	**namibisch**
Nepal	**Nepal**	**Nepalese**	**Nepalesin**	**nepalesisch**
Netherlands	**die Niederlande**	**Niederländer**	**Niederländerin**	**niederländisch**
New Zealand	**Neuseeland**	**Neuseeländer**	**Neuseeländerin**	**neuseeländisch**
Nicaragua	**Nicaragua**	**Nicaraguaner**	**Nicaraguanerin**	**nicaraguanisch**
Niger	**Niger**	**Nigrer**	**Nigrerin**	**nigrisch**

	Country	*Inhabitant*	*Female inhabitant*	*Adjective/language*
Nigeria	**Nigerien**	**Nigerianer**	**Nigerianerin**	**nigerianisch**
Norway	**Norwegen**	**Norweger**	**Norwegerin**	**norwegisch**
Pakistan	**Pakistan**	**Pakistani, Pakistaner**	**Pakistanerin**	**pakistanisch**
Palestine	**Palästina**	**Palästinenser**	**Palästinenserin**	**palästinensisch**
Panama	**Panama**	**Panamene**	**Panamenin**	**panamenisch**
Papua New Guinea	**Papua-Neuguinea**	**Papua-Neuguineer**	**Papua-Neuguineerin**	**papua-neuguinesisch**
Paraguay	**Paraguay**	**Paraguayaner**	**Paraguayanerin**	**paraguayanisch**
Persia	**Persien**	**Perser**	**Perserin**	**persisch**
Peru	**Peru**	**Peruaner**	**Peruanerin**	**peruanisch**
Philippines	die **Philippinen**	**Philippiner**	**Philippinerin**	**philippinisch**
Poland	**Polen**	**Pole**	**Polin**	**polnisch**
Portugal	**Portugal**	**Portugiese**	**Portugiesin**	**portugiesisch**
Puerto Rico	**Puerto Rico**	**Puertoricaner**	**Puertoricanerin**	**puertoricanisch**
Qatar	**Katar**	**Katarer**	**Katarerin**	**katarisch**

	Country	*Inhabitant*	*Female inhabitant*	*Adjective/language*
Romania	**Rumänien**	**Rumäne**	**Rumänin**	**rumänisch**
Russia	**Russland**	**Russe**	**Russin**	**russisch**
Rwanda	**Ruanda**	**Ruander**	**Ruanderin**	**ruandisch**
Samoa	**Samoa**	**Samoaner**	**Samoanerin**	**samoanisch**
Scotland	**Schottland**	**Schotte**	**Schottin**	**schottisch**
Senegal	**Senegal**	**Senegalese**	**Senegalesin**	**senegalesisch**
Seychelles	**die Seschellen**	**Sescheller**	**Seschellerin**	**seschellisch**
Sierra Leone	**Sierra Leone**	**Sierraleoner**	**Sierraleonerin**	**sierraleonisch**
Slovakia	**Slowakien**	**Slowake**	**Slowakin**	**slowakisch**
Slovenia	**Slowenien**	**Slowene**	**Slowenin**	**slowenisch**
Solomon Islands	**die Salomonen/Salomon-Inseln**			
Somalia	**Somalien**	**Somalier**	**Somalierin**	**somalisch**
South Africa	**Südafrika**	**Südafrikaner**	**Südafrikanerin**	**südafrikanisch**
Spain	**Spanien**	**Spanier**	**Spanierin**	**spanisch**
Sri Lanka	**Sri Lanka**	**Srilanker**	**Srilankerin**	**srilankisch**

	Country	*Inhabitant*	*Female inhabitant*	*Adjective/language*
		Singhalese	**Singhalesin**	**singhalesisch**
		Tamile	**Tamilin**	**tamilisch**
Sudan	**der Sudan**	**Sudanese**	**Sudanesin**	**sudanesisch**
		Sudaner	**Sudanerin**	**sudanisch**
Surinam	**Suriname**	**Surinamer**	**Surinamerin**	**surinamisch**
Sweden	**Schweden**	**Schwede**	**Schwedin**	**schwedisch**
Switzerland	**die Schweiz**	**Schweizer**	**Schweizerin**	**schweizerisch**
Syria	**Syrien**	**Syrer**	**Syrerin**	**syrisch**
		Syrier	**Syrierin**	
Tajikistan	**Tadschikistan**	**Tadschike**	**Tadschikin**	**tadschikisch**
Taiwan	**Taiwan**	**Taiwanese**	**Taiwanesin**	**taiwanesisch**
Tanzania	**Tansania**	**Tansanier**	**Tansanierin**	**tansanisch**
Thailand	**Thailand**	**Thailänder**	**Thailänderin**	**thailändisch**
Tibet	**Tibet**	**Tibetaner**	**Tibetanerin**	**tibetanisch**
		Tibeter	**Tibeterin**	**tibetisch**

	Country	*Inhabitant*	*Female inhabitant*	*Adjective/language*
Togo	**Togo**	**Togoer**	**Togoerin**	**togoisch**
Tonga	**Tonga**	**Tonganer**	**Tonganerin**	**tonganisch**
Tunisia	**Tunesien**	**Tunesier**	**Tunesier**	**tunesisch**
Turkey	**die Türkei**	**Türke**	**Türkin**	**türkisch**
Turkmenistan	**Turkmenistan**	**Turkmene**	**Turkmenin**	**turkmenisch**
Uganda	**Uganda**	**Ugander**	**Uganderin**	**ugandisch**
Ukraine	**die Ukraine**	**Ukrainer**	**Ukrainerin**	**ukrainisch**
United Arab Emirates	**die Vereinigten Arabischen Emirate**			
United Kingdom	**das Vereinigte Königreich**			
United States	**die Vereinigten Staaten (die USA)**			
Uruguay	**Uruguay**	**Uruguayer**	**Uruguayerin**	**uruguayisch**
Uzbekistan	**Usbekistan**	**Usbeke**	**Usbekin**	**usbekisch**
Vatican (City)	**der Vatikan, die Vatikanstadt**			
Venezuela	**Venezuela**	**Venezolaner**	**Venezolanerin**	**venezolanisch**
Vietnam	**Vietnam**	**Vietnamese**	**Vietnamesin**	**vietnamesisch**

	Country	*Inhabitant*	*Female inhabitant*	*Adjective/language*
Virgin Islands	**die Jungferninseln**			
Wales	**Wales**	**Waliser**	**Waliserin**	**walisisch**
Yemen	**Jemen**	**Jemenit**	**Jemenitin**	**jemenitisch**
Zaire	**Zaire**	**Zairer**	**Zairerin**	**zairisch**
Zambia	**Sambia**	**Sambier**	**Sambierin**	**sambisch**
Zimbabwe	**Simbabwe**	**Simbabwer**	**Simbabwerin**	**simbabwisch**

Index

Index